. . . Foliis tantum ne carmina manda,
ne turba volent rapidis ludibria ventis . . .

—Virgil, *Aeneid* VI.74-75

# A Splendid Wickedness
## *and Other Essays*

David Bentley Hart

William B. Eerdmans Publishing Company
Grand Rapids, Michigan

Wm. B. Eerdmans Publishing Co.
2140 Oak Industrial Drive N.E., Grand Rapids, Michigan 49505

**Library of Congress Cataloging-in-Publication Data**

Names: Hart, David Bentley, author.
Title: A splendid wickedness and other essays / David Bentley Hart.
Description: Grand Rapids, Michigan: Eerdmans Publishing Company, 2016.
Identifiers: LCCN 2016003796 | ISBN 9780802872647 (pbk.: alk. paper)
Subjects: LCSH: Theology.
Classification: LCC BR118 .H3645 2016 | DDC 230 — dc23
LC record available at http://lccn.loc.gov/2016003796

www.eerdmans.com

*For Francesca Murphy, John Betz & John Cavadini*

# Contents

# Preface

When I compiled my earlier collection of essays *In the Aftermath:
Provocations and Laments*, I chose to use the texts I had originally
written rather than the versions that had already appeared in print, which
had often been edited to fit into a particular format. I have elected to do
the same here. This is not because I have had much cause to complain
over the years where editors are concerned; none that I have worked with
has ever been of the intrusive sort, and all have allowed me free rein with
my prose (no matter how often it might curvet or bolt). Even so, there are
differences between the unpublished and published versions substantial
enough that in many cases I have been unable to resist rescuing omitted
passages or images or turns of phrase from the oblivion of my hard drive.
I cannot say with absolute confidence that one version is superior to the
other in any given instance, but I can say which conforms more nearly
to my original intentions. And I should also mention that a few of the
pieces included herein have never appeared in print before now, and that
I include them out of sheer vanity. The truth is that essays of this sort —
composed sometimes in haste, always in connection with some particular occasion, rarely with any larger project in view — have the form of
ephemera: songs written on leaves and then carried away to become the
*ludibria* of the rushing winds. But I believe that the form belies the content,
and that each piece collected here possesses enough intrinsic interest to
merit preservation. True, they remain occasional essays, and their topics,
rather than following any continuous pattern, were dictated by momentary fancies of my own or the inspired suggestions of an editor. But there
are several dominant and recurring themes that, I like to think, lend these
pages a certain unity of purpose. Admittedly, as often happens when one

is producing *occasional* prose at a *regular* rate, there are a few detours into the obscure or the trivial, and a few signs of inadvertency. But perhaps I am too vain to part with those either, and I hope readers will charitably regard them as ornamental virtues of the text rather than as essential vices.

Most of these pieces appeared originally in *First Things*, either the print or online editions. Of those appearing previously in print, the exceptions are as follows:

"Brilliant Specialists" (*The Baseball Research Journal*, Fall 2010)
"America and the Angels of Sacré-Cœur" (*The New Criterion*, December 2011); reprinted in *Future Tense: The Lessons of Culture in an Age of Upheaval*, ed. Roger Kimball (Encounter Books, 2012)

All pieces are reprinted with permission.

This volume's "Coda" is a paper I delivered at a conference at the University of Notre Dame in December of 2013; while there, in a moment of desperation (an editor at *First Things* had informed me by e-mail that my column for the next issue was overdue), I extracted several paragraphs and rearranged them into a Back Page article. I include the complete text here (in addition to its reduced version) simply because I particularly enjoyed writing and delivering it and think that it works best in its entirety. It also constitutes for me one of the oddest memories I have of any conference in which I have taken part. The gathering had been summoned by the formidable (and rather magnificent) Francesca Murphy, who, in her ceaseless search for ways to make academics behave like interesting human beings, had hit upon the novel notion that the participants should deliver papers not *about* the figures they had been assigned to discuss, but *as* those figures. She then conscripted me to prepare a paper on — or, rather, by — Charles Baudelaire. I consented (though perhaps it would be more accurate to say I obeyed), and decided I had better speak as Baudelaire's ghost, so that I could rely upon his *Journaux intimes* as a sort of master key to all his works. What no one thought to tell me until it was too late was that I was the only one of the conference participants who had agreed to the conceit of impersonating rather than merely talking about the person of whom he or she had been asked to provide a treatment. So, while everyone else there delivered a fairly standard paper of the academic kind, I alone was left to make a spectacle of myself. Not being particularly shy, I did not mind the distinction; but it did introduce an unexpected note of the surreal into what was otherwise a very delightful, very informative, but also very normal academic affair.

My thanks to all the editors I have worked with, and most especially Rusty Reno of *First Things*. Thanks also to Bill Eerdmans, not only my publisher but a generous and indefatigable friend. My thanks also to my research assistant at St. Louis University, a gifted young scholar named Jacob Prahlow, for assembling this volume for me and for preparing it for submission.

Finally, as a personal note, I entreat all readers of good will or kindly temperament, to pray for me and my family. I suffered a considerable blow to my health in the first months of 2014, and I need all the help God might give as I try to recover.

# ONE

# The Gnostic Turn

**M**y son was still too deeply immersed in his thousandth or so reread-ing of *The Wind in the Willows* to take an immediate interest in the copy of Antoine de Saint-Exupéry's *The Little Prince* that I had just res-cued for him from the chilly hinterlands of my library, so I decided to read it again myself. Memory, I found, had not really altered the story in my mind, but also had not quite prepared me for its total effect. I am no less susceptible to the tale's charm than most of its readers are, I can honestly say, or to its fetching dreamlike atmosphere; but I still came away from the experience thinking that there is something rather mystifying about the perennial appeal of this book.

It is, for one thing, a deeply melancholy little fable, and while this is hardly a surprising quality in a book written by so incurably wistful an author — or at so dreadfully dark a moment in the world's history (1943) — it is certainly a surprising quality in a children's book of such enduring popularity. Children, as we all know, are quite capable of enjoying grim or frightening or perverse stories, and do not mind being a bit disturbed by what they read; but one generally does not expect them to have much of an appetite for tales that are morose, or pervaded by adult nostalgia, or freighted with spiritual disenchantments. *The Little Prince* is all of these. It is, moreover, a somewhat dated piece, what with its crowded gallery of slightly annoying symbolist personifications — the proud rose, the fox who wants to be tamed, the serpent who brings eternal sleep — all of which probably seemed exquisitely profound to a rather romantic French writer reared in the long lavender shadow of Maurice Maeterlinck, but all of which now, on too pitilessly close an inspection, possess little more than a quaint pasteboard bathos. (Though, to make a clean breast of things, I actually like all those bits.) My error may, of course, lie in assuming that it is in fact children, rather than their parents, who are the principal admirers of the work. I honestly do not recall what my reaction to it was when I was, say, seven; but I know that what fascinates me about it now is the enigmatic but fairly obvious Christian Gnostic allegory at its heart. The Little Prince is — if not a savior figure — nonetheless a bearer of a higher wisdom, blessed with a positively transcendent innocence, too pure for our fallen reality, and so no more than a temporary sojourner here on earth. He comes to us out of an eternal childhood and, for that very reason, has never been rendered foolish by experience. His own world contains both good and evil seeds, we are told, but he is without fault. He even, in descending into our world, passes through the planetary spheres, pausing briefly at each to converse with its reigning archon: the king who imagines himself ruler of all things, the vain man who demands only adoration, the drunkard sunk in shame, the heartlessly calculating man of business, the harried and miserable lamplighter, the explorer who never leaves his study — all quite absurdly self-important and all trapped within their fated roles.

Then, to one lone, eccentric, and somewhat unworldly man, stranded in the desert, he brings enlightenment, and that of a rather thin and impalpable variety: the knowledge that somewhere above this world a divine child is laughing and the ability therefore to hear (as others cannot) the laughter of the stars. Then the Little Prince departs again, even more mysteriously than he came; unable to ascend again to his true home while still burdened by an earthly body, he must submit to the serpent's bite; and the next day even his body has vanished.

Perhaps this is precisely what the book's admirers really like about it — or, at least, what most of the adults and a few particularly lugubrious children like about it. After all, its sadness is a sadness that emanates from the inescapable dilemma of the modern spiritual imagination. In a sense, a certain "Gnostic turn" is inevitable for us today when we attempt to find our way toward the transcendent, inasmuch as we begin all our spiritual journeys now in a world from which the transcendent has been forcibly expelled, and not as a result of mere cultural prejudice.

The world we inhabit — the world our imaginations know and within which our deepest desires must move — is the world after Darwin (and Marx and Freud and a host of other prophets of disenchantment, but first and foremost Darwin); we simply cannot now (if we are paying attention) imagine a universe whose grandeurs and mysteries unambiguously lead the reflective mind beyond themselves toward a transcendent order both benign and provident. There was a time, perhaps, when nature really did seem to speak with considerable eloquence of a good creator and a rational creation. Formal and final causes were everywhere visible, guiding material and efficient causes toward their several — yet harmoniously interwoven — ends. The endless diversity of nature was an elaborate, gorgeous, and glittering hierarchy, rising from the dust to heights beyond the merely cosmic, comprising worms and angels within a single continuum of articulate splendor. That was a while ago, however.

Whether or not Darwinism is really quite the "universal solvent" that Daniel Dennett and others believe it is, and whether or not, logically considered, it really does away entirely with the need for some concept of final or formal causes, at the level of general cultural imagination it has certainly drawn a veil for us between experience of the world and knowledge of God. Nature, as many of us cannot help but see it now, no matter how much we may delight in its intricacies and beauties and dangers, is primarily an immense and mindless machine that generates poignantly ephemeral life out of a perpetual chaos of violence and death. And, far from constituting a rational continuum, obedient to what Arthur Lovejoy liked to call the *principium plenitudinis* (that is, the metaphysical law that no possible level of existence can be absent within a complete cosmic order), nature's diversity appears to us now as only the fortuitous result of a combination of spontaneous material forces and enormous spans of time. Whereas, for example, an ape's morphological proximity to a man could once have appeared to educated minds as evidence of a perfect arrangement of graded eidetic kinds within an ideal universe, that same similarity appears to us now to be chiefly the residue of a random series of divergences and ramifications and attritions within a phylogenic series, guided only by chance and material necessity. A likeness within difference that at one time could be seen as the line of demarcation between angelic intellect and bestial impulse is now the humbling reminder of an arbitrary division of fortunes within a single mammalian family; the ape does not just point upward toward us; he also draws us down again into the mire of animal organism.

Now, this is not to say that many of us cannot feel quite at peace with this state of affairs. I, for one, rejoice in the knowledge of my kinship with the gentle and venerable mountain gorilla, and suspect that — of the two of us — I may be the more honored by the association. Moreover, I do not really believe that an acknowledgment of the fact of special evolution obliges me to abandon the instinctive Platonism of my nature that tells me that goodness, truth, and beauty still infuse all of creation with a transcen-

3

dent purpose, one that includes both me and my distant simian cousin. But even I, reflecting on the vast torment and ruin of nature, cannot help at times slipping into a slightly Manichaean mood and wondering whether he and I are not both together involved in some great tragic cosmic drama in which good and evil, light and darkness, even spirit and matter ceaselessly vie with one another. At such moments, when looking for a source of spiritual comfort, my eyes do tend to turn somewhat upward and away from the world.

Hans Jonas defined the special pathos of Gnosticism as the unearthly allure of the call from beyond, the voice of the stranger God that resonates within the soul that knows itself to be only a resident alien in this world. And he saw this as a pathos peculiarly familiar to us in this the age of "unaccommodated man." This is undoubtedly correct, but it should also be said that this "call of the stranger God" is itself only one modality of a more general summons audible to all persons (except those who have laboriously deafened themselves to it), more or less at all times. It is that same experience of wonder at the sheer unexpectedness and mystery of existence that Plato and Aristotle called the beginning of philosophy, or the same primordial agitation of desire that Augustine described as the unquiet heart's yearning for God. The distinctive note that shifts this summons into a Gnostic register, however, is that of alienation from the world; and this is largely a matter of cultural circumstance.

It is undoubtedly the case that it is our shared imaginative grammar that determines for us how and to what degree we can reconcile our native human longing for the divine with our love of the things of earth. In a more hospitable cosmos than ours now appears to be, it was much easier to be at home in the world and to believe that that which lies farthest beyond us is also that which lies most deeply within all things; in such a cosmos, transcendence is the mystery at once of the far and the near. But the modern perspective seems to shatter that unity; for us, to a greater degree than for most of our more distant ancestors, the beyond is only beyond, and transcendence is a kind of absence or impenetrable paradox, announced to us not so much in the splendor and order of nature as in our alienation from it.

This is why so much of the art of the modern age, high and low, so often treats of spiritual longing in Gnostic terms. French literature — being at once the richest and most diseased of any nation — provides the most vivid examples, produced by believers and unbelievers alike: Hugo, Huysmans, Anatole France, Mallarmé, Verlaine, Bernanos, and, of course, Baudelaire (whose inner sense of a certain "Gnostic paradox" generated a poetry at once fervently pious and blasphemously decadent). The novels of Patrick White (especially *Riders in the Chariot*) might be the most striking recent specimens of high Gnosticism in English letters. At a considerably more popular level, a great deal of science fiction, written or cinematic, turns again and again to Gnostic themes. A particularly famous example would be David Lindsay's atrociously written, but oddly absorbing, *A Voyage to Arcturus* — to which one should subjoin a mention of Harold Bloom's virtual plagiarism thereof, the even more unreadable *The Flight to Lucifer*. And of science fiction films constructed around Gnostic themes — implicit or explicit — there is already a notable tradition: George Lucas's 1971 film *THX 1138*, for instance, or the *Matrix* trilogy. Two films written by Andrew Niccol — 1997's *Gattaca* and 1998's *The Truman Show* — were both consciously Christian Gnostic fables; the latter especially was an affecting expression not only of a certain Gnostic paranoia regarding the nature of reality, but of faith in a spiritual dignity in the soul that transcends the world (it even ends with a rather splendid and moving confrontation between the hero, the one "true man" in the tale, and the demiurge of the universe from which he seeks escape).

My final observation, I suppose, would be this: Our longing for transcendence is inextinguishable in us, and the appeal of the transcendent to our deepest natures will always be audible and visible to us in some form — first and finally in the form of beauty — and will continue to waken in us both wonder and an often inexpressible unhappiness. But in an age such as ours, within the picture of the world that now prevails, that beauty must seem more ambiguous, more beleaguered, and the call of transcendence more elusive of interpretation, like a voice heard in a dream. In the absence of that scale of shining mediations that once seemed seamlessly to unite the immanent and the transcendent, the earthly and the heavenly, nature and supernature, we are nevertheless still open to the same summons issued in every age to every soul; but it must for now come to us as something more mysterious, tragic, and terrible than it once was.

# TWO

# On Butterflies and Being

We are living this year in a cottage in the forest, halfway up the slope and under the slightly furrowed brow of a green mountain whose ridge forms our western horizon, and over which the brief twilight rises in the evening as a pale gold thinly fringed with dark amethyst. The days are filled with the incessant clamor of stridulating and timbalating insects, to which at night — undiminished — is added the mighty song of the upland chorus frog (*Pseudacris feriarum*, for those with a taste for taxonomic Latin) and the sweet belling of the Cope's gray tree frog (*Hyla chrysoscelis*). Earlier in the summer, the woods were full of fireflies, but they are gone now. The only regularly invited visitors to our rustic retreat are ruby-throated hummingbirds — who come for the red nectar in the two feeders hanging on either side of the house — and a large assortment of butterflies — whom we entice to our porch with sprays of purple hyssop. The deer come unbidden, usually in the dawn.

The most numerous of the butterflies — or, at any rate, the most conspicuous — are the common swallowtails, or *Papilioninae*, of which I have seen two varieties here. There is the splendid black swallowtail (*Papilio polyxenes*), whose sable wings are adorned with markings of yellow and iridescent blue; the female is especially lovely, with her lavish train of shimmering sapphire; and on each of the hindwings of either sex there is a single russet ocellation with a black "pupil." Then there is the eastern tiger swallowtail (*Papilio glaucus*), of which the male is always a bright jonquil yellow striped and bordered with black, but of which the female is either yellow or (more alluringly) black with glittering azure hindwings. There are few sights more purely enchanting up here than that of a yellow male and a black female sailing and fluttering about one another in the erratic

6

choreography of their courtship *pas de deux*, before finally achieving the fragile stillness of consummation on some leaf or blossom or bending frond. All of us less graceful beasts, it is hard not to think, should be envious of the sheer ethereal delicacy of that lepidopterogamy.

All right, well, I suspect that with that last word I've gone a bit too far; so perhaps I should leave off painting the scene and simply get to the story I want to tell — which does indeed involve a butterfly, but not a swallowtail, of any hue. The lepidopteron in question was, rather, a red admiral, or — a few last flourishes of Linnaean jargon — a *Vanessa atalanta*, a butterfly that does not really belong to the admiral subfamily (*Limenitidinae*) of the brushfoots (*Nymphalidae*) at all, but belongs instead to the true brushfoot subfamily (the *Nymphalinae*). It is a gorgeous creature: black with lashings of white on the upper forewings, faintly tinged with ashen blue at its outer and inner tips, and strikingly marked with broad bands of ember red across the centers of its forewings and along the skirts of its hindwings. I have seen it only once since arriving here. What made that lone sighting remarkable to me, though, was neither the butterfly's beauty nor its comparative rarity in these woods, but the eerily perfect timing of its appearance.

I was sitting on my porch with two volumes I had recently acquired, both by Vladimir Nabokov: a first edition of *Pale Fire* in good condition, which is not very hard to find, and that Holy Grail of Nabokoviana, a first printing of the 1970 volume *Poems and Problems* in absolutely immaculate condition, bearing not so much as a single scuff mark on its jacket. And I had just flipped to that haunting passage in the former where John Shade is about to cross the road to his death and a "Red Admirable" (Nabokov preferred the older form of its common name) emerges suddenly from the junipers and shrubs and whirls around the poet "like a colored flame" flashing and vanishing amid the sunbeams, then briefly settles on his sleeve, and then hastily disappears into the shadows of the trees, when a red admiral came coasting toward me, performed three elegantly gliding circumvolutions of my head, briefly came to rest on the arm of my chair, and then flew off again and quickly disappeared in the shadows of a Chinese tulip tree.

The coincidence alone would have been enough to astonish me, but the event was rendered considerably more uncanny by the particular significance of that butterfly in the text. Red admirals constitute a recurring motif throughout *Pale Fire*, and many attentive readers have concluded (rightly, I believe) that the one who appears at that point in the novel is a kind of revenant of John Shade's dead daughter Hazel, either attempting to warn him of the danger across the way or to welcome him over the threshold of the next life. Nabokov, as is well known, was a fairly firm believer in the immortality of the soul, as well as a believer in fate, and he tended to think that the patterns of our lives are in large part shaped and guided by the spiritual community of those who have gone before us. In the strange, often tragic, but also often beautiful symmetries of his own life he thought he could discern the clear workings of these benign presences, close about us at all times, hiding and yet revealing themselves in the exquisite intricacies of nature and art. He certainly would have been pleased by the potently exact synchrony of my experience on my porch and would surely have refused to ascribe it to chance; and I have to admit that, for a brief tremulous moment, I wondered if his spirit had not been teasing me, in a way simultaneously obvious and impenetrable.

There are any number of fascinating aspects to the curious interaction and equally curious demarcation that existed between Nabokov the lepidopterist and Nabokov the artist. As a scientist, he affected to be completely indifferent to the aesthetic splendor of the creatures he studied; and, as a novelist, he affected to despise facile symbolisms. But it is clear from his writings that his love of lepidoptera was in part fired by the mysterious grandeur of a holometabolous species whose life cycle seems to encompass a magical passage from death to greater life — from the earthbound groping of the larva (in Latin, after all, a word for "ghost" or "funerary mask"), through the golden entombment of the chrysalis, to the winged liberty and polychromatic glory of the fully formed *imago* (the true "image"). An Atlas moth breaking from its cocoon at the end of his early story "Christmas," for instance, clearly figures as an intimation of life beyond death.

A more interesting feature of Nabokov's interest in butterflies for me, however, and of his entire career as a naturalist, was his intuition — at once metaphysical and aesthetic — that between nature and art there is no ultimate formal difference. Though not in any conventional sense a religious man — his only answer in an interview to the question of whether there is a God was to hint that he knew far more than he could say — he was certain that the natural world exhibited innumerable signs of conscious and even somewhat whimsical artistry: morphological games, almost, patterns of mimicry and delightful complexity that exceeded any purely evolutionary warrant, and that spoke of a sort of creativity whose rationale was ultimately aesthetic. Nature, no less than art, and no less (for that matter) than the mysteriously guided lives of individual men and women, seemed to him a work of supreme intelligence, conjuring enchantments purely for the sake of enchantment.

One has to be careful to make the proper distinctions here. There was nothing in Nabokov's vision of reality that would have brought his thinking into the vicinity of the current "Intelligent Design" movement, with its logically and epistemologically unverifiable arguments regarding "irreducible complexity" and its crude mechanistic deism and its all-too-immanent god of the gaps. For Nabokov, nature's "design" was something he thought he perceived in the sheer surfeit of the beautiful over the needful, and in the specular play of formal likenesses and variations among species. It was an aesthetic judgment on the whole of the natural order, not an empirical claim about certain portions of its machinery.

It is hard to know what to make of the more "spiritualist" elements of Nabokov's beliefs. Perhaps they might be dismissed as the quaint residue of a certain Silver Age Russian hermeticism, or perhaps as just too idiosyncratic to provide a philosophy for any but the very particular sensibility that harbored them. Whatever the case, his beliefs certainly endowed him with a limitless capacity for happiness, one that never failed him even in the darkest period of his life, when his family's vast estates had been seized by the Bolsheviks and he was forced to live the life of an impoverished émigré for decades on end. According to him, he was always able to find life to be a delightful "surprise," and for this reason he was always able to see something more shining through the veils of the ordinary.

And it is this quality of "surprise" that lends depth and poignancy (and delight) to all of Nabokov's art. Whatever else one makes of his peculiar metaphysics, it is clearly an expression of that most original of human intuitions regarding existence, known to every reflective child, and forgotten only by adults who have coarsened their intellects through moral indifference or "realist" dogmatism: the awareness that the very familiarity of the world of beings is saturated by the infinite strangeness of the fact of being as such. His was nothing other than the ancient Platonic and Aristotelian sense of *thaumazein* — of original rational wonder at existence — transcribed into a new key. As Wittgenstein said (a pronouncement the implications of which even some of his most avid admirers seem not to notice), it is not *how* things are, but *that* they are, that constitutes "the mystical." While the Intelligent Design theorist wants us to ponder the (actually incalculable and therefore imponderable) probabilities in *how* the world is ordered, a simpler and yet immeasurably richer perspective enjoins us to feel awe before the sheer there-ness — the sheer inexplicable *that*-it-is — of intelligibility and complexity and grandeur.

This is a consciousness of things more aesthetic than empirical and more spiritual than aesthetic, but at every level it is an experience of beauty — which is to say, an experience of the utter nonnecessity, the absolute fortuity, of being. Heidegger, in an infuriatingly terse paragraph in the "epilogue" of his "Origin of the Work of Art," correctly rejects as inadequate those static understandings of beauty that say it resides simply in form and order and a certain splendor (*quod visum placet*), and insists on the ontological dimension of the beautiful. No object, however striking, is beautiful as a sheer sensuous effect (that is nothing but a neurological agitation), nor even as an object of intellectual comprehension; it is beautiful because, in addition to these things, there is the mysterious surprisingness of its existence, by which it discloses to us being in its advent, or being as *event.* The experience of the delightful needlessness of the beautiful awakens us to the needlessness of the existence of things, to their ontological contingency, to the failure of their "essences" (conceived statically) to account for their existence. In this moment, we are aware — not always reflectively or speculatively, admittedly — of the difference between being and beings; and so long as we dwell in that apprehension, we cannot fall prey to that excruciating confusion that makes someone like, say, Richard Dawkins incapable of grasping the difference between the mystery of existence and the question of origins. The philistine hath said in his heart . . .

At any rate, this is what I take to be the profoundest truth in Nabokov's belief in nature's secret artistry: that sheer sense of surprise at the beautiful that — when we seek it, but more often when we do not — reminds us of a deeper surprise that inhabits our consciousness at all times, but of which we are usually oblivious, distracted as we are from being by beings. The surfeit of the beautiful over the necessary is a revelation of the surfeit of being over beings. It is an enigma written as plainly upon the surface of a twig or a brick as upon the wing of a butterfly; but only the greatest artist or saint has the ability to see it with equal ease in all circumstances. Even if my encounter with that *Vanessa atalanta* was nothing more than a wildly amusing coincidence, or even if it was one of those exquisitely unanticipated patterns that Nabokov's kindly ghosts weave into the fabric of quotidian existence, the most significant lesson to be learned from it is that — as we all know — every butterfly is a *Papilio mysteriosus*, an emblem and an emissary of being in its infinite familiarity and infinite strangeness, and all things properly contemplated remind us that, of themselves, they cannot be. And yet they are.

# THREE

# Tolstoy and Dostoevsky (and Christ)

I have had this experience three times now, on three different occasions, in admittedly similar circumstances, but not similar enough to explain the coincidence: I am speaking from a podium to a fairly large audience on the topics of — to put it broadly — evil, suffering, and God; I have been talking for several minutes about Ivan Karamazov, and about things I have written on Dostoevsky, to what seems general approbation; then, for some reason or other, I happen to remark that, considered purely as an artist, Dostoevsky is immeasurably inferior to Tolstoy; at this, a single pained gasp of incredulity breaks out somewhat to the right of the podium, and I turn my head to see a woman with long brown hair, somewhere in her middle thirties, seated in the third or fourth row, shaking her head in wide-eyed astonishment at my loutish stupidity. It is not, I hasten to add, the same woman on each occasion; it is, apparently, a single ideal type in three distinct instantiations. My assumption in each case is that she is an American convert to Eastern Orthodoxy, probably from the Episcopal Church, whose defection to the Christian orient was in large part inspired by reading *The Brothers Karamazov* at an impressionable age, and so she simply cannot imagine what depraved aesthetic criteria could prompt anyone to deliver himself of so bizarre an opinion.

I understand her distress, of course. I love the wild tumults and tourbillions of Dostoevsky's fiction as much as anyone, and I acknowledge that he was a more profound thinker than Tolstoy in any number of ways, and was blessed (or cursed) with far greater perspicacity and a far more terrible consciousness of the perversity of the human will. But, that said, is there really any plausibly disputable question as to which of these men was the greater writer: which, that is, produced books that — in their individual parts and in their totality — are more accomplished, more capacious, more sophisticated, more true to experience, and more beautiful? Certainly the consensus of most educated and literate Russians over the years has been preponderantly on Tolstoy's side. And, as much as Bakhtin may have taught us to admire Dostoevsky's "polyphonic poetics," most judicious readers of Russian — like the great Prince D. S. Mirsky — have recognized in Tolstoy's art the kind of serene sublimity and fullness of vision that place it naturally and worthily in the company of Shakespeare's plays, Dante's *Commedia*, and the Homeric epics. It is certainly no denigration of Dostoevsky's genius to admit that the same cannot — or, at any rate, should not — be said of his books, at least not as works of *art*.

In any event, I was recently reminded of my encounter with that woman — those women, rather — while reading Boris Jakim's new translation of *Notes from Underground* (Eerdmans, 2009), which is quite splendid and which should certainly now be regarded as the standard version in English. No other translator to this point has captured the frantic, nervous, querulous, acid, and occasionally coarse tone of the Russian original nearly so well. In Jakim's rendering, the voice of the Underground Man achieves something of the startling novelty it no doubt had in the ears of those who first heard it, when the book made its debut and a new, altogether indispensable fictional personality entered the canon of modern literature. Once again, the Underground Man appears before us as the perfect compendium of every spiritual pathology of the modern age; his resentments, irrationalities, rationalizations, contradictions, perversities, protests of innocence, admissions of guilt, fits of self-laceration, displays of moral impotence, self-justifications, self-accusations — all of it rings out with extraordinary immediacy. None of it, though, is quite *real*.

I do not mean that it is not "realistic." Realism is a worthless standard to apply to any work of art, and what we call realism is as often as not a cheap parlor trick, a mediocre writer's attempt to distract us from his lack of poetic range by flaunting an overdeveloped talent for mimicry or an unrestrained appetite for inventories of inconsequential detail (Zola comes to mind). At the same time, one must acknowledge that part of the special enchantment of the novel, considered as a distinct literary form, is the illusion it can create of a fully realized world; a truly great novel is like a magic mirror, whose surface reflects not only the appearances but also the souls of living men and women. Precisely because of its special combination of immensity and intimacy, it affords its author room, scope, time for the subtlest gestures and finest strokes of psychological portraiture. And among the very few novelists who have succeeded at keeping all the forces of the novel in balance — the great and the small, the epic and the homely, the architectonic and the decorative — Tolstoy is unsurpassed. Dostoevsky, on the other hand, is brilliant wherever extreme effects are called for, but almost hopeless at creating a substantial world around the delightful clamor of his characters' voices, or at creating a credible psychological personality behind any of those voices.

This last claim, I know, will strike many readers as patently ludicrous. After all, even in his own time Dostoevsky was acclaimed as a brilliant psychologist. Nietzsche thought him unrivaled in the field. And it would indeed be foolish to deny how perfectly Dostoevsky captures certain states of mind or certain traits of character. The exaggerated heartiness of Raskolnikov in the presence of the police, for instance, summons up some recollection in each of us — usually from childhood — of how it feels to be guilty of something whose penalty we dread and yet too clumsily anxious to hide that guilt. And all of Dostoevsky's better characters are vivid and rich, and we feel we know them by the ends of their tales. It is not, however, the accuracy of Dostoevsky's psychological observations that I would question, but — again — the credibility of the personalities by which they are illustrated. We recognize a single character called Prince Myshkin as an aesthetic effect; we become familiar with the style of his presentation and the sound of his sentences; we know his innocence, his fragility, and his ardor. Similarly, each of the Karamazov brothers stands out for us as a fictional constant running through the texture of the novel. Their words and actions are seemingly consistent. But, if we look too closely, we will inevitably come to see that, however brilliantly Dostoevsky has fused together an ensemble of psychological convulsions and habits of temperament in each of these characters, the result of that fusion is in most cases a creature that could never exist outside of the novel. One cannot enter into these characters; when one attempts to do so, they dissolve back into multiplicity. Not one of them is as plainly, poignantly, unexceptionally alive as, say, Pierre in *War and Peace*.

This is not a reproach. I am not even sure it would have constituted much of an artistic triumph if Dostoevsky had succeeded in producing a fuller illusion of reality for characters of such opulently farraginous mental states. Far better, perhaps, to allow them to occupy the realm of the grotesque and exorbitant, of the fantastic and febrile. As mere personalities, they might be perfectly insufferable; but, as the fabulous psychological chimeras they are, their grand absurdity and pathos often cast a new (if somewhat lurid) light back upon the ordinary world of our experience. In a wonderfully concise passage in his 1940 preface to Adolfo Bioy Casares's

*The Invention of Morel*, Jorge Luis Borges — taking issue with Ortega y Gasset's elevation of "psychological" fiction over the "fantastic" — offers a devastating critique of the pretensions of a great deal of modern "psychological realism": "The Russians and their disciples have demonstrated, tediously, that no one is impossible. A person may kill himself because he is so happy, for example, or commit murder as an act of benevolence. Lovers may separate forever as a consequence of their love. And one man can inform on another out of fervor or humility. In the end such complete freedom is tantamount to chaos. But the psychological novel would also be a 'realistic' novel, and have us forget that it is a verbal artifice, for it uses each vain precision (or each languid obscurity) as a new proof of realism."

We can, of course, recognize any number of Russian writers in this caricature, including Tolstoy. After all, it is Levin in *Anna Karenina* who — married to the woman he loves, the father of a new child, living on his estate in his beloved countryside — has to avoid lengths of rope and loaded guns lest his personal spiritual crisis cause him suddenly to seize on any opportunity to kill himself. But, without question, the writer Borges's words most immediately bring to mind is Dostoevsky. And this raises a question.

What precisely does it mean, really, when we call Dostoevsky a psychologist? Frankly, I suspect that what we often mean is that his characters are violently contradictory, and since we know that the human mind often contradicts itself, the more contradictory his characters become, the more psychologically profound their depiction must seem to us. The Underground Man is a wonderful invention, and we would be poorer without him; but, as a fictional personality, he is only a vast collection of antic gestures, a tour de force of contradictions, and the nearer his wild emotional and intellectual oscillations approach a state of absolute incoherence, the more we are persuaded that he is a genuine psychological "type," whose mysteries Dostoevsky has disclosed to us.

Personally, I prefer not to read Dostoevsky as a psychologist at all, while still acknowledging the genius of his phenomenology of certain extreme states of spiritual perturbation. Indeed, I prefer to ignore the very category of "psychological fiction" as an error of judgment. I do admire, however, any writer who can create the beautiful effect of an emotionally, intellectually, and spiritually complete and vivid and utterly believable personality. And, in this, Tolstoy's art so far surpasses Dostoevsky's that any comparison can only be invidious. I can think of two very good examples of what I mean off the top of my head, both of them from *Anna Karenina*. One is the scene in which Dolly is on her way to visit Anna at

14

Vronsky's estate in the country; as she travels, the narrative takes us into her thoughts, which are perfectly ordinary: her anxieties as a mother, principally, and as a wife, and her moral uncertainties; but it is all rendered with such confident and seemingly omniscient artistry that one almost feels as if one has momentarily become this woman, and can think and feel as she does; and more than one female critic has called attention to how well Tolstoy succeeds here at imagining his way into the worries and regrets of a wife and mother. And the other example is the startlingly brilliant and heartbreaking passage in which Tolstoy describes the thoughts and internal apprehensions of Anna's child Seryozha in the long days after his mother went away — a scene that is more or less indescribable and that one must read to appreciate. In either case, Tolstoy's ability to immerse himself entirely in a seemingly real consciousness other than his own and then emerge again appears utterly effortless (though obviously it is not). Both of these scenes — as well as innumerable others like them in Tolstoy's fiction — are simply far beyond Dostoevsky's range as a writer; he could never have produced anything remotely like them. And both scenes possess a "psychological" truth that no mere "psychology" could ever approach.

It might be protested, I acknowledge, that I am simply expressing the disposition of my own private sensibility. After all, the two novelists are, as George Steiner so well argued in his *Tolstoy or Dostoevsky*, very different in their intentions, techniques, and (above all) artistic temperaments. Tolstoy, for instance, is an "epic" writer, whose books overflow with physical details and frequently threaten to overflow their own narrative structures and become as vast and as inconclusive as life itself, while Dostoevsky is a "dramatic" writer, whose books are full of fraught and urgent voices, at times almost disembodied, trapped in situations of immediate and pressing crisis, and surrounded by a physical world usually having no more substance than a collection of painted canvasses or pasteboard silhouettes at the back of the stage. And so on. But I am convinced that this is a matter not of *personal* taste — I love drama as much as epic, in the abstract, and I probably enjoy Dostoevsky's books as much as Tolstoy's, if in a very different way — but simply of *good* taste. The truth is that Tolstoy, as an epic writer, is majestically brilliant at his craft, while Dostoevsky, as a dramatic writer, has his many moments of genius (Mitya and Grushenka's night together just before Mitya's arrest, for instance), but all too often falls into the worst conventions of nineteenth-century melodramatic theater. There are too many passages in Dostoevsky's fiction that one simply has to tolerate, for the sake of the whole, and all too often they are crucial passages.

One that I find especially difficult to endure is the climactic conversation between Raskolnikov and Sonya in book 4 of *Crime and Punishment*, with its unremittingly forced portentousness and the embarrassingly obvious (but entirely unconvincing) device of Raskolnikov asking Sonya to read the story of the raising of Lazarus in John's Gospel — which culminates in one of the most egregious displays of authorial heavy-handedness in the history of serious literature. In the Constance Garnett translation: "'That is all about the raising of Lazarus,' she whispered severely and abruptly, and turning away she stood motionless, not daring to raise her eyes to him. She still trembled feverishly. The candle-end was flickering out in the battered candlestick, dimly lighting up in the poverty-stricken room the murderer and the harlot who had so strangely been reading together the eternal book."

That, I suppose, is just in case the reader had failed to notice. One almost feels that three or four exclamation marks might have been inserted at that juncture as well, just to make absolutely certain we get the point. It is hard at such moments not to feel the justice in Vladimir Nabokov's remark that Dostoevsky often seemed to write with a bludgeon.

Of course, in making so much out of my encounters with that oddly recurrent (yet oddly variable) woman in the third or fourth row, I am probably engaging in the wrong argument. I should remember that, in many circles, a preference for Dostoevsky over Tolstoy is practically de rigueur on purely ideological grounds. Among converts to Orthodoxy, for instance, as well as among many cradle Orthodox of a particularly rigorist kind, Dostoevsky is especially honored for having held firmly to Chalcedonian orthodoxy and having introduced the greater world to the figure of Father Zosima, from whom all the light of Eastern Christian contemplative spirituality shines out; and, more generally, among Christians of many confessions, Dostoevsky is revered as a prophet, the great Christian anti-Nietzsche, the voice of ancient Christian truth crying out in the spiritual desert of the modern West. Tolstoy, by contrast, was practically a liberal Protestant, who thought of Jesus principally as a divinely inspired teacher of moral truth; he was not only indifferent to, but also scornful of, dogmatic tradition; he was even excommunicated, for goodness' sake.

Fair enough, I suppose. I would observe, however, that there are all kinds of orthodoxy and all kinds of heresy. It is true that Dostoevsky personally assented — despite occasional episodes of doubt — to the creeds of the ancient church, and that he believed deeply in the mystical and sacramental traditions of the Orthodox Church, and that in general his vision of things was shaped by traditional Christian understandings of sin and redemption. That said, it is also true that his Chalcedonian orthodoxy was often almost inextricably confused with a dark, semipagan mysticism of the "Russian Christ" and of Russian blood and soil, and that he nursed slightly deranged fantasies of an Eastern Christian crusade to recapture Constantinople by violence, and that his virulent and contemptible anti-Semitism was anything but an accidental feature of his moral philosophy. Tolstoy, on the other hand, despite his creedal heterodoxy, at least believed that, say, the Sermon on the Mount should be taken quite literally, and that Christ's injunction to love our enemies and Paul's claim that, in Christ, there is neither Jew nor Greek (and so forth) meant that Christians really ought not to kill Turks or hate Jews. If we were really to make conformity to Christian teaching our chief criterion of comparison between the two men, I would still hesitate to concede Dostoevsky the advantage.

Anyway, that is neither here nor there, I suppose. The claim on my part that always elicits that same gasp of dismay from that same quarter of the audience is a purely aesthetic claim. It is quite possible to acknowledge Dostoevsky's greatness as a novelist, and to concede his unquestionable preeminence as a moral and religious philosopher among modern thinkers, and to marvel at how uncannily accurate his predictions regarding the modern age were proved to be by the events of the twentieth century, and still think Tolstoy the far greater writer. This is only, after all, a relative evaluation made between two figures of monumental accomplishments, neither of whom has ever been threatened by many plausible rivals in his special field of achievement. Even so, it seems to me nothing but simple justice to grant the one his prophet's mantle and his tragic wisdom, but still to grant the other the supremacy of his art.

# FOUR

# Saint Shakyamuni

In 1571, the Doge of Venice presented King Sebastian of Portugal with certain relics of Saint Josaphat of India (including, if memory serves, a fragment of his spine). This was a lavish gift, to say the least. No legend of the late Middle Ages and the early modern period was more famous throughout the entire Christian world than the tale of Barlaam and Josaphat, nor were there very many saints more beloved than its eponymous protagonists. Their joint feast — celebrated on 27 November in the West and 26 August in the East — was observed with a special relish by Christians of every land. Josaphat in particular was revered as the very archetype of the holy prince, a child of the blood royal who was willing to forswear all the power and wealth of his earthly kingdom for the sake of the kingdom of God. The surrender of any portion of his sacred remains was no small gesture.

Alas, the relics were not authentic, though the doge had no way of knowing this (and I doubt King Sebastian was ever any the wiser). They could not be, for the simple reason that there never was a Christian King Josaphat in India. It would not, however, be entirely correct to say that either he or his story was simply the invention of pious imagination, as was, say, Saint Christopher. There was, in fact, a real person — a very famous person, as it happens — behind the figure of the Christian saint; he simply was not a Christian. He was, rather, the man who in his own day came to be called Shakyamuni — "sage of the Shakya clan" — but whose given name tradition records as Prince Siddhartha of the house of Gautama: in short, the Buddha.

It is actually not very difficult to trace out the process by which the story of the Buddha's youth and enlightenment was transformed into what was for centuries one of the most popular and influential of Christian legends. At least, a fairly clear history of textual transmission can be reconstructed, with only a few insignificant lacunae. The original of the narrative was no doubt one of the standard Indian versions of the Buddha's life — perhaps the *Lalitavistara* — which entered into Persian literature, almost certainly at some point in the sixth century, in the form of a story entitled *Bilauhar and Budisaf.* This latter name is simply the Persian rendering of the word "bodhisattva," which means "enlightened being" and is used of one who is on the way to Nirvana (or, in the Mahayana, one who is on the way but who holds back to devote himself to the salvation of other beings). The story, it appears, was especially favored by the Manichaeans. By the eighth century, when Persia was the seat of the Abbasid Caliphate, a translation of the story had appeared in Arabic under the title *Kitab Bilawhar wa-Yudasaf,* the "Book of Bilawhar and Yudasaf."

It was not, however, until the tenth century that the two principals in the tale were "baptized" by some unknown Georgian translator, who produced a version of the book in his native tongue and transformed it — by really only the most superficial of cosmetic alterations — into a story about the Christian communities of India: the tale of *Balahvar and Iodasaph* (known also simply as the *Balavariani*). Then, at some point in the early eleventh century (or thereabouts), the story made its way to Constantinople and became the Greek legend of *Barlaam and Iodasaph* (later erroneously attributed to John of Damascus), which in 1048 was translated into Latin as *Barlaam and Josaphat.* Thus a new and wonderfully picturesque hagiographic legend became the common property of all Christian peoples. And thus, under the many veils acquired in the course of his millennial narrative migrations — or perhaps one should say transmigrations — the "bodhisattva" of the Shakyas became the "Josaphat" of the Christians, and the Buddha entered incognito into the calendar of Christian saints.

The tale's popularity is easy to understand. It is simply a very good story, and rather moving. At least, this is true of — among the Christian renderings — the Georgian text, which is far more artistically assured and uncluttered than its successors. The Greek version is often ponderously didactic, interlarded as it is with edifying discourses elaborating upon the purer and simpler spiritual discourses of the earlier translation. The story begins with a certain King Abenes (Abenner in the Greek), whose realm once upon a time lay somewhere in India, and who — out of zeal for his native gods — instituted a policy of persecution against the Christians under his rule, inspired in part by the conversion and obstinate fidelity of one of his knights to the alien creed.

At the birth of Abenes's son Iodasaph, two court astrologers produce two quite incompatible prophecies regarding the child's future; one says the boy will come to be one of the most powerful rulers of his age, while the other says the boy will become a spiritual leader who will guide others upon the path of truth. To assure that the former prophecy will prove correct rather than the latter, Abenes has a city of pleasure built in which Iodasaph is to be reared without any exposure to suffering, privation, age, or death. He then orders the expulsion of all Christians from his kingdom. With the aid of one of his tutors, however, Iodasaph — now grown — learns of his father's desire to shield him from a true understanding of the world; so, journeying out one day from his city, Iodasaph becomes acquainted with the full spectrum of human misery — blindness, infirmity, poverty, age, death — and with the truth of its inevitability for all men and women.

He then turns for instruction to a Christian hermit named Balahvar, who, defying Abenes's decree, enters Iodasaph's house and relates to the prince a series of parables. These take up about a third of the book, as it happens, and are quite marvelous; taken together, moreover, they constitute a fairly exotic confection, being as they are equal parts Buddhist and biblical in content. (The third and best of the parables, incidentally — the story of the elephant, the dragon, and the mice — was one Tolstoy cited as contributing profoundly to his own spiritual awakening.) Iodasaph is converted and Balahvar departs.

Abenes is enraged when he learns of what his son has done, and employs every means at his disposal to sway Iodasaph from the path of renunciation. With the help of a heathen ascetic named Thedma, he finds a man who looks exactly like Balahvar to "debate" the priests of the old religion publicly, but Iodasaph is not deceived by the impostor (who, in fact, is soon himself converted to Christianity). Abenes then offers Iodasaph a ravishingly beautiful woman for his wife, and Iodasaph is tempted to accept; but, warned in a dream of the perdition he is courting, he ultimately resists. Finally, Abenes cedes half his kingdom to his son, and this Iodasaph accepts, as it allows him to provide a safe haven for the Christians of his lands.

Abenes is finally so impressed with the justice and wisdom of his son's regime that he too converts to Christianity and abdicates his throne in his son's favor. Even the Hindu sage Thedma, after a period of resistance, yields to the gospel. After Abenes passes away, Iodasaph desires to retreat to the wilderness as a hermit, but this he must delay doing for a variety of reasons. At last, however, he is able to join Balahvar in the wild, and the two thereafter live together a life of prayer and self-abnegation, at least until Balahvar dies. Iodasaph continues on in the ascetic life for several years more, until he too dies.

There is, I suppose, no great moral to be extracted from the curious history of the legend of Barlaam and Josaphat, apart perhaps from the rather banal and ordinary observation that the partitions between religious cultures in the premodern world were far more porous than we typically tend to imagine, and the channels of literary and cultural influence far wider. For me, though, the entire episode (for want of a better word) prompts two trains of reflection, each of which terminates in a fairly pregnant question.

First, it is rather remarkable — as any reader of the *Balavariani* with a knowledge of both Christianity and Buddhism should note — how purely and even exquisitely Buddhist the entire religious atmosphere of the story is. The spiritual counsels around which the book is built all concern the transience of earthly pleasure, the unreality of common experience, and the impermanence of all things; and salvation is presented throughout entirely in terms of renunciation and enlightenment. At times, there is not even the thinnest superimposition of Christian motifs upon the surface of the text. What then might we conclude about the spiritual temper of much of the Christianity of the Middle Ages and early modern period, and its relative affinity with the spiritual temper of Indian Buddhism, from the ease with which Buddhist teachings could be absorbed without scandal, or even any sense of strangeness, by the Christian cultures of both East and West after the tenth century?

And, second, surely there is some quality of irrevocability in any declaration of sainthood. Admittedly, Josaphat was never the object of any formal process of canonization — which is a process, apparently, for which there is no provision for revocation. Thus he does not linger on in the Roman calendar in the embarrassing manner of Pope Marcellinus, who was made a saint more or less as a result of a clerical error, but who there is good reason to believe was actually an apostate during the emperor Diocletian's persecutions of the church (not to worry: an entirely apocryphal account of Marcellinus's martyrdom was later inserted into the *Liber pontificalis*, which squares all accounts nicely). Nevertheless, he was revered by Christians for many hundreds of years, his feast was observed with liturgies and masses, and his relics were treasures of great cities and gifts of mighty princes. What then might we make of the delightful oddity that, in a sense, and admittedly under a foreign guise, the Buddha was for centuries venerated by Christians as one of their more beloved saints?

I confess, I should like to make quite a great a deal of it, though that is merely a matter of personal temperament. I sometimes think I am possessed of an *anima naturaliter buddhistica*. Certainly the *Dhammapada* and Shantideva's *Bodhicaryavatara* occupy suspiciously high positions on my list of favorite spiritual readings. But even those of us who feel not the slightest stirring of spontaneous reverence at the sight of a particularly grand Buddharupa or at the distant knelling of Asian temple bells might still pause to ask ourselves whether the story of this legend's long metamorphic journey from East to West — from *dharma* to evangel, so to speak — is not some kind of example of the irony of providence.

# FIVE

## The Secret Commonwealth

As All Souls' Day nears, spare a piteous thought, if you will, for the poor Rev. Robert Kirk, who lived from 1644 to 1692, and whose mortal remains rest — or do they? — in his parish kirkyard in Aberfoyle, a Scottish village lying near the Laggan River and at the foot of Craigmore. The great slab of his gravestone is in much the same condition as most of the other funerary markers that survive from the seventeenth century in those latitudes: smoothed and darkened by the winds and rains of three centuries, brindled with dark green and pale glaucous lichens, gently sunken to one side by a slight subsidence in the soil, and bearing an inscription ("Robertus Kirk, A.M. / *Linguæ Hiberniæ Lumen*"), now worn down to a shallow and barely legible intaglio of milky gray. Such is the sad impermanence of stone. Perhaps it does not matter all that much, however; the marker may be only a cenotaph, when all is said and done. Local legend has it that there is nothing more interred beneath that slowly dissolving monument than a coffin filled with rocks, the good reverend's body having been spirited away by fairies soon after his sepulture, to be kept till the end of time in their mansions beneath Doon Hill (the Anglicized version, I assume, of *"dun sitheen"* or "fairy knoll"), by which device they also keep his soul imprisoned in the great pine that grows on the hill's crest. Another, less terrible version of the same story says that Kirk is not so much a prisoner of the fairies as an ambassador, able to convey messages between two realms that over the years have become increasingly estranged from one another. Whatever the case, the great tree of Doon Hill is still called the Minister's Pine, and one to this day can occasionally find bright strips of cloth — upon which wishes have been written — strewn about it or tied to the branches of surrounding trees.

If the legend is true (and I, as any sane man ought, choose to believe it is), Rev. Kirk was the victim not only of the spite of a notoriously capricious folk, but of his own curiosity. A scholar trained at St. Andrew's and Edinburgh, a master of Celtic tongues, the author of the Gaelic Psalter of 1684, a theologian and student of antique lore, Kirk's greatest intellectual achievements were as a natural scientist (so to speak) of the hidden realm. Thus he is best remembered for his treatise of 1691, *The Secret Commonwealth of Elves, Fauns, and Fairies*. There is some dispute regarding whether a published edition of this work was actually indited in Kirk's time, or whether instead Sir Walter Scott's edition of 1815 was its first true appearance in print; but the form in which it is best known now is in Andrew Lang's critical edition of 1893 (which the always indispensable Dover Publications has recently made available again at a reasonable price). In any event, it was not long after completing this book, which may have revealed more than was prudent, that Kirk met his end. He had trespassed perhaps once too often upon the clandestine counsels of the Unseelie Court and so, on one of his frequent nighttime walks upon Doon Hill — which lay between his parish and his house, and which he was convinced was an entranceway into the other land — he simply fell into a swoon and died (or appeared to die).

His true fate would have remained unknown, however, had not Kirk, shortly after his obsequies, made a posthumous visit in a vision to his cousin, Graham of Duchray, in order to relate what had actually happened and to entreat his cousin to assist him in escaping his captors. At the time of Kirk's death (or perhaps one should say abduction), his wife had been with child and, in the time since, she had been delivered of a son; Kirk promised that he would appear as a phantom at the child's baptism and that, if his cousin would at that moment throw an iron knife at the apparition, Kirk would be released from his bondage. Graham of Duchray came prepared on the day, but the actual sight of his cousin's ghost — which did indeed appear — so froze him with wonder that he forgot to do as he had been bidden until it was too late. And so Kirk vanished again, and his spirit returned to the pine on Doon Hill.

Sad though Kirk's fate was, we should remember that he was neither the first nor the last naturalist to fall prey to the species he studied, and we should be glad that we still have the fruit of his researches to hand. *The Secret Commonwealth* rewards frequent readings, even by persons so fanatical in their prejudices as to refuse to believe its reports (such tragically deluded souls can treat the book as only a compendium of folklore, if they must, and still profit from it). Kirk's real concern, as it happens, is not simply the fairy realm, but those rare mortals privileged with the ability to see its inhabitants with their own eyes. It is, to a great extent, a treatise on the "second sight," a gift Kirk believed to be the special possession of a very few — a great many of whom were, like Kirk himself, seventh sons — and to be demonstrable not only from anecdote, but also from Scripture. Not to everyone do the "peaceable folk" appear, it seems, but a wealth of anecdotes — principally anecdotes concerning remarkable instances of foreknowledge on the part of recognized seers, or concerning their encounters with the specters of persons who had died far away — proves that there are those who, from birth, are able to pierce the veil within which the fairy realm is hidden. And these persons, says Kirk, are of the same family as the prophets of ancient Israel, and of all prophets in all lands and among all peoples.

That said, one does learn quite a lot of elfin lore from Kirk. He relates stories of cruel mischief, tells of the fairies' wicked habit of carrying away new mothers to act as wet nurses to fairy infants, recalls tales as well of their frequent benignity, discourses on the moral character of the "subterranean people," explains how each of us is attended through life by an ethereal double who sometimes lingers on in this world after we die, and so on. These beings are, says Kirk, nothing but those elemental guardians of the nations who, according to the New Testament, have been appointed as wardens in the earth, but who frequently forget their roles and resist the sway of God. They are dangerous, but not evil; they are, rather, morally neutral, like the forces of material nature.

One aspect of Kirk's investigations I find especially interesting is the purely autochthonous quality he ascribes to the second sight. Once removed from his native heath, says Kirk, a prophet loses the virtue that allows him to see the other world, and he becomes as blind to preternatural presences as any other mortal. He is like Antaeus raised up off the earth. Not only is every fairy a *genius loci*, every seer is a *vates loci* with a strictly limited charter. And the reason it pleases me to learn this is that it allows me to offer a riposte to an English friend of mine — a famous theologian whose name (which is John Milbank) I should probably withhold — who has quite a keen interest in fairies, and who regards it as a signal mark of the spiritual inferiority of America that its woods and dells, mountains and streams, are devoid of such creatures. In proof of this, he once cited to me the report of some English traveler in the New World who sent back a dispatch from Newfoundland (or somewhere like that) complaining that there were no fairies to be found in these desolate climes. But, ah no, I can say (having read Kirk), of course some displaced Sassenach wandering in the woods of North America would be able to perceive none of their ethereal inhabitants, as any faculty he might have had for seeing them would have deserted him. And, anyway, anyone familiar with the native lore of the Americas knows that multitudes of dangerous and beneficent manitous haunt or haunted these lands. They may lack some of the winsome charm of their European counterparts, not having been exposed to centuries of Greco-Roman and Christian civilization; and they may therefore be somewhat more Titanic than Olympian in their general character and deportment; but they certainly do not merit disdain or a refusal to acknowledge their existence.

Anyway, so as not to wax too facetious, let me make three observations about Kirk, and then a final observation about his way of seeing the world. First, it is certainly the case that he undertook his researches into folklore out of a genuine interest in the traditions of the Celtic north, and also out of what appears to be a deep conviction that those traditions touch upon a real dimension of vital intelligence or intelligences residing in the world all about us, occasionally visible and audible to us, but for the most part outside the reach of our dull, earthbound senses. Second, though, there is good reason to believe that he wrote *The Secret Commonwealth*, and placed so strong an emphasis on scriptural attestations of the reality both of elemental spirits and of the second sight, because he lived in the days of the early modern witch-hunting craze, when more than a few harmless Scottish country folk who innocently dabbled in the lore of their culture had found themselves arraigned by Presbyterian courts for practicing the black arts; Kirk may very well have been attempting to enter a brief in behalf of these unfortunate souls, by providing a theological warrant for their beliefs. And, third, it may be that such a theological warrant really could be found in the Bible, and Kirk was simply a more careful reader than most other Christians on this matter; after all, though Christian tradition came soon to abominate all the lesser spirits venerated or feared in pre-Christian culture as just so many demons, this was not the view taken of them in the Pauline corpus; there they appear as perhaps mutinous deputies of God, part of the compromised cosmic hierarchy of powers and principalities, whom Christ by his resurrection has subdued, but not *necessarily* as servants of evil; Colossians 1:20 even speaks of them as being not only conquered by Christ, but reconciled with God.

Finally, though, and perhaps a mite perversely, I want to urge the essential sanity of Kirk's approach to reality. One need not believe in fairies to grasp that there is no good reason why one ought not to do so. To see the world as inhabited by these vital intelligences, or to believe that behind the outward forms of nature there might be an unperceived realm of intelligent order, is simply to respond rationally to one of the ways in which the world seems to address us, when we intuit simultaneously its rational frame and the depth of mystery it seems to hide from us. It may be that the apprehension of such an unseen order, when it comes in the form of folklore about fabulous beings, has been overlaid by numerous strata of illusion — but so what? Everything we know about reality comes to us with a certain alloy of illusion, not accidentally, but as an indispensable condition. Even the dreariest Kantian can tell you that our ability to know the world depends upon those transcendental qualities the mind impresses upon it before it can impress them upon the mind, and that all perception requires the supreme fictions of the synthetic a priori. At the most primordial level of consciousness, the discrimination between truth and fantasy — if, by truth, one means the strictly empirically verifiable — becomes merely formal. Moreover, even if one suspects this is not a matter so much of illusion as of delusion, again that is of no consequence. A delusion this amiable is endlessly preferable to boredom, for boredom is the one force that can utterly defeat the will to be, and so the will to care at all what is or is not true. It is only some degree of prior enchantment that allows the eye to see, and to seek to see yet more. And so, deluded or not, a belief in fairies will always be in some sense far more rational than the absolute conviction that such things are sheer nonsense, and that the cosmos consists in nothing but brute material events in haphazard combinations. Or, I suppose, another way of saying this would be that the ability of any of us to view the world with some sort of contemplative rationality rests upon the capacity we possessed as children to see in everything a kind of articulate mystery, and to believe in far more than what ordinary vision discloses to us: a capacity that endows us with that spiritual *eros* that allows us to know and love the world, and that we are wise to continue to cultivate in ourselves even after age and disillusion have weakened our sight.

So, again, spare a thought for the soul of the good Rev. Robert Kirk, imprisoned in the great pine atop Doon Hill.

# SIX

# The Poetry of Autumn

We rhapsodize about "New England autumns," and for good reason; but, really, autumn anywhere in the deciduous forests of North America, especially in the East — from upper Canada to the deep South — is magnificent, and far outshines anything the Old World has to offer. In those years in which I've found myself in some corner of Europe during the fall, I have never been able to suppress a certain feeling of disappointment at the limited palette nature employs there for what is surely my favorite of the seasons. This isn't to say European autumn isn't lovely enough, with its muted light and drifting mists and pale flavescence. But the chromatic spectrum is narrow. For the most part, the trees pass from a darker to a more limpid green, and then to light gold, and then to ocher and brown, before their branches are stripped bare. There are occasional bright flashes of red and maroon amid the tawny pallor, though mostly from imported species of flora. But, to an eye accustomed to the endlessly varying hues of America's autumn, it all seems a little insipid.

Perhaps it's only because I come from the east coast of North America that I think fall the most poetical of months. Of course, every season is a season *for* poetry, and every season has been the subject *of* poetry; but I tend to think of this time of year as the most intrinsically poetic in nature. This may just be because of the contrasts in color: all that purple, crimson, scarlet, orange, cadmium, gold, and so forth, shifting and intermingling against a backdrop of luminous gray; it all seems like such a perfect coincidence of gaiety and melancholy, exuberance and death. Or perhaps it's because of a certain strange quality in the air that imbues everything with an additional tincture of mystery: whole days washed in a kind of opaline twilight, the sun blanched to a cold silver by ubiquitous clouds, wood smoke floating through soft rains, and so on. Or perhaps it's simply because, as the temperature drops, one spends more time inside, ideally by a fire, and so has more time to devote to reading poetry.

Whatever the case, now that fall is fully upon us, and I — in my forested retreat — can spend far more than my fair share of idle hours wandering about among the trees, I've begun making lists in my head of my favorite poems about autumn. There's far too much to choose from, of course, for this to be a useful occupation, unless one is compiling one of those ephemeral anthologies that show up now and again, always already on sale, at Borders or Barnes and Noble (which I'm not). But it's an enjoyable pastime, and innocuous, and so I thought I might offer a brief extract here, and solicit additional suggestions.

In English, obviously, *the* autumnal poem is Keats's "Ode to Autumn," whose images, cadences, mood, and music seem more evocative of the season's feel than any other lyric in the language. It's probably too well known to need quoting, but there's no harm in recalling at least the first stanza:

Season of mists and mellow fruitfulness,
Close bosom-friend of the maturing sun;
Conspiring with him how to load and bless
With fruit the vines that round the thatch-eaves run;
To bend with apples the mossed cottage-trees,
And fill all fruit with ripeness to the core;
To swell the gourd, and plump the hazel shells
With a sweet kernel; to set budding more,
And still more, later flowers for the bees,
Until they think warm days will never cease,
For Summer has o'er-brimmed their clammy cell.

For all its archetypal supremacy, however, Keats's poem is not necessarily any more distinguished than a great many others in the English canon. A case can be made that Thomas Hood's "Autumn" is every bit as accomplished, and every bit as successful in conveying a sense of the dying year's somber beauty. Again, the first stanza:

I saw old Autumn in the misty morn
Stand shadowless like silence, listening
To silence, for no lonely bird would sing
Into his hollow ear from woods forlorn,
Nor lowly hedge nor solitary thorn; —

Shaking his languid locks all dewy bright
With tangled gossamer that fell by night,
Pearling his coronet of golden corn.

This is splendid, as are all the verses that follow. And Edward Thomas's "October" is a quiet tour de force. To quote only its first lines:

The green elm with the one great bough of gold
Lets leaves into the grass slip, one by one, —
The short hill grass, the mushrooms small milk-white,
Harebell and scabious and tormentil,
That blackberry and gorse, in dew and sun,
Bow down to. . . .

Some of the finest autumnal poetry in English, moreover, is the simplest. I have a certain tender regard for Walter Savage Landor's "Autumn":

Mild is the parting year, and sweet
The odour of the falling spray;
Life passes on more rudely fleet,
And balmless is its closing day.

I wait its close, I court its gloom,
But mourn that never must there fall
Or on my breast or on my tomb
The tear that would have soothed it all.

And growing up has done nothing to diminish my admiration for Robert Louis Stevenson's "Autumn Fires":

In the other gardens
And all up the vale,
From the autumn bonfires
See the smoke trail!

Pleasant summer over
And all the summer flowers,
The red fire blazes,
The grey smoke towers.

Sing a song of seasons!
Something bright in all!
Flowers in the summer,
Fires in the fall!

That, as far as I'm concerned, is pure genius.

When I turn to poetry in French, I have to admit, the pickings become slimmer — and I say this as a confirmed Francophile. In fact, for the most part French poetry is far poorer in nature verse than English poetry. Why this should be, given the beauty of the French landscape, it's hard to say. Perhaps it's because Romanticism arrived so late, and in such a decadent form, in France. The sheer severity of French classicism was often peculiarly inhospitable to any but the most urbane of themes. All the lovely, austere, exact Alexandrines of the French Golden Age stage taken together do not possess the power of four or five lines from *A Midsummer Night's Dream* to summon up either the delicacies or the grandeurs of nature. And later French verse, to a greater degree than the English, remained largely a poetry of the city. These are generalizations, of course, susceptible of endless qualification.

But it seems to say something that two of the most famous French poems to mention autumn in their titles — "Sonnet d'automne" and "Chant d'automne," both by Baudelaire — have practically nothing to do with nature at all, and everything to do with the poet's arrested emotional development. In the first, the actual season appears only in the closing lines: "Crime, horreur et folie! — Ô pâle Marguerite! / Comme moi n'es-tu pas un soleil automnal, / Ô ma si blanche, ô ma si froide Marguerite?" ("Crime, horror, and madness! — O pale Marguerite! Are you not, like me, an autumnal sun, O my Marguerite, so white, so cold?") And the second uses autumn as little more than a metaphor for every morose discontent and hysterical premonition the poet can wring out of his own pathologies: "Bientôt nous plongerons dans les froides ténèbres; / Adieu, vive clarté de nos étés trop courts! / J'entends déjà tomber avec des chocs funèbres / Le bois retentissant sur le pavé des cours" ("Soon we shall plunge into the cold shadows; Farewell, delightful brightness of our too short summers! Already I hear the wood already falling, with a funereal shock, resounding over the courtyard pavement"). And the mood gets sicklier from there on.

Probably the best-known French poem about autumn, at least among English readers, is Verlaine's "Chanson d'Automne," which is so limpidly simple as to verge on the dainty, and whose gauzy effect no translation can really capture:

Les sanglots longs
Des violons
De l'automne
Blessent mon cœur
D'une langueur
Monotone.

Tout suffocant
Et blême, quand
Sonne l'heure.
Je me souviens
Des jours anciens,
Et je pleure.

Et je m'en vais
Au vent mauvais
Qui m'emporte
De çà, de là,
Pareil à la
Feuille morte.

(The long sobs of the violins of autumn wound my heart with a monot-onous languor. // Stifling everything, and wan, when the hour sounds, I recall the old days and I weep. // And I depart with the ill wind that carries me away, now here, now there, just like a dead leaf.)

This is all right, I suppose, in a tenuous, *Gymnopédies* sort of way, but somewhat lacking in the cider-soaked merriment of harvest time.

The specimens to be found in German seem, on the whole, to offer a somewhat richer range of feeling and color. Goethe's "Herbstgefühl" ("Autumn Emotion") strikes just the right balance between wistfulness and celebration:

Fetter grüne, du Laub,
Am Rebengeländer
Hier mein Fenster herauf!
Gedrängter quellet,
Zwillingsbeeren, und reifet
Schneller und glänzend voller!
Euch brütet der Mutter Sonne
Scheideblick, euch umsäuselt

Des holden Himmels
Fruchtende Fülle;
Euch kühlet des Mondes
Freundlicher Zauberhauch,
Und euch betauen, ach!
Aus diesen Augen
Der ewig belebenden Liebe
Voll schwellende Tränen.

(A fuller green, you leaves, up here to my window, along the grape trellis!
Swell more crowdedly, indistinguishable berries, and ripen more quickly
and more fully gleaming! On you broods the mother sun's parting glance,
all around you rustles the lovely sky's fruitful abundance; you are cooled
by the moon's kindly and magical breath, you are bedewed — ah! — by the
tears overflowing from these eyes of eternally enlivening love.)

I very much like Lenau's "Herbst," which has all the valedictory melancholy of Baudelaire's poems, but without the morbidity. But it hardly
evokes the season at all. And the same is true of Hölderlin's "Der Herbst,"
despite a lovely line about the ghost of rain appearing again in the sky.

Perhaps the most strangely affecting piece of autumnal verse in German is Rilke's "Herbsttag," "Autumn Day," which fully displays his ability
to infuse the ordinary with an indefinable quality of mystery:

Herr: es ist Zeit. Der Sommer war sehr groß.
Leg deinen Schatten auf die Sonnenuhren,
und auf den Fluren laß die Winde los.

Befiehl den letzten Fruchten voll zu sein;
gieb innen noch zwei südlichere Tage,
dränge sie zur Vollendung hin und jage
die letzte Süße in den schweren Wein.

Wer jetzt kein Haus hat, baut sich keines mehr.
Wer jetzt allein ist, wird es lange bleiben,
wird wachen, lesen, lange Briefe schreiben
und wird in den Alleen hin und her
unruhig wandern, wenn die Blätter treiben.

(Lord: it is time. The summer was too long. Lay your shadow across the
sundials, and let loose the winds upon the meadows. // Bid the last fruits to

be full; give them two more southerly days, urge them on to fullness and chase the final sweetness into the heavy wine. // Whoever has no house already will build none now. Whoever is now alone will long remain so, will waken, read, write long letters, and in the lanes will restlessly wander, here and there, while the leaves blow about.)

Anyway, only a very small selection, to be sure. For what it's worth, my favorite poem about autumn, I think — and the one with which I shall close — is Blake's "To Autumn": a very early piece, practically a *juvenilium*, and largely devoid of the peculiar magic of his later, more hermetic verse. Of course, there is the characteristic transformation of its subject into an allegorical persona, which — along with a few other details — marks it as distinctively Blakean (but only just). As for why I would place it first in my affections, it is difficult to say. One never really knows why some poems affect one more than others of arguably equal or superior quality. The diction is a bit rough, even for Blake, and the scansion is somewhat thorny. But it captures something otherwise ineffable in the way the fall feels to me, especially in its personification of the season as a figure who is essentially (in the most proper sense of the word) jovial.

O Autumn, Laden with fruit, and stain'd
With the blood of the grape, pass not, but sit
Beneath my shady roof; there thou may'st rest,
And tune thy jolly voice to my fresh pipe,
And all the daughters of the year shall dance!
Sing now the lusty song of fruits and flowers.

"The narrow bud opens her beauties to
The sun, and love runs in her thrilling veins;
Blossoms hang round the brows of Morning, and
Flourish down the bright cheek of modest Eve,
Till clust'ring Summer breaks forth into singing,
And feather'd clouds strew flowers round her head.

"The spirits of the air live in the smells
Of fruit; and Joy, with pinions light, roves round
The gardens, or sits singing in the trees."
Thus sang the jolly Autumn as he sat,
Then rose, girded himself, and o'er the bleak
Hills fled from our sight; but left his golden load.

# SEVEN

# Imprisoned

This is, in a sense, a footnote or an addendum to a column I wrote in 2009 for *First Things Online* called "The Gnostic Turn."

For my sins, I suppose, I subjected myself last week to all six hours (counting commercials) of the AMC-ITV "remake" of the late 1960s television series *The Prisoner*. To persons *d'un certain âge*, there should be little need to explain what the original series was. Somewhat dated in some of its features now, perhaps, and not to everyone's taste, it was probably — at its best — the most perfectly realized fantasy ever to appear within the deadening confines of episodic television drama.

Conceived by, occasionally written and directed by, and starring the Anglo-American actor Patrick McGoohan (born in New York, raised in Ireland and England, he lived his later years in California), *The Prisoner* was the seventeen-episode tale of a recently resigned secret agent's abduction and imprisonment in a surreal community called the Village, governed by some mysterious power on one side or other of the Cold War, or perhaps on both sides, or perhaps on neither (we never find out really). It is a community that values and ruthlessly enforces social, mental, and civic conformity, and whose inhabitants have no names, but only numbers assigned to them from above. The protagonist of the tale — called simply "Number 6" throughout — has been brought to the Village, at least putatively, so that his captors can learn why he left the secret service; he, however, refuses to divulge anything; and the drama from week to week consists mostly in the attempts of the community's leader, Number 2 (played by a different actor almost every episode), to overcome Number 6's resistance, on the orders of the unseen Number 1.

Actually, lest I give a false impression of my age, I should note that I was only four (if I have the dates right) when *The Prisoner* first aired on American TV. My brothers — both of whom are considerably older than I, and even now hobbling into contented senility — got far more from it on its first run. My earliest recollections of the program all center around Rover, the large white rubber bubble (a mechanism or organism of some sort) that chases down and nearly asphyxiates those who attempt to escape the Village. It was only in subsequent airings during the 1970s that the series made a deeper impression on me. But from fairly early on I was able to recognize the allegory at the heart of the story. The Village was, primarily if not exclusively, a satire upon the modern world. The various attempts of its masters to bend Number 6 to their will almost all depend upon the manipulation of the principal forces of conformity by which the contemporary world — at least, seen from a healthily paranoid perspective — functions: politics, psychology, advertising, drugs, and so forth. And Number 6 represents the indomitable — if not necessarily victorious — sovereign soul, captive but raging in its chains, but also perhaps (it is hinted at the end) a collaborator in its own imprisonment.

Much of the program reflected both the intellectual stance and personality of its creator. Patrick McGoohan was a very likable but fairly flinty soul, by all accounts, with a gift for playing characters with a very sharp edge; he was also a believing Catholic with a deep streak of Christian humanism in his vision of reality, whose moral convictions were firm and nonnegotiable. An old story says that he turned down the role of James Bond because he objected to a "hero" whose chief accomplishments were killing and copulating at random. His most famous character before Number 6 was John Drake (who, incidentally, may actually be the same character as Number 6), the protagonist of *Danger Man* (or, as it was called in this country, *Secret Agent*), far and away the most intelligent entry in the fanciful espionage genre of the sixties; and it is remarkable now, when one reviews that program, that its central character — a handsome man in a dangerous line of work — is entirely devoid of any impulse toward brutality or promiscuity. And yet, for many of us who came of age watching him, McGoohan was the very quintessence of what it was to be cool.

Anyway, this is a very roundabout way of getting to my more immediate subject, which is last week's miniseries, in which Jim Caviezel played "6" and Ian McKellen "2" (in this version, the same character throughout). My interest in the program is that of a cultural pathologist only. As a piece of entertainment or a work of fiction, it was utterly and irredeemably dreadful. Told in a willfully incoherent fashion, of the sort that film-school graduates mistake for artistic, and culminating in an altogether annoying conclusion, its principal flaw was that it was excruciatingly dull. The first virtue of the original series, which continues to recommend it even to those who are indifferent to its moral allegory, was that its individual episodes were — with a few exceptions only — extremely diverting in their sheer cleverness, with in each case a well-crafted plot inevitably ending in an ingenious twist. By contrast, the new version was a dreary amble alongside an entirely uninteresting and diffuse lead character through a series of disconnected and tedious situations, whose narrative and moral logic was impossible to discern, or at any rate too boring to be worth trying to discern.

What was interesting, however, were certain of the ideas that inspired — but were never properly realized in — the story. In this telling of the tale, the allegory has become consciously Gnostic. The Village, as it turns out in the end, is not some actual place in our world, but a realm deep within the layers of the subconscious, created or discovered by a dreaming woman who has the power of drawing the subconscious selves of other persons into its meshes. Its purpose is a kind of psychotherapy, by which imperfect or damaged persons in this world are repaired through being captured, strictly controlled, and re-created from within. Its coercions and terrors are all guided by some great moral rationale, as conceived by Mr. Curtis (the terrestrial original of "2") and his wife, the dreamer who holds the inner realm together.

The Gnostic themes, moreover, are not hidden. It is made clear that the Village contains two sorts of persons: those born there, who can never leave because it is their only home, and those who come from the other world, "up there," who cannot remember their true home but who nevertheless often long for escape. The secondary world in which the action occurs is in some sense illusory, the work of the demiurgic "2," who insists that there is no other world beyond the Village, and his wife, the dreaming Sophia who first descended into the previously unexplored abyss of the deep unconscious; in another sense, it is entirely real, as it has the power to contain within itself the inmost personalities (or souls) of those whom it has ensnared — or whom it has rescued, perhaps. There is even a brief harrowing-of-hell scene, very badly done, as well as a vision of the underlying nothingness (the Gnostic *kenoma*) above which the illusory world of the Village is suspended. And then, what's more . . .

Well, actually there is not much more. It was boring to watch and it is boring to recount. Having gotten hold of a number of Gnostic motifs, the writer of the program (Bill Gallagher) seems not to have known how to do anything interesting with them. Instead, the story simply stumbles toward a faintly nihilistic ending in which Michael (the terrestrial original of Number 6) is convinced by Mr. Curtis to take his place and to keep the Village running. Curtis does this by playing upon Michael's compassion, showing him how hopelessly psychologically wounded one of the characters from the Village is in this world, and how impossible it would be to save her from her suffering if she were taken out of the Village. And so, at the end, Number 6 becomes Number 2, or becomes Number 1 (one or the other), and at the end takes control of Curtis's organization in this world while also taking over the supervision of the Village in the other. And this despite the fact that Number 2 is not only a ruthless tyrant in the world of the Village, but is also — we learn, or seem to learn — quite willing to kill people in this world to keep his operation going.

This may be intended as tragedy, or as irony, or as realism; it is hard to say, because one does not care about any of the characters in this version of the story, so one cannot sustain the effort of thinking about them for very long. What is disquieting about this particular denouement, however, is that one cannot be certain that, for the writer, this was not simply the corner into which he had painted himself. The Gnostic elements in the allegory were always there *in nuce* in the original series, perhaps (and were occasionally quite explicit, as in the very best episode of all, "Dance of the Dead"), but were made intelligible by the essentially humanist (by which I mean Christian humanist) protest at the core of the story, the absolute and bloody-minded refusal of Patrick McGoohan to concede any moral ground to the forces of dehumanizing conventionality, even (and especially) those that represented themselves as therapeutic. The original version of *The Prisoner* started from the exhilarating moral certitude that there is something inviolable in the soul worth jealously preserving against the temptations of a world that all too easily dulls the conscience and offers comfortable conformity in place of spiritual liberty. Its ending involved certain moral and narrative ambiguities, but it left one with a sense of moral victory all the same, because it seemed to insist, against various modern social pieties, that it is better to be a broken and suffering person than a contented and functioning number: better the fallen image of God than a fully working part of the system.

I am not at all sure, however, that the new version presents us with difficult questions or ambiguous answers, rather than confused answers to foolish questions. At the end of the tale, Number 6 seems to have been converted to the position that the Village is not ideal, but may have to do until a better way of fixing people comes along, and until then it is a project that can perhaps be conducted in the right way. Perhaps we are meant to see this as a defeat, a final moral subversion of our main character, a bitter comment on the temptation to play God for the sake of others — the final and most irresistible temptation of the noble heart — but that is not the impression one gets. It is just as plausible to see this way of ending the story as a reflection of the uncertainty of its writer's position. Once a therapeutic purpose has been established for the Village, how precisely can one reject the Village as a whole? After all, if it succeeds in knitting together certain broken souls, it might well be a defective but necessary corrective to a suffering world. If McGoohan's Number 6 represented an ultimate rejection of the therapeutic, come hell or high water, this new Number 6 may very well represent a complete uncertainty regarding what true liberty or true personality is, and what the relation between the individual and society ought to be, and whether human suffering might best be cured by subjection to the regime of the therapeutic. At the end of the original series, Number 6 destroys the Village; at the end of this revisionist version, he rescues the Village from destruction. Then again, maybe I am mistaken and the whole thing is meant as a delightful Origenist allegory, from which one should conclude that this world is in fact a place of therapy for fallen souls, to prepare them to return to the divine. Really, one can read it in any number of ways. But, again, as I have already indicated, one really does not care all that much by the end. Before one can be moved to deep reflection by a story, the story must succeed *as* a story.

That said, the experience of watching the program — punctuated howsoever it was by my frequent expostulations of "Why the hell am I watching this?" — did leave me with one observation and one question. The observation is simply the one that I made in my earlier column at some length: that the return of the Gnostic imagination is in some sense an inevitable circumstance for us, in our disenchanted world, and this should tell us something both about the nature of spiritual yearning and about the nature of the world in which we are now obliged to explore that yearning. The question, though, which I find slightly disquieting, and which does not presuppose any particular conclusions regarding the intentions of the writer of the miniseries, is whether it is possible for Gnostic discontent to coexist peaceably with a certain degree of nihilistic resignation: That is, can the sense that we are imprisoned in a world that defies the aspirations of the soul lead naturally toward a decision for reconciliation with that world and suppression of the soul's aspirations — or, more simply, a decision against salvation and for therapy? I mean, is this a genuine imaginative and moral possibility? And, I suppose, all things considered, that it is.

# EIGHT

# The Sanest of Men

We are now a few weeks into the Chinese New Year (a year of the tiger, elementally specified as metal, metaphysically specified as *yang*), and this seems a fairly auspicious time to pay tribute to one of my favorite of Chinese culture's immortals: the great poet T'ao Ch'ien (AD 365–427), also known by his birth name, T'ao Yüanming. Revered as the father of the high tradition of Chinese poetry, T'ao is also regarded as something of a great sage, and has been claimed, at various times, by Confucian, Taoist, and Ch'an (Zen) traditions (and the last even though he was not a Buddhist). Popular legend even occasionally names him as one of the figures in the iconic image of the Three Laughing Sages, sometimes as the Confucian, sometimes as the Taoist; and some scholars of Chinese Buddhism accord him an absolutely seminal importance in the evolution of the peculiar sensibility of Zen. All of which, I suspect, he would have thought rather silly.

T'ao was not a prolific writer; he left behind only a small collection of verse, a few short essays, and a single letter written to his son. In his own day his poetry was scarcely noticed. But the great efflorescence of Chinese poetic culture during the Tang and Sung dynasties sprang, in large part, from the rediscovery of T'ao, both as a poet and as an ideal. The greatest writers of China's poetic golden age regarded him as the absolute virtuoso of "the natural voice," almost magically able to combine the subtle and the simple in verse that was most lyrical precisely where it appeared least adorned. "On the outside," remarked the great Sung poet Su Shi (Su Tung-p'o), "it is withered, but on the inside abundant. It seems plain, and yet is truly beautiful." It was T'ao, more perhaps than anyone else, who bequeathed to classical Chinese literature its most central aesthetic values: immediacy, limpidity, and a veneration of nature.

All of this is cause enough to celebrate the man. My own reason for calling attention to T'ao just at the moment, however, is my firm conviction that he may have been simply one of the sanest human beings who ever lived.

I want to be clear here. Sanity is not sanctity (indeed, the latter often requires the forfeit of the former), and T'ao was neither a saint nor a mystic; his wisdom, which was deep, was nevertheless of a thoroughly earthly and ordinary variety. He scrupulously avoided, in fact, the only path of spiritual liberation on offer in his day. Hui Yüan, the Buddhist abbot of Lu Mountain, was so anxious to win T'ao over that he even allowed wine (the poet's one notorious weakness) to be served on monastery grounds; but, while T'ao was happy to drain his cup when visiting the monks, he still declined to embrace the *dharma*. He was temperamentally averse to asceticism or inflexible regimens, and he valued the joys of family and household far above the prospect of a salvation so laboriously won.

Which is very much to my point. The essence of mental and spiritual health is, after all, to care deeply about a very few, particularly precious, and intimately familiar things, and to regard the rest of reality with generous indifference. Of course, if everyone were sane, in this sense, nothing would ever get done — which would, I suppose, be a bad thing. We seem to have some need, for instance, for politicians, at least under our current system. Considered rationally, however, only a person who is somewhat deranged could ever possibly care enough about politics to want to participate in its processes; anyone able to read a piece of legislation with interest is already a tad demented, and anyone willing to write a piece of legislation clearly suffers from a minor obsessive psychosis. So, God bless them, but God spare us their derangement.

T'ao was entirely devoid of whatever spiritual malady or degeneracy of the soul it is that makes certain persons ambitious for political office. In fact, he assumed the cognomen Ch'ien — "Recluse" — in middle age precisely to give notice that he would never resume any of the official responsibilities or titles that had occasionally been thrust upon him as a younger man, both by the accidents of his birth and by the exigencies of poverty. Born of a distinguished family of classically educated Confucian scholars, trained to serve in the administrative class of the Middle Kingdom, he preferred farming; but for many years he could not make his farm solvent.

At the age of twenty-nine, he reluctantly took up a post in his local provincial government, near Hsün-yang; but bureaucracy and the intolerably deferential protocols of office soon drove him back to his farm. Financial necessity forced him again into public service from 395 to 400, but he again fled home in 401 and managed for a while to wring a bearable subsistence from the soil. In 405, however, an injury made the exertions of farming too difficult, and friends prevailed on him to return to public service. So he accepted the position of government magistrate in P'eng-tse.

He held this, his last government post, for a tenure of only eighty days. Soon after taking up his seal of office, he dictated that all the government fields in his jurisdiction be planted exclusively with glutinous rice used for making wine (though his wife soon convinced him to plant a sixth of the fields with a comestible variety instead). Otherwise, he discharged his responsibilities conscientiously, but not avidly; and he still could not bend his nature to official ceremony. When his assistant one day informed him he would have to fasten up his girdle to pay his respects to a visiting government inspector, T'ao groaned and remarked that he would not bow and scrape to some oaf just to earn a few bushels of rice. That same day, he resigned.

Thereafter, for more than twenty years, he politely refused every entreaty to return to public life, and devoted himself only to what he loved: farming, poetry (which, he said, he wrote only for his own amusement), the perennial cycles of the natural world, the transitory music of familial affection, and wine. Everything else he did his best to ignore. He chose obscurity over preeminence, poverty over wealth, and family over society. He was, the records report, almost boundlessly contented. In those years, he was not a sociable man, but there was no one whose society was more eagerly sought. One of his friends, just for the pleasure of his company, once even laid a "honeyed" trap for him — a table decked with cups and a flagon of wine, set up along a path where T'ao often walked — knowing that this was the only thing that could detain the poet for more than a few moments.

The virtue that T'ao ultimately refined to utmost perfection was *hsien*, "idleness." Not "laziness," that is (farming is no occupation for the indolent), but rather a condition of deep peacefulness and interior quietude. *Hsien* is not exactly detachment, since it flows most properly from genuine attachment to the right things, nor is it any kind of spiritual austerity. It is simply an inability to be agitated by trifles or distracted by irrational appetites, and the sublime capacity for total contentment in doing nothing when nothing is what needs to be done.

Around this still center within himself, this abiding *hsien*, T'ao cultivated a character that was gentle but never mawkish or servile, humorous but never cruel, proud but never arrogant or pompous, and sensualist but never depraved or avaricious. He made room for his appetites (which were moderate) without being enslaved by them. He could certainly drink too much now and then, but usually drank only enough to bedizen the world with an amiable glow. And he was blessed with a deep and sympathetic kindness. His one surviving letter rather touchingly enjoins his son to be kind to a peasant boy who works on the farm, "for he too is someone's son."

In any event, for all that he craved rustic obscurity, T'ao ultimately became one of the indispensable pillars supporting the "gold and jade palace" of Chinese cultural identity. Indeed, but for his want of worldly ambition, this would not have happened. He died largely impoverished, but left behind a joyful and inextirpable cultural memory, a particularly delightful pattern of the ideal man, and a small body of perfectly accomplished art; and he was able to do all this because — again — he was so imperturbably and incorrigibly sane.

# NINE

# A Perfect Game

In his later philosophy, Heidegger liked to indulge in eccentric etymologies, because he was certain that there were truths deeply hidden in language that can be discovered only by delving down into the roots of certain words. It is one of the more beguilingly magical aspects of his thought, and therefore — to my mind — one of the more convincing. Consider, for instance, the wonderful ambiguity one finds in the word "invention" when one considers its derivation. The Latin *invenire* means principally "to find," "to encounter," or (literally) "to come upon." Only secondarily does it mean "to create" or "to originate." And even in English, where the secondary sense has now entirely displaced the primary, the word retained this dual connotation right through the seventeenth century.

This pleases me for two reasons. The first is that, as an instinctive Platonist, I naturally believe that every genuine act of human creativity is simultaneously an innovation and a discovery, a marriage of poetic craft and contemplative vision, which captures traces of eternity's radiance in fugitive splendors here below by translating our tacit knowledge of the eternal forms into finite objects of reflection, at once strange and strangely familiar. The second is that the word's ambiguity helps me to formulate my intuitions regarding the ultimate importance of baseball.

Stay with me here.

I occasionally find myself wondering what the final tally of America's contribution to civilization will be once the nation has passed away (as, of course, it must). Which of our *inventions* will endure intact and continue to astonish the children of future ages? We shall, of course, have made our contributions to political philosophy, technology, literature, music, the plastic and performing arts, cuisine, and so on. But how much of these can we claim as our native inventions, rather than merely our peculiar variations on traditions that long antedate the country? And how many will persist in a pure form, rather than being subsumed into future developments? Jazz, perhaps, but will it continue on as a living tradition in its own right, or simply be remembered as a particular period or phase in the history of Western music, like the baroque or Romanticism?

My hope, when all is said and done, is that we will be remembered chiefly as the people who invented — who devised and thereby also, for the first time, discovered — the perfect game, the very Platonic ideal of organized sport, the "moving image of eternity" *in athleticis*. I think that would be a grand posterity. I know there are those who will accuse me of exaggeration when I say this, but until baseball appeared, humanity was a sad and benighted lot, lost in the labyrinth of matter, dimly and achingly aware of something incandescently beautiful and unattainable, something infinitely desirable shining up above in the empyrean of the ideas; but, throughout most of the history of the race, no culture was able to produce more than a shadowy sketch of whatever glorious mystery prompted those nameless longings.

The coarsest and most common of these sketches — which has gone through numerous variations down the centuries without conspicuous improvement — is what I think of as "the oblong game," a contest played out on a rectangle between two sides, each attempting to penetrate the other's territory in order to deposit some small object in the other's goal or end zone. All the sports built on this paradigm require considerable athletic prowess, admittedly, and each has its special tactics, of a limited and martial kind; but all of them are no more than crude, faltering lurches toward the archetype, entertaining perhaps, but appealing more to the beast within us than to the angel.

In a few, peculiarly favored lands, more refined and inspired adumbrations of the ideal appeared. The Berbers of Libya produced *Ta Kurt om el mahag*, and the British blessed the world with cricket; but the running game in both is played between just two poles, and so neither can properly mirror the eternal game's exquisite geometries, flowing grace, and sidereal beauties. And then there is that extended British family of children's games from which baseball drew its basic morphology (stoolball, tut-ball, and, of course, rounders); but these are only charming finger-paint renderings of the ideal, vague and glittering dreams that the infant soul brings with it in its descent from the world above before the oblivion of adulthood purges them from memory; they are as inchoately remote from the real thing as a child's first steps are from ballet. In the end, only America succeeded in plucking the flower from the fields of eternity and making a garden for it here on earth. What greater glory could we possibly crave?

YOU NEED NOT SMIRK. I admit that my rhetoric might seem a bit excessive, but be fair: something about the game elicits excess. I am hardly the first aficionado of baseball who has felt that somehow it demands a "thick" metaphysical — or even religious — explanation. For one thing, there is the haunting air of necessity that hangs about it, which seems so difficult to reconcile with its relatively recent provenance. It feels as if the game has always been with us. It requires a whole constellation of seemingly bizarre physical and mental skills that, through countless barren millennia, were not only unrealized but also *unsuspected* potencies of human nature, silently awaiting the formal cause from beyond that would make them actual. So much of what a batter, pitcher, or fielder does is astonishingly improbable, and yet — it turns out — entirely natural. Clearly baseball was always intended in our very essence; without it, our humanity was incomplete. Willie Mays was an avatar of the divine capacities that lie within our animal frames. Bob Feller's fastball was Jovian lightning at the command of mortal clay.

And there is something equally fateful, as has been so often noted, in the exact fittingness of the game's dimensions: the ninety feet between bases, the sixty and a half feet between the pitching rubber and the plate, that precious third of a second in which a batter must decide whether to swing. Everything is so perfectly calibrated that almost every play is a matter of the most unforgiving precision; a ball correctly played in the infield is almost always an out, while the slightest misplay usually results in a man on base. The effective difference in velocity between a fastball and a changeup is infinitesimal in neurological terms, and yet it can utterly disrupt the timing of even the best hitter. There are Pythagorean enigmas here, occult and imponderable: mystic proportions written into the very fabric of nature, of which we were once as ignorant as of the existence of other galaxies.

How, moreover, could anyone have imagined (and yet how could we ever have failed to know) that so elementary a strategic problem as serially advancing or prematurely stopping the runner could generate such a riot of intricate tactical possibilities in any given instant of play? Part of the deeper excitement of the game is following how the strategy is progressively altered, from pitch to pitch, cumulatively and prospectively, in accordance with both the situation of the inning and the balance of the game. Comparing baseball to even the most complex versions of the oblong game is like comparing chess to tiddlywinks.

And surely some account has to be given of the drama of baseball: the way it reaches down into the soul's abysses with its fluid alternations of prolonged suspense and shocking urgency, its mounting rallies, its thwarted ventures, its intolerable tensions, its suddenly exhilarating or devastating peripeties. Even the natural narrative arc of the game is in three acts — the early, middle, and late innings — each with its own distinct potentials and imperatives. And because, until the final out is recorded, no loss is an absolute *fait accompli*, the torment of hope never relents. Victory may or may not come in a blaze of glorious elation, but every defeat, when it comes, is sublime. The oblong game is war, but baseball is Attic tragedy.

ALL THIS POINTS beyond the game's physical dimensions, toward its immense spiritual horizons. When I consider baseball *sub specie aeternitatis*, I find it impossible not to conclude that its essential metaphysical structure is thoroughly idealist. After all, the game is so utterly saturated by infinity. All its configurations and movements aspire to the timeless and the boundless. The oblong game is pitilessly finite: wholly concerned as it is with conquest and shifting lines of force, it is exactly and inviolably demarcated, spatially and temporally; having no inner unfolding narrative of its own, it does not end, but is merely curtailed, externally, by a clock (even overtime is composed only of strictly apportioned, discrete units of time).

Baseball, however, has no clock; rather, terrestrial time is entirely subordinate to its inner intervals and rhythms. And, although the dimensions of the diamond are invariable, there are no fixed measures for the placement of the outfield walls. What would be a soaring home run to dead center in St. Louis falls languidly short in Detroit, like a hawk slain in midflight. A blow that would clear the bleachers at Wrigley Field is transformed into a single by the icy irony of Fenway's left field wall, while a drowsy fly ball earns four bases. Even within a single park — Yankee Stadium, for instance — there is an often capricious disproportion between the two power alleys.

All these variations, all these hints of arbitrariness, are absolutely crucial to the aesthetics and moral metaphysics of the game, because they remind us that fair territory is in fact conceptually limitless, and extends endlessly beyond any outfield walls. Home plate is an open corner on the universe, and the limits we place upon the game's endless vistas are merely the accommodation we strike between infinite possibility and finite actuality. They apprise us, yet again, that life is ungovernable and pluriform, and that *omnia mutantur et nos mutamur in illis*. They speak both of our mortality (which obeys no set pattern or term) and of the eternity into which the horizons of consciousness are always vanishing (the primordial orientation of all embodied spirit). And something similar is true of the juncture of infield and outfield, where metaphysics' deepest problem — the dialectical opposition but necessary interrelation of the finite and the infinite — is given unsurpassable symbolic embodiment.

Now, when I speak of baseball's "idealism," it is principally Platonism I have in mind: Greek rather than German idealism. But I have to admit that many of the aspects of the game I have just mentioned seem to speak not only of the finite's power to reflect the infinite, but of a kind of fated, heroic human striving *against* the infinite. There are few spectacles in sport as splendid and pitiable as the batter defiantly poised before all that endless openness. We know that even the most majestic home run is as nothing in such vastness, but this somehow lends a far more moving grandeur to those rare Homeric feats that linger on in our collective memory: Babe Ruth in Detroit in 1926, Frank Howard in Philadelphia in 1958, Mickey Mantle in New York in 1963, Frank Robinson in Baltimore in 1966, and so on.

No other game, moreover, is so mercilessly impossible to play well, or affords so immense a scope for inevitable failure. We all know that a hitter who succeeds in only one-third of his at bats is considered remarkable, and that one who succeeds only fractionally more often is considered a prodigy of nature. Now here, certainly, is a portrait of the hapless human spirit in all its melancholy grandeur, and of the human will in all its hopeless but incessant aspiration: fleeting glory as the rarely ripening fruit of overwhelming and chronic defeat. It is this pervasive sadness that makes baseball's moments of bliss so piercing, this encircling gloom that sheds such iridescent beauty on those impossible triumphs over devastating odds — so amazing when accomplished by one of the game's gods (Mays running down that ridiculously long fly at the Polo Grounds in the 1954 World Series, Ted Williams going deep in his very last appearance at the plate), and so heartbreakingly poignant when accomplished by a journeyman whose entire playing career will be marked by only one such instant of transcendence (Ron Swoboda's diving catch off Brooks Robinson's bat in the 1969 Series).

Really, the game has such an oddly desolate beauty to it. Maybe it is the grindingly long 162-game season, which allows for so many promising and disheartening plotlines to take shape only to dissolve again along the way, and which sustains even the most improbable hope past any rational span; or maybe it is simply the course of the cosmic seasons, from early spring into midautumn: nature's perennial allegory of human life, eloquent of innocent confidence slowly transformed into wise resignation. Whatever it is, there is something of twilight in the game, something sadder and more lyrical than one can quite express. It even ends in the twilight of the year: all its many stories culminate in one last prolonged struggle in the gathering darkness, from which one team alone emerges briefly victorious, after so long a journey, and then everything lapses into wintry stillness, hope defeated, the will exhausted, O dark, dark, dark, all passion spent, silent as the moon, and so on. And yet, with the first rumor of spring, the idiot will is revived, the *conatus essendi* stirs out of the darkness, *tanha* awakens and pulls us back into the illusory world of hope and longing, and the cycle resumes.

All that said, though, one should not mistake the passing moods that the game evokes for the deeper metaphysical truths it discloses; one must not confuse tone color with the guiding theme. Ultimately, baseball's philosophical grammar truly is Platonist, with all the transcendental elations that that implies. This is most obvious in the sheer purity of its central action. In form, it is not a conflict between two teams over contested ground; in fact, the two sides never directly confront one another on the field, and there is no territory to be captured. Rather, in shape it is that most perfect of metaphysical figures: the closed circle. It repeats the great story told by every idealist metaphysics, European and Indian alike: the purifying odyssey of *exitus* and *reditus*, *diastole* and *systole*, departure from and ultimate return to an abiding principle. What could be more obvious? The game is plainly an attempt to figure forth the "heavenly dance" within the realm of mutability; when play is in its full flow, the diamond becomes a place where the dark, sullen surface of matter is temporarily transformed into a gently luminous mirror of the "supercelestial mysteries." Baseball is an instance of what the later Neoplatonists called "theurgy": a mimetic or prophetic rite that summons (or invites) the divine graciously to descend from eternity and to grant a glimpse of itself within time. No — seriously.

I AM NOT NEARLY as certain, however, that baseball can be said to have any discernible religious meaning. Or, rather, I am not sure whether it reflects exclusively one kind of creed (it is certainly *religious*, through and through). Its metaphysics is equally compatible and equally incompatible with the sensibilities of any number of faiths, and of any number of schools within individual faiths; but, if it has anything resembling a theology, it is of the mystical rather than the dogmatic kind, and its doctrinal content is nebulous. At its lowest, most cultic level, baseball is hospitable to such a variety of little superstitions and local pieties that it almost qualifies as a kind of primitive animism or paganism. At its highest, more speculative level, it tends toward the monist, as a consistent idealism must.

In between these two levels, however, the possibilities of religious interpretation are numberless, and it may require the eyes of many kinds of faith to see all of them. My friend R. R. Reno sees a bunt down the first base line, in which the infield rotates clockwise while the runner begins his counterclockwise motion, as a clear evocation of Ezekiel's vision of the divine chariot's living wheels, and so an invitation to *merkabah* mysticism. A Buddhist acquaintance from Japan, however, sees every home run as a metaphor for the *arahant* who has successfully crossed the sea of becoming on the raft of *dharma*.

Of course, the mental and physical disciplines of the game are clearly contemplative in nature. No one could, for instance, no matter how fine his eyesight or physical coordination, hit a major league pitch with a cylindrical bat if there were not some prior attunement on his part to the subtle spiritual force that flows through all things, a sort of Zen cultivation of the mindless mind, in which the impossible is accomplished because it somehow simply accomplishes itself in us. Japan's greatest hitter, Sadaharu Oh — whose hitting coach, Hiroshi Arakawa, was a disciple of Morihei Ueshiba, the founder of Aikido — even wrote a book on his discovery of the Zen way of baseball. But there are contemplatives and adepts in all major religious traditions.

One could, I suppose, conclude that baseball is primarily Western in its religious orientation, on the shaky grounds that the game as we know it has a somewhat eschatological logic: within the miniature cosmos of the park, the game must be played down to its final verdict, and cannot end before judgment is passed. No one, I think, doubts that Yogi's most oracular formula, it ain't over till it's over, is a perfectly condensed statement of what for us are the game's highest spiritual and dramatic stakes. And yet the Japanese will play to a draw with equanimity, content at the last simply to let go, so that all forces can reach equilibrium; and I do not believe their version of the game is necessarily any less elegant or profound than ours.

There are, however, at least two respects in which I suppose baseball could be said to speak to, and speak out of, an essentially biblical vision of reality. Firstly, there is simply its undeniable element of Edenic nostalgia: that longing for innocence, guileless play, the terrestrial paradise — a longing that it both evokes and soothes. Bart Giamatti, though, wrote so famously and so well on this topic that I have little to add. I shall only observe that the ballpark is a paradise into which evil does occasionally come, whenever the Yankees are in town, and this occasionally lends the game a cosmic significance that it would not be improper to call "apocalyptic." This, in fact, is why that dastardly franchise is a spiritually necessary part of the game in this country; even Yankees *fans* have their necessary role to play, and — though we may occasionally think of them as "vessels of wrath" — we have to remember that they too are enfolded in the mercy of providence.

And, secondly, the game is, for many of us, a hard tutelage in the biblical virtues of faith, hope, and love. Here, admittedly, I am drawing on personal spiritual experience, but can do so out of a vast reservoir of purgative suffering. My team, you see, is the Baltimore Orioles. In my youth, I was full of wicked pride. The Orioles, for nearly the first two decades of my life, were the envy of the baseball world: winning more games than any other franchise, the only team with a winning record against the Yankees, awash in Gold Gloves and Cy Young Awards, a team that was often said to be "magic." In those days — the days of Frank and Brooks, Powell and Palmer, Blair and Buford, Eddie and the rest — it was almost unimaginable that a season would pass without a pennant race, or that New York would not tremble before us.

And now?

These — and I shall close on this thought — are the great moral lessons that only a game with baseball's long season and long history and dramatic intensity can impress upon the soul: humility, long-suffering, dauntless love, and inexhaustible faith in the face of invincible misfortune. I could no more abandon my Orioles now than I could repudiate my family, or my native heath, or my own childhood — even though I know it is a devotion that right now brings only grief. I know, I know: Orioles fans have not yet suffered what Boston fans suffered for more than twice the term of Israel's wanderings in the wilderness, or what Cubs fans have suffered for more than a century; but we have every reason to expect that we will. And yet we go on. The time of tribulation is upon us, and we now must make our way through its darkness guided only by the waning lights of memory and the flickering flame of hope, not knowing when the night will end, but sustained by the sacred assurance that whosoever perseveres to the end *shall* be saved.

# TEN

## Julian Our Contemporary

When he died from a spear wound in June AD 363, while on campaign in Persia, the emperor Julian was only thirty-two years old. His reign as Augustus had lasted just nineteen months. His great project to restore the ancient faith of the "Hellenes" and to turn back the inexorable advance of the "Galilean" religion perished with him; what some had briefly hoped might be the first stirrings of a glorious revival of perennial truth now turned out to have been only the last spasm of a dying age. If anything, his reforms only hastened the Christianization of imperial culture, by inaugurating a new and anxious epoch of politically imposed religious uniformity. Objectively speaking, then, Julian's reign was at most a minor episode, poignantly and flickeringly ephemeral, leaving nothing of permanent significance behind — a momentary stammer in history's verdict, meriting little attention. And yet, perhaps precisely because he stands out as so fruitless an anomaly in the narrative of Western history, he continues to exercise a rare fascination over historians, philosophers, theologians, and artists (to take nothing away from his considerable personal gifts).

For the Christians of late antiquity and the Middles Ages, of course, he was the great "Apostate," a sort of vicar of Satan on earth. The sort of restrained admiration for him one finds in a few antique Christian writers was soon swept away by lurid legends of Julian the sorcerer, who tore out children's hearts or ripped fetuses from their mothers' wombs in order to perform feats of black magic; or of Julian the demoniac, who pledged himself to the devil in exchange for worldly dominion; or of Julian the persecutor, steeped in the blood of the martyrs. For certain Renaissance humanists, on the other hand — Lorenzo de Medici in particular — Julian's enmity to the church was only the unfortunate consequence of those virtues that made him so intelligent, forceful, and estimable a prince. For various playwrights of the Golden Age theater of the late sixteenth and early seventeenth centuries, as well as some of the playwrights in the Jesuit colleges of Germany, he was a kind of tragic hero, deeply deceived of course, but destroyed more by the susceptibilities of a noble nature than by any inclination toward evil. To certain rationalists, *Aufklärer*, and *philosophes* of the eighteenth century, he was philosophy's lonely champion, defiantly raising the torch of reason one last time amid the gathering gloom of the Christian "dark ages." To a few Romantics, he was a proud rebel against the morbid tyrannies of religion. And, in the twentieth century, he became whatever took a writer's fancy: for Nikos Kazantzakis an existentialist knight of the absurd, for Gore Vidal a deeply introspective and sexually adventurous enemy of Christianity's rigors and repressions, and so on.

Of course, Julian did not kill babies or practice goetic magic. Neither was he on speaking terms with the devil. Christians under his reign generally had little cause to fear for their lives. On the other hand, while he was a gifted ruler, his errors of judgment were legion, his hatred of the Christians often degenerated into childish spite, and he was destroyed more by callow egotism than by tragic hubris. Far from being any sort of rationalist, he was a particularly credulous religious enthusiast, who delighted in blood sacrifice, magic, astrology, and mystery; when he tried his hand at philosophy, the results were embarrassing. Not only was he not a rebel against religion's chilly moralism; the faith he preached was notable principally for its joyless austerity. If anything, his sense of the absurd was dangerously underdeveloped. And there is a great likelihood that he died a virgin. Of course, had he lived longer, time's slow levigations might have burnished his virtues and worn away at his vices; but the record is not encouraging on that score. During his year and a half in power, his malice toward the "Galileans" increased the more his pagan revival faltered, and his measures against the younger faith, official and unofficial, became increasingly vindictive; he even had two soldiers executed for refusing to remove the Christian *labarum* from their standards. His treatment of cities that did not, to his mind, appreciate him adequately — such as Caesarea and Antioch — was marked by petulance and cruelty. In his final months, moreover, deluding himself that he was a second Alexander, he rejected Persia's embassy of peace and led an invasion that was as pointless as it was unwinnable. By the end, despair had made him capriciously cruel; he even ordered the decimation of three cavalry squadrons whose only crime was that they had lost a few men in an ambush.

Having said all this, however, I have to admit that I myself am one of those who find Julian to be an utterly absorbing, and even oddly attractive, personality — for any number of reasons. Chief among them, I suppose, is his sheer naïveté, his obviously earnest belief that he could communicate his deep spiritual fervor to his contemporaries, his certainty that the fire of general pagan devotion could be rekindled with only a little effort. I find it oddly moving. His hatred of Christianity rose out of an always deeper reserve of genuine, guileless affection for the beauty and nobility of the pre-Christian order, and a profound faith in its invincible vitality. There was none of Nietzsche's world-weary viciousness and ironic detachment in him. I find it impossible not to be affected, moreover, by the simple pathos of Julian's protest against what he saw as his culture's progressive abandonment of the traditions that had sustained it from time immemorial. From his giddy eminence, he could look back over countless centuries of civilization, at a history of incomparable achievements in philosophy, the arts, law, warfare, and civil administration. He also could look back to religious customs that mediated between the human and natural orders, that guarded innumerable sacred sites where human and divine stories intermingled, and that bore witness to a cosmos in which, as Thales said, "all things are full of gods." But he could also see, all about him, temples deserted or destroyed, the gods not only forsaken but deprecated as demons, and the entire ethos of the empire slowly melting away. If nothing else, it is a pathos that some might find strangely familiar.

We now also live in the twilight of an ancient civilization, and many of us occasionally deceive ourselves that the course of history can be reversed. Christendom is quite gone, and the Christian culture of the West seems irrevocably destined for slow dissolution. The arts it inspired, the moral grammar it shaped, the shared stories and convictions by which it bound peoples together seem surely to belong to a constantly receding past. So, at the very least, those restive souls who feel some sort of reverence for that civilization — even those prepared to grant all the evils and failures inextricable from its history, and even those who acknowledge the deep corruption of the gospel it entailed — should be able to understand Julian's anxiety, indignation, and implacable hostility toward the "Galileans." Perhaps now, then, having had to suffer the trauma of modernity, both for good and ill, reflective Christians might be prepared to recognize that strange, compelling, and rather deluded man — Christian history's most notorious "apostate" — as someone who, as best he could, strove to "keep the faith."

# ELEVEN

# Eschatology as Entertainment

King K'inich Kan Bahlum II reigned in Baalak from AD 685 until his death in 702. Like his father before him, the great K'inich Janaab Pakal, he was responsible for many of the most glorious architectural and artistic achievements of Mayan civilization's "classical period," including the completion of the great pyramidal Temple of Inscriptions in Palenque, on one of whose walls he left a legend predicting that his dynasty would last until 21 October 4772. I have always been impressed by the absolute precision of these old Mayan prophecies, I have to say: never any vague predictions of nameless catastrophes occurring at uncertain hours — "In the time of great sorrow, when the moon is in the third house and the curlew's nest is empty, a dark fortune will descend upon the house of Tarquinio" or anything like that — but only exactly dated auguries of specific events. Of course, I would be considerably more impressed if, in addition to their precision, they had occasionally exhibited some tendency toward accuracy (which, alas, turns out not to have been the case). Kan Bahlum's dynasty, for instance, died out sometime in the early ninth century. We need not quibble, though — and what's four millennia here or there, anyway? — because the most interesting thing about Kan Bahlum's prophecy is that it refers to an event that will occur exactly 2,759 years and ten months *after* 21 December 2012, which is supposedly the day on which, by the reckoning of the Mayan long calendar, the current "Great Cycle" of 5,125 years (which began in 3114 BC) will reach its end. And the reason this is so interesting is that we have just recently entered a period of popular fascination with this date, or at least with the year 2012, which will almost certainly become more intense over the next thirty-six months or so. According to any number of recent books, articles, television programs, and viral videos, as well as one particularly cretinous film, this is when the classical age Mayans predicted the world will end, or at least suffer a cataclysm of such enormous proportions that the vast majority of life on earth will perish. And yet here was Kan Bahlum, ever the sunny optimist, it seems, confidently asserting that his family's reign in Palenque would continue on unbroken for better than twenty-seven centuries beyond that mark.

There is no mystery here, really. The truth of the matter is that the ancient Mayans understood 2012 as the terminal year not of the cosmos or the planet, but of a calendrical rotation. There is clear evidence that they did indeed regard every transition from one Great Cycle to another as something quite momentous, with some greater mystical or cosmic significance, but they certainly did not see it as ushering in the end of time. In fact, the Mayans do not seem to have had any real concept of the end of time. Rather, they had an insatiable predilection for large numbers arranged in magnificently intricate mathematical schemes, as well as an equally insatiable fascination with astronomy; and these two appetites in combination produced marvelous and fantastical myths and monuments and vaticinations, all embraced within a vision of time as a kind of endless epochal spiral, rather like Yeats's system of "gyres," but on a far greater order of magnitude. For them, as for other Mesoamerican cultures of pre-Christian times — such as the Aztec, Toltec, and, more distantly, Hopi — time was apparently conceived as a complex system of circles, but not circles of total cosmic recurrence of the sort one finds in Stoicism or certain schools of Platonism or Hinduism. The Mayans appear rather to have thought in terms of a regular, natural, and continuous succession of distinct aeons, each with its own special character, and each leading to the next according to some deep and inscrutable law of spiritual evolution. And the Great Cycles themselves were seen as being contained within other, larger cycles, and those perhaps in larger cycles still, of unimaginably vast duration, and so on indefinitely, all together playing their gyratory roles in the grand, elaborate, circumvolving dance of eternity.

There could scarcely be a more drastic confusion of categories, therefore, than the application of eschatological themes to what is in essence a mythology of perpetual periodic regeneration within natural time. It is probably an inevitable mistake for modern Westerners, however; it is the result of what might be called our "Zoroastrian heritage." At least, according to tradition, it was Zarathustra (who lived, according to the best current estimate, sometime in the eleventh or tenth century BC) who brought about the great divergence in Aryan culture between Persian and Bharatan — or Avestan and Vedic — religion, and who first clearly framed the cosmic narrative that would come in time to dominate all the great faiths of the Near East: the story of a universal struggle between good and evil, light and darkness, God and the devil, played out along the axis of a single linear history, and culminating in a final overthrow of and judgment upon evil, a general restoration of cosmic order, and the arrival of a cosmic savior (or Saoshyant). It was a version of this story, it is generally assumed, that migrated into the Judaism of the postexilic or "Persian" period, producing Jewish apocalyptic literature and sects and giving shape to eschatological expectations that would appear again, with distinctive variations, in Christianity and Islam. But, really, the material history of such eschatological motifs is not very important (and only someone prone to the genetic fallacy could imagine that that history tells us anything regarding the truth or falsehood of eschatological expectations). It simply is the case that for all of us who have been raised within the fold of one of the "Abrahamic" faiths, or at least within a culture formed by such a faith, it seems perfectly natural to think in terms of a last day: of a catastrophic, or redemptive, or catastrophic *and* redemptive, conclusion to the narrative of history and nature as we know them. Our imaginations are haunted by the prospect of a final age of tribulations and terrors — wars and rumors of war, wormwood and fire, desolation and wrath — and at the same time enticed by visions of creation's final restoration, the cessation of worldly suffering, the vindication of virtue, and the inauguration of an endless age of peace and joy.

The pathos of the eschatological, however, is not indigenous only to Near Eastern prophetic religion, or to creeds that think exclusively in terms of the "arrow of time." Many systems of thought that involve some idea of eternal recurrence presume that the end of each cosmic revolution will be announced by an age of decline and depravity, which will grow progressively worse until a final calamity consumes the universe. The last, bleak dawn of each world-age, just before Vishnu wakes from his demiurgic slumbers and everything returns into him again, and the nuptial play (*lila*) of Ishvara with Maya reaches one of its caesuras, is a "Kali Yuga," a brief interval — say, a mere 432,000 years or so — of demonic vice and cosmic degradation, when knowledge of eternal *dharma* will dwindle away, God will be forgotten, evil will run rampant through the earth, wars will multiply, lust and dissipation will go unrestrained, and piety will wither away. And, of course, any mythology of genuine *recurrence* must necessarily presume a periodic annihilation of the cosmic order, so that the cycle can begin anew. Thus, for the Stoics, every Great Year must end in a universal *ekpyrosis*, or conflagration, in which the divine fire that pervades all things resumes the universe into itself again. The conviction or, at any rate, apprehension that "time must have a stop" is part of the common conceptual property of the whole Indo-European world. And that, in itself, explains a great deal regarding certain persistent motifs in the Western popular imagination. It does not, however, explain everything.

I realized this several weeks ago when my young son was deeply disturbed by a two-minute conversation he happened to see on television. The fault was entirely mine: I thought I had turned on one of his beloved nature programs on the National Geographic Channel and had walked away before I realized that I had mistakenly turned to one of those cable channels that specializes in "investigative" programs about UFOs, undiscovered monsters hiding in mountains or forests or inland seas, the Holy Grail, the secret "histories" of the Templars or the Masons, and things of that sort. On this occasion, the topic was the impending extermination of almost all life on earth, scheduled to arrive in 2012, when — or so a pale, angular, ectomorphic, slightly epicene, and rather debauched-looking fellow with an Austrian or Hungarian lisp and a thin, sibilant, phlegmily emphysemic voice was informing us — a vast increase in solar electromagnetic emissions will induce a reversal of the planet's magnetic poles; this will apparently bring about earthquakes of unprecedented scale, tsunamis large enough to inundate entire continents, the collapse of every conventional structure in the inhabited world, and so on (or something like that). When I became aware of my mistake, I switched over to the belugas or penguins or katydids or whatever it was that we were supposed to be watching, but not before my son had been visibly shaken. Ignore this dainty *mitteleuropäisch* degenerate, I told my son; he's just a nasty charlatan spouting lies in order to make a bit of cash by playing on people's anxieties or morbidities. My son already knew this, though; what had bothered him was the weird, sadistic pleasure the odd little goblin seemed to take in prognosticating "such horrible things." Happily, though, the salamanders or eels or elk or whatever they were soon intervened and restored my son to equanimity.

There is a question here worth pondering, though. Why are chiliastic and apocalyptic fantasies such inexhaustible sources of popular entertainment, especially now? What is it that draws us, or a great many of us at least, to the idea of a world shattered and scorched and whelmed by the seas, and to the thought of civilization reduced to savagery in a single day? And, more importantly, why is the prospect of that day's *imminence* one of the most tantalizing elements in these fantasies? Of course, I suppose we would not really be entertained by them very much at all if we really believed them. But, still, there has been such an abundance of post-Armageddon novels, works of "nonfiction," films, television stories, "documentaries," and so forth over the past four or five decades that the whole genre seems now to enjoy the sort of popularity that once attached to westerns or romantic musicals. This is especially true of cinema; since the birth of the nuclear age, there has been a broad and incessant flow of films set in the aftermath of doomsday, usually with some bitter but redoubtable survivor of the cataclysm at its center — Gregory Peck, Ray Milland, Edward Judd, Charlton Heston, Mel Gibson, Will Smith, Viggo Mortensen, Denzel Washington, and on and on — attempting to make his way, alone or at the head of a small troupe of fellow survivors, through the wastes. The larger market for eschatological fantasy, moreover, crosses almost every demographic cultural boundary, albeit with significant variations. For some, the postapocalyptic genre is simply a subcategory of the horror genre, and as such has no grander function than to inspire little macabre thrills of unease or *Schadenfreude*, and is best served up with a generous complement of cannibals, zombies, mutants, or things of that sort. For the more morally serious, it has a graver, more minatory purpose, and should apprise us, as ponderously and as sanctimoniously as possible, that nuclear war, environmental devastation, genocidal pandemics, swarms of omnivorous nano-robots, and dangerous experiments on subatomic particles are very bad things that ought to be avoided on most occasions. Then again, for certain evangelical Christian fundamentalists, "end times" fantasy is a kind of licit pornography, absorbed with unhealthy relish; the deeply perverted *Left Behind* novels are a splendid example of the pathology and its degrading symptoms. And there are other variations as well. But I suspect that, underlying all the superficial differences, some essentially uniform impulse of the imagination is at work, some species of shared desire or fear.

Not to say that I have any clear notion of what exactly it is. It may simply be the result of history, of course. The latter half of the twentieth century was hardly an encouraging period for persons of sanguine temperament; in one sense, our shared visions of the impending eschaton might be nothing more than memories of the recent past allegorically inverted into fabulous premonitions of the near future. And, certainly, the past six or seven decades have given all of us sufficient cause for anxiety regarding the extreme fragility of civilization, and just as much cause to wonder whether civilization still exists in any form other than a residual collection of cultural habits and souvenirs. That, however, explains only the element of collective therapy in these fantasies, not the great pleasure they seem to afford many people (at least, apart from the momentary pleasure of emotional release). Perhaps their appeal reaches down to a more fundamental level, one either more basically physiological or more obscurely metaphysical, or perhaps both at once. One of the few ideas of Freud's that I have ever found remotely interesting — and then, admittedly, more for its poetic than its empirical value — is the notion he developed in *Beyond the Pleasure Principle* of a constant tension in each of us between the will to life and the will to death. Perhaps when we fantasize about the destruction of the world that we know we are merely allowing Thanatos a brief, playful period of predominance over Eros, so that once the crueler god has been served we can return to the task of living temporarily relieved of the restive weight of material existence. Perhaps there really is some sort of primordial agitation at the heart of the experience of finite being that longs for final repose even as it resists extinction, some tension in the organic ferment of animal life between the elation of persistence and the yearning to subside into the peaceful oblivion of inert matter. Or, to borrow Bergson's terminology, perhaps our susceptibility to the allure of apocalypse is just one psychic register of the constant fatigue that our *élan vital* suffers as it strives against lifeless matter's gravity, and a sign of some urge lurking at the physical roots of consciousness to lapse gratefully again into restful nothingness.

On the other hand, the popularity of eschatological fables may, much more simply, proceed from a fairly understandable desire to know how any story ends (and, of course, now we have some inkling of how that ending might plausibly be brought about). We all suffer from the often intolerable knowledge that each of us occupies only a vanishingly minuscule particle of terrestrial time, and that most of us are not destined to play any conspicuous role in the great drama of history. In many of us, surely, there must be some tacit impulse to rebel against the indignity of our own transience and seeming irrelevance; and maybe that impulse is somewhat soothed when one allows oneself to aggrandize one's brief moment in the light by imagining that it coincides with the end of time. Then again, of course, it is also true that very few of the stories we tell about the end of the world are actually about the end of the world. That is to say, most of them are about the end of the world as we know it, but not the total extinction of the human race or life on earth. There is usually a saving remnant, a small community intent upon surviving the devastation and beginning the human story — and the cycle of history — anew. These are not so much "Zoroastrian" tales, really, as tales of cosmic recurrence, pitched in a somewhat violent and apocalyptic key.

This suggests to me the hopeful thought that some substantial part of the appeal of such stories lies not in the satisfactions they offer to some latent death-instinct in us, or to some malicious appetite for destruction, or to some egoistic desire to subsume the destruction of the world under one's own death, or even to plain morbidity and nihilism, but in a curiously subdued but persistent longing for innocence — the bright golden innocence of the desert. Perhaps what draws many of us to the poetry of annihilation is the thought of a world of sublime simplicity, purged of politics, taxes, national and corporate interests, social coercions, and private ambitions: a world without the ambiguities or structures of sin. In utter desolation there is a kind of purity, the fertility of the fallow time before Eden, the simple chaos from which a blameless new order of things might arise. It would, at any rate, be pleasant to conclude — in good Christian Platonist fashion — that since even our most vicious desires spring from and only distort a more original desire for the good, we cannot really be entertained by the spectacle of universal destruction without simultaneously longing, even if at only the most deeply hidden levels of consciousness, for a world redeemed "as by fire" and returned to the innocence of pure possibility.

But who knows, really? I certainly don't. This much, though, seems certain to me: whatever it is that makes eschatological fantasy so entertaining for so many people, it really is in extraordinarily bad taste for television producers to summon up leering trolls from the grottoes of the Danube to scare children just before bedtime; and it is a grave injustice to implicate the poor, defenseless, long-departed classical age Mayans in depraved fables about impending cosmic destruction. The world, I think we can confidently predict, will not end in 2012. Kan Bahlum II — however wrong the rest of his prophecy may have proved to be — certainly got that part right.

# TWELVE

## . . . Of Hills, Brooks, Standing Lakes, and Groves . . .

A few days ago I was walking along the woodland trails of the national park near my home with my son Patrick and dog Roland (I think I have that the right way around). When we had set out, the sky was overcast, traces of the morning's mist were still drifting among the trees, and the gold, scarlet, and stubborn green of the foliage around us was gently glistening from the previous night's rain. But by the time we had reached the rise in the trail that lies almost exactly midway along our accustomed path, where a clearing to the left over a steeply descending slope allows us to look down on the lake at the park's center, the mist was gone; and, as we paused there, sunlight broke from the clouds overhead just as a gust of wind sent hundreds of pale yellow leaves from the poplars on the opposite side of the lake swirling high over the water in a vast dancing spiral. All at once, everything was shining: the lingering droplets of rain shaken down on us from the branches above flashed iridescently in the air; the lead-gray lake was changed to a radiant, silvery blue; Roland's nose became positively resplendent in its glossiness.

Autumn is the most beautiful and most mysterious of the seasons, at least to me, just as twilight is the most beautiful and mysterious part of the day. There is something so hypnotically uncanny about these liminal times — between summer and winter, between day and night — partly because of the obliging softness of the light, which lends such depth and subtlety to the world's colors, and partly because of the strange feeling of suspense that pervades them. Everything seems to hover tremulously in a state of pure transformation, slowly passing from one fixed condition to another — from seething torpor to icy dormancy, from light to darkness. There is a haunting sense that everything has been briefly displaced from any proper order, that almost anything might happen, that strange, lovely, and mighty forms are moving just behind the surface of reality. These are the times when one is most immediately aware of the numinous within nature.

This, at any rate, was what I said to my son — in very different terms — as we stood there looking down over the lake, and he agreed with me heartily. Then he observed that a forest is always a mysterious place, no matter what the season, and I had to concede the point, with a discreet thrill of paternal pride. But then he remarked that this must be why people used to believe there were spirits of the trees and streams, before science discovered that there are no such beings. I was stunned; his words pierced me to the core. Where on earth, I wondered, had he acquired this dreadful superstition? Who had corrupted his eleven-year-old mind with the abominable nonsense that science had somehow "discovered" the nonexistence of nature spirits, or that modern empirical method could ever possibly be competent to do such a thing? Suppressing my alarm as best I could, I quickly interrogated him, and within a few moments had learned the title of the offending school text. Then, as we resumed our stroll, I assured him patiently but emphatically that it was all so much sordid twaddle, and that we have absolutely no warrant for assuming that we know any better than our distant ancestors on this score: indeed, they may have been far better attuned to the deeper truths of nature than we now are. He was pleased to be corrected. (Roland merely heaved a longanimous sigh.) As far as Patrick was concerned, the matter had been settled; but I have to admit that the episode continues to trouble me. It is not that I expect my son never to be exposed to any of the conceptual confusion or magical claptrap of his age; and I trust his native intelligence to disabuse him of the worst of it. But it is still depressing to think how much conceited gibberish has become simply part of the received wisdom of our time.

It puts me in mind of a particularly annoying witticism that one occasionally encounters in the current popular debates between atheists and theists: the orgulous infidel waves his hand contemptuously and announces that he believes neither that there is a God nor that there are fairies at the bottom of his garden — or (a slight variation on the theme) observes that everyone in the room is an unbeliever when it comes to Thor or Baal, and that the atheist is simply an unbeliever in one god more. There are two reasons for treating such remarks with indignant disdain: the obvious one and mine. The obvious one, of course, is that only a simpleton could mistake these two orders of conviction for specimens of the same kind of belief. A person who believes in fairies or in Thor may or may not be mistaken about certain finite objects within the cosmos; a person who believes in God may or may not be mistaken about being, the nature of existence itself, the logical possibility of any world, the moral meaning of the universe, and so on. The former kind of belief concerns facts of experience, the latter truths of reason, and to suggest that they occupy the same conceptual or existential space is either to confess one's own stupidity or willfully to engage in cheap rhetorical thuggery.

That though, as I say, is obvious. *My* reason for taking exception to such remarks is perhaps somewhat more precious, but still quite sincere. Simply enough, what if there *are* fairies at the bottom of one's garden? Or, more precisely, what the hell is so irrational in believing there are or might be? One may be in error on the matter, naturally — one may just have misread the signs — but one cannot justly be accused of having committed any trespass against logic. Nothing gives us warrant to imagine that, on account of our grasp of various organic processes, we have succeeded in lifting the veil of Isis.

Well, I blame Francis Bacon. I know, I know: one can talk of Christianity's "desacralization" of creation, or of the Enlightenment having delivered humanity from the terrors of the "demon-haunted world," but all of that is misleading. Perhaps Christianity chased the gods and sprites away, or forced them to assume different forms, but it never did so entirely. And, after all, Paul never suggested that the elemental powers or ethereal principalities were illusions; he merely claimed that they had been made subject to Christ. The author of Colossians even seems to say that they have now been reconciled to God. As for the Enlightenment, whatever one imagines that might be, on this issue it marks not an advance from ignorance to understanding, but only a mutation of conceptual paradigms. And the principal author of that mutation, at least as an explicit and systematic intellectual project, was Bacon. It was he who chose to establish his new model of the sciences by proscribing any consideration of formal and final causes, and to approach all of nature as something analogous to a mindless machine, and to accept as knowledge only the kind of comprehension that gives one the power to control and manipulate that machine. And, for better and worse, it was a remarkably successful project, as every new successful therapy for a previously fatal disease and every new weapon of mass murder reminds us.

In Bacon's defense, of course, one could argue (charitably, if not quite accurately) that he was principally recommending only a revision of scientific method: by prescinding from formal and final causality, the sciences are able to submit their conjectures to the verdict of empirical data alone.

Properly understood, this should mean that the sciences, in order to move upon a very narrow path of experimental progress, must willingly forfeit any right to pronounce upon metaphysical or spiritual questions. But, unfortunately, the mechanical philosophy soon ceased to be a matter merely of method and became instead a metaphysics in its own right, and so mistook itself for the one thing it can never possibly be: an exhaustive picture of reality. As a consequence, much of our culture has now been reduced to a condition of such savagery that educated persons really adhere to the degrading belief that the cosmos is indeed only a kind of machine. Ours is what Heidegger called the time of technology, the "age of the world-picture," in which all of nature has been "en-framed" as a reserve of inert resources awaiting exploitation by the will to power. The name we seem now to have settled on for this philosophy is "naturalism," which comes in any number of reductionist forms (the most incoherent, absurd, and yet logically inevitable of which is called "eliminativism").

There are two great problems with naturalism. The first is that it is obviously false, if for no other reason than it is radically incomplete as a philosophy of the whole of things. The one thing that a naturalist view of reality cannot encompass is being itself, the very existence of nature; nature, by definition, is what already exists, and no investigation of its *innate* causes can penetrate the mystery of its ontological contingency. Thus naturalism is always surrounded and permeated and exceeded by that which is, quite literally, *super naturam*; and naturalism can be held as a philosophy only to the degree that one fails or scrupulously refuses to notice this surd of the supernatural, this ever deeper mystery behind and beyond all the lesser mysteries of natural order. The second problem is that naturalism, being a false picture of things, is inevitably destructive of nature, both cosmic and human. I mean not only that the age of technology has, as we all know, given us the power to ruin the world about us with magnificent profligacy. I mean also that it makes it all but impossible for human beings to inhabit the natural world as participants in its gratuity, greatness, and enchantment. And this is rather tragic, because all of civilization — quite literally *all* of it — springs up in the space between mortals and the mystery of the divine within and beyond the things of earth. But to find that space — that clearing in the forest — we must first consent to be servants, not simply masters. The works of our hands have to be the way in which we respond to the summons of the ever deeper mystery within things, born out of a primordial human capacity for wonder that never presumes to know more than it can know, and that never tries to determine in advance what may or may not reveal itself. And any deafness to this summons, or any arrogant forgetfulness of this mystery, is the deepest, most barbarous irrationality of all.

Or so I would argue, and with greater precision if this column were not already too long. But I have a journey to make this evening, and we must go for our daily walk in the woods before I leave. With any luck, we may catch a glimpse of a nymph or hamadryad, though I have no expectation that we will. Neither Patrick nor I can recall ever having seen one; and whatever Roland knows he keeps hidden in the fastness of his heart.

# THIRTEEN

# Brilliant Specialists

*Hub Fans Bid Kid Adieu: John Updike on Ted Williams.* By John Updike. The Library of America (2010). $15.00, hardcover. 64 pages.

It is hard not to begin this review with the phrase "This slender volume . . ." (in fact, I avoided doing so only by pulling the coy trick of
beginning it the way I just did). But this *is*, in fact, a very slender volume,
and the few pages it comprises are only sparsely populated by text; it's
more an oversized postcard, really. Other than a very brief author's preface and a short coda distilled from a few other of his fragmentary jottings
on Williams, the book contains only the text of Updike's celebrated 1960
*New Yorker* essay (with the footnotes he added in 1965), recounting Ted
Williams's final game (played at Fenway, against the Orioles) and the
splendidly improbable home run he hit in his last at bat. In the case of
this volume, however, the minimalist approach has worked beautifully.
A compact and handsome fiftieth anniversary tribute to what many regard as one of the best baseball essays ever written, it is at the same time a
pleasant, slightly accidental commemoration of its author, who died only
last year.

Baseball has generated a richer, deeper, and more sustained literary
tradition than any other sport. Only cricket has produced books of comparable literary quality, and the best of these — C. L. R. James's masterpiece
of social philosophy *Beyond a Boundary*, Hugh de Selincourt's gossamer
eclogue *The Cricket Match* — have been slightly eccentric rarities; there
is no large continuous school of cricket writing, and the cricket essay has
never become a recognized genre all to itself. The literature of baseball,
however, is a crowded and distinguished field, and so it really is a consid-

erable achievement for any single short piece of baseball writing to have acquired the sort of mythic luster that attaches to the Updike essay. It is especially impressive, perhaps, in that it is really the only piece of baseball writing Updike ever did.

Of course, according to Updike, he was not really writing about baseball at all, but rather about Williams, his boyhood hero. Perhaps this is true; but, even so, some of the more famous passages capture the poetry of the game so exquisitely that they have to stir something in any lover of the game: "baseball, with its graceful intermittences of action, its immense and tranquil field sparsely settled with poised men in white, its dispassionate mathematics, seems to me best suited to accommodate, and be ornamented by, a loner. It is an essentially lonely game." And, even when reflecting specifically on Williams, Updike occasionally shows what looks like an aficionado's eye for detail, as when he calls attention to the qualitatively peculiar trajectory of some of Williams's low, squarely struck, continuously rising home runs. (My father has often regaled his sons with the golden legend of that trajectory — specifically a home run Williams hit in the old Oriole Park late in his career, a shot that took a foot-long splinter out of one of the wooden seats over the right field wall, still apparently on the ascent when it did so.)

I SUPPOSE the question one ought to ask — since the Library of America has gone to the trouble of producing a single volume edition of what remains, at the end of the day, only a diverting "occasional" essay — is whether the piece really holds up well fifty years along. In a way — but only in a very impressive way — it does not. The truth is that it's been set apart in a class of its own for so long that it no longer needs to be measured against other specimens of baseball writing to ensure its reputation; one measures it now against itself, and against the memory of it that one has from previous readings. Picking it up again this time around, I couldn't help but notice that it has a somewhat slighter feel about it than I remembered it having. I thought I recalled it as being just a bit longer, more lyrical, more suspenseful in its buildup to that final plate appearance, more saturated with the light and colors of late September. But that in itself is a kind of tribute to the essay: it clearly has an evocative power, and generates a kind of emotional atmosphere, that lingers on and that far exceeds what's immediately evident on the page.

In the end, it really is the nonpareil baseball essay it's reputed to be. Nothing about it seems dated. (Well, almost nothing: it *is* momentarily arresting to come across a merely anonymous mention of "the Orioles third baseman" — and, really, by late 1960 most serious followers of the game were well aware of who that was.) Only a few sentences seem overly mannered; for the most part, Updike had already, at only twenty-eight years of age, achieved the sparkling ease of his mature style. And all the famous, oft-repeated phrases still ring out with a crystal tone: "the tissue-thin difference between a thing done well and thing done ill"; or "that intensity of competence that crowds the throat with joy"; or "when a density of expectation hangs in the air and plucks an event out of the future"; or "immortality is nontransferable"; or, of course, "Gods do not answer letters."

And, perhaps most importantly, the high points do not tower over the rest of the essay. It's a model of elegant writing throughout. Even the brief précis of Williams's career with which Updike sets the scene is graceful; only the most interesting and salient statistics are cited, and always in order to cast light on the strangely remote character of the man who amassed them. Then the narrative proper begins, and proceeds at just the right pace; the story almost seems to tell itself. Of course, in a sense it did tell itself. How Updike would have finished the tale if Williams had weakly flied out in the eighth is hard to imagine. He might not have written about the game at all; or he might have dwelled longer on its soft autumnal sadness, and tried to write it with even greater poignancy. Whatever the case, it would have lacked that last, faintly magical moment that draws the whole story — not only the story of that day, but the story of Williams's entire career — to its achingly symbolic denouement.

IN LONG RETROSPECT, it seems to me that Updike and Williams were oddly suited to one another, and it's something of a fortunate accident that their careers briefly converged in one unexpectedly exquisite magazine article. This may seem like a less than gracious observation, but I mean it as very high praise indeed: soberly and honestly considered, each man was a brilliant specialist — by which I mean, each was supremely skilled in one vital facet of his craft, and merely better than ordinary at all its other aspects. Williams was a pure hitter of almost uncanny ability, of course, with that fluid, oddly dipping and rising yet perfectly timed swing of his: a dead pull hitter in the live ball era who ripped heroically at everything inside, and yet who could still post averages with which Ty Cobb or Rogers Hornsby would have been quite contented come the fall. It almost defies belief, frankly. And yet, at everything else in the game he was unexceptional. On the bases or in the field, he discharged his duties well enough, and he kept himself in good athletic trim throughout his playing days; but it was only with the bat that he stood apart from other players.

Similarly Updike was, at his best, an altogether magnificent prose stylist. There are many, many passages in his collected works that rival or surpass the best work of just about any other English language writer of the twentieth century; there are whole paragraphs and chapters of almost delirious beauty. And yet he never really wrote a great book. Even the very best of his novels (such as *The Centaur*) and the most accomplished of his short stories (such as the early Maples stories) always somehow seemed to add up to less than the sum of their glittering sentences and ingenious metaphors. They were good novels and good stories, diverting and clever, and sometimes astonishingly good in many of their individual parts; but they were never masterpieces.

That, though, is not a criticism. The careers of both Williams and Updike serve as excellent reminders that, in most walks of life, only a very few of us are capable of doing anything as near to perfection as humanly possible. For anyone, though, who does have the ability, concentrating upon that one extraordinary skill or gift, even at the price of doing everything else (at most) only a little better than average, is the surest way to achieve genuine greatness. And, having achieved it, such a person should certainly be regarded not only with admiration, but also with a little awe.

# FOURTEEN

# Anarcho-Monarchism

The only thing I know that J. R. R. Tolkien and Salvador Dali had in common — or rather, I suppose I should say, the only *significant* or *unexpected* thing, since they obviously had all sorts of other things in common: they were male, bipedal, human, rough contemporaries, celebrities, Catholics, and so on — was that each man on at least one occasion said he was drawn simultaneously toward anarchism and monarchism. In the case of Dali, it was probably a meaningless remark, since almost everything he ever said was; whenever he got past the point of "Please pass the butter" or "That will cost you a great deal of money," he generally gave up any pretense of trying to communicate with other people. But Tolkien was, in his choleric way, giving voice to his deepest convictions regarding the ideal form of human society — albeit fleeting voice. The text of his sole anarcho-monarchist manifesto, such as it is, comes from a letter he wrote to his son Christopher in 1943 (forgive me for quoting at such length):

> My political opinions lean more and more to Anarchy (philosophically understood, meaning the abolition of control not whiskered men with bombs) — or to "unconstitutional" Monarchy. I would arrest anybody who uses the word State (in any sense other than the inanimate real of England and its inhabitants, a thing that has neither power, rights nor mind); and after a chance of recantation, execute them if they remained obstinate! If we could go back to personal names, it would do a lot of good. Government is an abstract noun meaning the art and process of governing and it should be an offence to write it with a capital G or so to refer to people. . . . Anyway the proper study of Man is anything but Man; and the most improper job of any man, even saints (who at any rate were at least

unwilling to take it on), is bossing other men. Not one in a million is fit for it, and least of all those who seek the opportunity. At least it is done only to a small group of men who know who their master is. The mediaevals were only too right in taking *nolo episcopari* as the best reason a man could give to others for making him a bishop. Grant me a king whose chief interest in life is stamps, railways, or race-horses; and who has the power to sack his Vizier (or whatever you dare call him) if he does not like the cut of his trousers. And so on down the line. But, of course, the fatal weakness of all that — after all only the fatal weakness of all good natural things in a bad corrupt unnatural world — is that it works and has only worked when all the world is messing along in the same good old inefficient human way. . . . There is only one bright spot and that is the growing habit of disgruntled men of dynamiting factories and power-stations; I hope that, encouraged now as "patriotism," may remain a habit! But it won't do any good, if it is not universal. (*The Letters of J. R. R. Tolkien*, ed. Humphrey Carpenter [Boston: Houghton Mifflin, 1981], pp. 63–64)

Last week, as I watched the waves of the 2010 Republican electoral counterinsurgency washing across the heartland, and falling back only at the high littoral shelves of the Pacific coast and the Northeast, I found myself reflecting on what a devil's bargain electoral democracy is. These occasional bloodless bloodbaths are deeply satisfying at some emotional level, whatever one's party affiliations, because they remind us of what a rare luxury it is to have the right and the power periodically to evict politicians from office. But, as is always the case here below in the *regio dissimilitudinis*, the pleasure is accompanied by an inevitable quantum of pain. The sweetest wine quaffed from the cup of bliss comes mingled with a bitter draft of sorrow (alas, alack). Tragically — *tragically* — we can remove one politician only by replacing him or her with another. And then, of course, our choices are excruciatingly circumscribed, since the whole process is dominated by two large and self-interested political conglomerates that are far better at gaining power than at exercising it wisely. And yet we *must* choose, one way or the other. Even the merry recreant who casts no vote at all, or flings a vote away onto the midden of some third party as a protest, is still making a choice with consequences, however small. And none of the other political systems on offer in the modern world are alternatives that any sane person would desire; so we cannot just eradicate our political class altogether and hope for the best (anyway, who would clean up afterward?).

Yes, I know: there are good and sincere souls who run for office, and some occasionally get in, and a few of those are then able to accomplish something with the position they assume, and some of those even remain faithful to the convictions that got them there. But, lest we forget, those are also the politicians who often create the greatest mischief. Sincerity, after all, is not the same as wisdom. A cynical poltroon of infinitely pliable principles is in many cases less a threat to liberty, justice, or peace than someone whose mind has been corrupted with "high" ideals or (worse yet) high *ideas*. As for all the others, the great majority of politicians — well, bear with me here for a moment. If one were to devise a political system from scratch, knowing something of history and a great deal about human nature, the sort of person that one would chiefly want, if possible, to exclude from power would be the sort of person who most desires it, and who is most willing to make a great effort to acquire it. By all means, drag a reluctant Cincinnatus from his fields when the Volscians are at the gates, but then permit him to retreat again to his arable exile when the crisis has passed; for God's sake, though, never surrender the fasces to anyone who eagerly reaches out his hand to take them. Yet our system obliges us to elevate to office precisely those persons who have the ego-besotted effrontery to ask us to do so; it is rather like being compelled to cede the steering wheel to the drunkard in the back seat loudly proclaiming that he knows how to get us there in half the time. More to the point, since our perpetual electoral cycle is now largely a matter of product recognition, advertising, and marketing strategies, we must be content often to vote for persons willing to lie to us with some regularity or, if not that, at least to speak to us evasively and insincerely. In a better, purer world — the world that cannot be — ambition would be an absolute disqualification for political authority.

One can at least sympathize, then, with Tolkien's view of monarchy. There is, after all, something degrading about deferring to a politician, or going through the silly charade of pretending that "public service" is a particularly honorable occupation, or being forced to choose which band of brigands, mediocrities, wealthy lawyers, and (God spare us) idealists will control our destinies for the next few years. But a king — a king without any real power, that is — is such an ennoblingly arbitrary, such a tender and organically *human* institution. It is easy to give our loyalty to someone whose only claim on it is an accident of heredity, because then it is a free gesture of spontaneous affection that requires no element of self-deception, and that does not involve the humiliation of having to *ask* to be ruled. The ideal king would be rather like the king in chess: the most useless piece on the board, which occupies its square simply to prevent any other piece from doing so, but which is somehow still the whole game. There is something positively sacramental about its strategic impotence. And there is something blessedly gallant about giving one's wholehearted allegiance to some poor inbred ditherer whose chief passions are Dresden china and the history of fly-fishing, but who nonetheless, quite *ex opere operato*, is also the bearer of the dignity of the nation, the anointed embodiment of the *genius gentis* — a kind of totem or, better, mascot.

As for Tolkien's anarchism, I think it obvious that he meant it in the classical sense: not the total absence of law and governance, but the absence of a political *archetes* — that is, of the leadership principle as such. In Tolkien's case, it might be better to speak of a "radical subsidiarism," in which authority and responsibility for the public weal are so devolved to the local and communal that every significant public decision becomes a matter of common interest and common consent. Of course, such a social vision could be dismissed as mere agrarian and village primitivism; but that would not have bothered Tolkien, what with his proto-ecologist view of modernity.

Now, obviously, none of this anarcho-monarchism is an actual program for political action or reform. But that is not the point. We all have to make our way as best we can across the burning desert floor of history, and those who do so with the aid of "political philosophies" come in two varieties. There are those whose political visions hover tantalizingly near on the horizon, like inviting mirages, and who are as likely as not to get the whole caravan killed by trying to lead it off to one or another of those nonexistent oases. And then there are those whose political dreams are only cooling clouds, easing the journey with the meager shade of a gently ironic critique, but always hanging high up in the air, forever out of reach. I like to think my own political philosophy — derived entirely from my exactingly close readings of *The Compleat Angler* and *The Wind in the Willows* — is of the latter kind. Certainly Tolkien's was. Whatever the case, the only purpose of such a philosophy is to avert disappointment and prevent idolatry. Democracy is not an intrinsic good, after all; if it were, democratic institutions could not have produced the Nazis. Rather, a functioning democracy comes only as the late issue of a decently morally competent and stable culture. In such a culture, one can be grateful of the liberties one enjoys, and use one's franchise to advance the work of more trustworthy politicians (and perhaps there are more of those than I have granted to this point), and pursue the discrete moral causes in which one believes. But it is good also to imagine other, better, quite impossible worlds, so that one will be less inclined to mistake the process for the proper end of political life, or to become frantically consumed by what should be only a small part of life, or to fail to see the limits and defects of our systems of government. After all, one of the most crucial freedoms, upon which all other freedoms ultimately depend, is freedom from illusion.

# FIFTEEN

# The Abbot and Aunt Susie

In the August/September 2010 issue of *First Things*, Matthew Milliner gave a delightful account of his visit to the Eastern Orthodox Monastery of St. Anthony in Arizona's Sonora Desert. At least, I quite enjoyed it — though, truth be told, I would have enjoyed it considerably more had it not included a brief exchange Milliner had with the monastery's abbot:

> "Is holiness possible outside the Orthodox Church?" I inquired. [The abbot] responded with tired eyes: "A measure of virtue perhaps, but holiness is not possible." The Orthodoxy on offer at St. Anthony's does not mince words.

No, apparently not. Jesus, of course, rather mysteriously asserted that the Holy Spirit goes wherever he will, so it is good of the abbot to provide a clarification on this point: the Holy Spirit may go wherever he likes, it seems, so long as he confines himself to the right neighborhoods. This is not, incidentally, the *official* teaching of the Orthodox Church (so few things are), and most Orthodox Christians would tend to regard it as the embarrassingly silly twaddle it is; but it is something that certain hardliners like to say. And, to be fair, I've heard something similar from one or two Tridentinist Catholics I've tripped over in a dark alley now and again.

Most of us know the rules here, of course: when some hoary-headed old mammal in monastic garb starts spouting nonsense of this sort, no matter how offensive we find it, we are supposed to shrug patiently and smile a gently ironic smile, reminding ourselves that a dash of curmudgeonly sectarian insularity is frequently the inevitable concomitant of deep piety. But I do not want to play along. The wonderful thing about holiness, when you really encounter it, is that it testifies to itself. This is not to say one can never be deceived; it's easy to mistake personal charisma for genuine grace, or to be misled by plausible charlatans — until, that is, one comes across the real thing, at a moment when one is open to it. Then one knows it for what it is: a quality of such lucid simplicity and moral beauty that one feels simultaneously deeply happy in its presence and ashamed of one's own failure to have realized it within oneself.

At any rate, I am quite convinced I have met a small number of truly holy persons in my life. Some were indeed Orthodox; some were even Orthodox monks. Others were Christians of other communions. And still others were not Christians at all. And, if I were to try to say who the first person was who made me aware of what genuine sanctity is, I think I would have to point to a woman who probably never even set foot in an Orthodox church. Her name was Mrs. Estelle Hayes, though in my childhood I only ever knew her as Aunt Susie, which was how my brothers spoke of her. She was a black woman who helped make ends meet by cleaning the homes of middle-class white people; having been born a little before the turn of the last century into the rigid caste system of segregated Maryland, she grew up without any opportunity for a more rewarding occupation than that. The name Susie had displaced her proper name when she was still a baby. She had been born at the southern end of Maryland's Eastern Shore, where the whistles of the steamships that sailed down the Chesapeake Bay from Havre de Grace and other ports were audible day and night. She had, it seems, a powerful set of lungs, and so her family started calling her after the ship with the loudest whistle of all, *The Susie.*

She entered my family's life well before I was born, and by the time I came along she had largely departed from it, so my own contact with her was as fleeting as it was moving. She had helped my father's mother keep house before my parents were married, and later began coming to help my mother once a week as well. She was still keeping things in order in the years when both my brothers were born, neither of whom ever had reason to suspect that she was not, in a strictly technical sense, one of his aunts. I never met her husband, Al Hayes, who was a professional gardener among other things, but my father often described him to me as a fine gentleman with a great salt-and-pepper beard and impeccable sense in clothes (including a fondness for spats); and once I overheard my father remark that Mr. Hayes's beard made him look a little like God. As I was about four at the time, I took this rather more literally than my father intended, no doubt, and for the next few years my mental picture of God was pretty firmly fixed as one of an older black man with a flowing white beard.

Aunt Susie had a strong and somewhat conservative personality, and a deeply generous nature; she was, most importantly, a fervent Christian who spoke of her faith with a great and convincing clarity. She had worked to earn registration as a practical nurse, and in the time she had free after cleaning houses and doing laundry, she devoted herself to the care of others, visiting elderly shut-ins and bringing food and basic medical assistance to those most in need. She was a physically strong woman, and seemingly indefatigable at the chores by which she earned her pay; but she was even more tireless at the end of the working day in performing works of Christian love. In her church, she was regarded as something of a saint. There was something about her, moreover, that convinced one that her prayers were of a more powerful variety than most. When my parents lived in a house on a hill above Ellicott City in Howard County, my father used to pick her up from and take her back to the streetcar in Catonsville just over the line in Baltimore County; and one evening, during a winter storm, the car went into a violent skid toward the tree line, and then just as suddenly straightened itself back into its lane before my father really had control of the wheel. Over the rapid beating of his heart, my father politely inquired of Aunt Susie whether she had just been praying, to which she calmly replied that she had indeed, and that the Lord had taken over from there. Coming from her, it seemed simply a plain statement of fact.

In any event, that was all a little before my time. During my childhood, I heard a great deal about Aunt Susie, but I did not meet her until she came to dinner when I was about ten. I was deeply impressed by the warmth and forthrightness of her character, and naturally addressed her — as I had always heard was correct — as Aunt Susie. But, thereafter, I saw little of her. My last encounter with her — one of the more indelible memories of my life — came a few years later, when she was dying in a somewhat dilapidated wing of the Women's Hospital in Baltimore. We went to visit her in her room, and found her in her bed, lying on one side, much frailer and much smaller than she had been in previous years. While we were there, a group of her parishioners from her church dropped in — to show their respect, dressed as though for church — and she insisted that we all pray together and join in some songs of praise. Since the charismatic movement had wafted through the icy halls of the Episcopal Church a few years before, my family actually knew the Pentecostal hymns that she wanted to hear, so we all joined hands around her and did as she asked. It would be quite impossible for me to explain what the hour we spent there was like, or what effect it had on me. I can only say that Aunt Susie spoke about her love of Christ in a very clear and confident way, with a power that the weakness of her voice did nothing to diminish. From that day to this I have never heard another profession of Christian faith that seized me with such irresistible force. I am not a very emotional person, as it happens, but I was almost overwhelmed by the unutterable beauty that emanated from her. Just as we were about to leave, Aunt Susie said that the Lord was telling her she would not see us again. We assured her that this was not so, and that we would be back before long, but she was quite certain that she was right, and so her last words to us had something of the quality of a valedictory blessing. And, of course, she was right; she died before we could make another visit to her bedside.

Anyway, I do not really imagine I can convey what I would like to about her in a short column of this sort. I only want to make clear why I cannot listen to remarks of the sort made by the abbot of St. Anthony's with quite the seemly equanimity I probably should, and why I see them as being a little blasphemous. To put the matter very simply, I am absolutely sure that Aunt Susie was a great woman, who probably did more good on many days of her life than most of us will ever really accomplish over the course of our lives. But, more than that, I am convinced that she was genuinely a woman of resplendent sanctity, and one from whom the good abbot — had he had the good fortune to have known her — might have learned a very great deal indeed about what true holiness is.

SIXTEEN

# A Forgotten Poet

Aimé Foinpré (1841–1880) died 130 years ago today (17 December), killed as he leapt from a second story window in Paris's seventh arrondissement to escape the wrath of a jealous husband; he was dead even before the raven-tressed cause of contention had hastily gathered up her clothes and fled from the room. It was a fittingly dashing and disreputable end for a man whose immense talent was exceeded only by his charm and lunatic recklessness. He is all but forgotten today, but in his time he exercised a subtle but substantial influence in French letters, and may indirectly have made a mark upon English-language literature as well. He was first and foremost a gifted classicist, and one whose special interest in late antiquity led him in the last fifteen years of his life to an ever-deepening fascination with Byzantine civilization. A distinguished graduate of the École Normale Supérieure, his reputation for frivolity and a tendency toward indiscretion had nevertheless denied him a university position; but somehow he was able to secure a position at a good *lycée* in a Parisian *commune*. He was also a poet, though his one volume of verse, published in 1878, appeared in a limited private edition of only two hundred copies and was never reprinted thereafter. The little book made the rounds in literary circles, however, and for a short period was celebrated by some of the finest writers of the age. Verlaine — not yet lost in a haze of absinthe and opiates — was deeply impressed. Anatole France was reportedly "alarmed" by the disorienting attractiveness of many of the poems. Villiers de l'Isle-Adam (whose judgments in such matters could admittedly be a bit capricious) compared the young classicist flatteringly to Baudelaire.

A promising debut but, alas, an abortive one. Had Foinpré devoted more of his energies to producing poetry and less to seducing beautiful women (at which he was quite prolifically accomplished) or to provoking fights with other men (over beautiful women) or to separating himself from beautiful women with calamitous theatricality (on account of other beautiful women), he might have accomplished a great deal more. Certainly had he not died so prematurely his literary posterity would not have fallen hostage to his deranged older sister, who as his sole living relative inherited his meager literary estate along with his library. Unable to understand that the writing of poetry has rarely been a path to fame and fortune, she would accept none of the terms publishers were willing to offer her to reprint her brother's verse, and she stoutly refused to yield on the point till she died in 1929. By then, her brother was remembered by almost no one. So he lived on only as a suppressed memory in *fin de siècle* French literature, though something of his sensibility continued to echo on at least into the late writings of Valéry. Moreover, there is some evidence that his poetry was stumbled upon by the young Robert Byron, who found in it further encouragement for his own adoration of all things Byzantine; if so, Foinpré might be accounted a distant influence on Yeats. But we should not grasp at straws, I suppose. As it turned out, his life was full of promise, but only promise.

At least, that has been so until now. At last, a sort of rediscovery of Foinpré is under way. A new critical edition of his poems — including six never before published — is being prepared in France, and I have been translating the poems for the American edition, scheduled to appear in the next two years. So, with my publisher's permission, I thought I might offer a few of those translations, just as a diversion (whether I am permitted to reproduce the new critical texts of the French edition, however, I do not know). The first is an early piece, written when he was in his midtwenties. Already, however, the Byzantine theme had become a central motif.

*"The Old Man Goes to Constantinople to Die"*
Upon the vision of those seas he cast
Himself when, full of days, he sought repose
Beyond dominions of the bitter past,
In habitations of the deathless rose.

Full eighty years and more his bent back knew;
His heart from grief had grown as cold as stone;
His eyes were pale, the adamantine blue
Of winter clouds, of ice and wind-stripped bone.

Those bleak November skies soon lost their drear
Albescence, and the seas their turbid gray,
As warmer winds outraced the changing year
And bore him on into an endless day.

He came to realms of porphyry and gold,
Of trees whose fruit were jewels, of sacred song,
Where harbor waters never knew the cold
At autumn's end, when northern nights grow long.

And so he there, in Wisdom's silver heart,
Below the ring of fire, fell down and prayed,
And saw the dome and Great Church break apart
And yield before the world that they portrayed.

Angelic flames now lit the heavens' vault;
He grew as still and changeless as the gold;
The lambent icons in his soul had wrought
New visions and new glories to be told.

The second is a sonnet, written, it seems, to express his frustra-
tion over his unsuccessful pursuit of one Renée Gautier, a lovely young
woman who was apparently a considerable scholar in her own right, with
a large knowledge of antique philosophy and religion, and whose interest
in Foinpré — much to the latter's consternation — never went beyond
conversation.

*"Hypatia"*

"The world is one, dear heart," she said, "and shines
Upon the burning mirror of the soul
Because the bright horizon of the whole
Gathers to its vanishing point the lines
Of sky and earth; so all things become signs,
While still the mind turns to its silent pole,
And once again is born the mystic foal
In time's wild grove, among the clustered vines."

"My love," said I, "perhaps, just as you say,
In mind the world and self are ever wed,
Each soul's a glass where fire and ocean play,

And cold stars gleam. . . . But come with me to bed:
For we are mortal flesh at close of day. . . ."
She smiled at me, and sadly shook her head.

I may have done Foinpré something of an injustice to this point,
however, by emphasizing only his satyriatic side. In fact, he was a man
of absorbing contradictions. Like Baudelaire, he was a dazzling combination of the devout and the profane. He was, in his odd way, a believing
Catholic, and each of his amorous adventures tended to be followed by a
brief penitential season, which always involved many candles and many
new resolutions, but which never had much effect on his private conduct.
Still, religious themes absolutely saturate his verse, and his two longest
poetic works are a pair of quasi-theological, slightly gnostic, deeply Alexandrian cycles of interrelated poems. One is about various icons he saw on
a journey through Italy and Greece in the summer of 1869, and the other
is a series of brief monologues attributed to various saints and — at the
conclusion — to the devil and Christ. I have chosen one piece from each.
From the former:

*The Fall of Lucifer*
*(Thessaloniki)*

No darkness falls across this golden noon,
And here no cloud or shadow mounts the wind;
Softly falls the dragon, through a ruined sky,
The region of the sullen southern stars.

A meteor, a silver strand of lightning
Upon the hazel dusk, he fell and fell,
Gold his hair and gold his eyes, such bright beauty
In sheer descent upon the torpid breeze. . . .

When, still delighting, sang the angels, sang
The stars. . . . The son of morning, fallen where
None can find him, who in the evening of
That age slipped down along the seam of night. . . .

Gone now, all glory, all that lovely bright
Magnificence: become the ember's glow,
The aftermath, the deep reproach of those
Cold, bleak, disconsolate, and empty heavens;

And now, amid a race who crave a God's
Miraculous sadness, terrible mirth,
The tawdry splendor of his glory's waste
Must wear another aspect than its own,

And he must walk the dismal floor of earth,
And range the fallow reaches of the sea,
And rule the turbulent and lifeless winds,
And hide in secret chambers in their hearts.

And from the latter a vaguely docetic lyric:

*II: John on Patmos*

My tongue was as a golden bird
Tangled in an emerald net,
My eyes were diamonds, my ears heard
His voice in silver echoes; yet
I knew no way to join the dance
Until the dancer took my hand,
And led me in a floating trance
When I could scarcely rise to stand.

Or so, when visions seized my soul,
It seemed; or when his gentle form
Amid the garden shadows, cold
And still (as when he calmed the storm
Upon the waters), fixed in prayer,
Became as pure and strange as light
Departing from the evening air
Before the melting blue of night.

I am as gold or emerald,
As twilit gems or moonlit silver,
Beyond all grief, transformed, and held
Within a cage of stars, and never
To leave this island washed by dreams;
I can recall as none else can
The otherness in him: he seemed
A shape more beautiful than man.

Anyway, I offer them for what they are worth. Every translation is also a betrayal, of course, so none of the defects of these verses as I have presented them here should redound to the discredit of the originals. I feel no contrition over my failings as a translator, however, because — to tell the truth — I just made all this up this past weekend.

FORGIVE ME. I lost the text of the column I wrote for today's *On the Square* due to technical difficulties just before I could send it in. At Christmastime, however, an amusement in which I engage for private entertainments is the composition of little literary pastiches, written in an "assigned" style, accompanied by short fictional vignettes for context. It is an idea we got from a number of Victorian writers. This year, the set subject was "Pretty English translation of poems by a forgotten French Symbolist poet," which leaves considerable scope for a certain sort of honey-glazed conventional versifying ("five-finger exercises," so to speak). I had the piece on hand when disaster struck. I suppose I might not have made the man such a libertine, given that Christmas is a church feast, and I may remove that — or mute it — before the day arrives; but it seemed the properly French thing to do. The poet's name, incidentally, is an elaborate joke (fifty cents if you can figure it out). Anyway, usually all this self-indulgent nonsense would be kept safely behind closed doors. But it occurred to me that it might make a rather amiably ridiculous gift, in keeping with the season. So, understanding the circumstances, take it as you will and have a merry and very blessed Christmas.

# SEVENTEEN

# An Infinite Passion

Atargatis, the "Syrian Goddess," was a demanding mistress. For one thing, her priests (the *galli*) could win their way into her affections only by emasculating themselves. According to *De Dea Syria*, attributed to Lucian of Samosata, any young man disposed to dedicate himself to her service in Hierapolis had to make this first and most extravagant oblation on one of her high holy days, in a fit of divine ecstasy, with a single economic slash of a sacred sword kept at her temple. After that, he would run naked and bleeding through the city streets until he found a home into which he felt inspired to fling the freshly severed jetsam. Any household thus "honored" was then required by religious decency to supply the new initiate with female attire and adornments. Now, admittedly, we all do our best to lay up treasure in heaven, and I suppose one ought not to cast too many peremptory judgments around regarding other people's pieties; but I think most of us can agree that this was a fairly exorbitant sum to place in escrow on an uncertain bargain. More to the point, pity the poor housewife or slave to whose lot it fell to take up the gauntlet (so to speak) from where it had been thrown down. Religious enthusiasts in every age have tended to make nuisances of themselves, granted; but even Jehovah's Witnesses showing up at the door at dinnertime do not impose themselves quite so inconsiderately and startlingly as that. And at that point, amazingly enough, the goddess's demands on her priests were only just beginning. Delighted as she no doubt was to have it proved to her yet again just how very, well, for delicacy's sake, let's just say *disarming* her admirers found her charms, her craving for constant reassurance was so jealous and ravenous that no gesture of allegiance, however irrevocable, could satisfy her for long. Thus her *galli* had to renew their sanguinary covenant with her at regular intervals, by whipping and lacerating them-selves mercilessly in public displays of votive zeal. And this meant that her importunities of the larger society were fairly unremitting as well.

Well before the latter half of the second century AD, when Lucius Ap-uleius painted his contemptuous portrait of the "Syrian" *galli* in his *Meta-morphosis* (or *Golden Ass*), the mysteries of Atargatis had migrated widely out into the empire. Wandering troupes of mendicant capon flagellants went about clad in outlandish motley, brandishing flutes and cymbals and tambourines, and harassing honest citizens with that most annoying expression of happy piety, singing in public. And, if Apuleius's views are representative of contemporary opinion, their self-inflicted incapacity did nothing to shield them from a reputation for vice. The *Metamorphosis* not only heaps disdain on their ritual antics and theatrical effeminacy, but depicts them as a society of charlatans, who collect alms only to subsidize a life of dissipation and sexual depravity. To Apuleius, plainly, Atargatis was just some vulgar demoness from the provinces, of low pedigree and untutored manners, whose worship was little more than a rude confidence game. Not that he really had much right to object in principle to the sect's practices. He certainly expresses no comparable distaste for Phrygian Cy-bele, the "Anatolian Mountain Mother" or "Great Idaean Mother of the Gods" — quite the reverse, in fact — even though Cybele's mysteries were probably the original template from which all other matrolatrous cults of excitable geldings were stamped. Her *galli*, at least those of the purest ob-servance, were pruned in exactly the same manner as their "Syrian" coun-terparts, if in a somewhat more ceremonious manner, and could boast a far more ancient lineage; her Corybants assailed the ears of passersby with their wails of frenzied hymnody and the din of cymbals and tambou-rines; and all her keener votaries generally behaved as one ought not to behave in polite settings. Initiation into her higher orders even involved being drenched in the gushing blood of a dying bull. By Apuleius's time, however, Cybele had long enjoyed the official adoration of Rome and, for all her irrepressible wildness, had become very respectable. She had been admitted into the company of recognized Roman deities as early as 204 BC and had become a favorite of many emperors from the time of Claudius onward; she had even been absorbed by the generous syncretism of the time into virtual identity with any number of the other mother goddesses thronging late antiquity's petticoat pantheon: Rhea, Artemis of Ephesus, Demeter, Bellona, and so on. She may have started out as a rustic Asiatic parvenue, but now she moved in the highest circles. Like the young Marie Antoinette stripped of her garish Austrian frills and flounces by the ladies of the French court and tricked out in the best Parisian fashions, it had taken only a few deft cosmetic alterations of costume to transform her from *gauche* to *à la mode*.

I SUPPOSE there must be some nasty psychological joke about certain boys and their mothers lurking in the tendency of many mother goddesses to demand so bindingly final a tribute from their more "favored" male worshipers. It is certainly something of a recurrent motif in the anthropology of religion. Even today in India, in fact, the goddess Bahuchara Mata is served by a community of *hijras*, or holy eunuchs (of the total ablation variety, horrifyingly enough). And, certainly, those of us born into religious traditions that grew up at the foot of Sinai, rather than of Ida or Sipylus or Meru, can take considerable comfort from the thought that our "patriarchal" creeds leave us — for the *most* part — physically intact. Not that our creeds are entirely free from any analogous excesses (at least, *slightly* analogous), over at the other, much more benign end of the same psychopathological spectrum. And I am not talking about Origen or any other early Christians who may have had themselves trimmed in the Alexandrian style for the sake of philosophical serenity; they were anything but religious ecstatics or enthusiasts. Rather, I mean some of the more peculiar manifestations of the ascetic or charismatic impulse in Christian history. A French scholar of hagiographies told me only last week, for instance, of one medieval saint who was able to embrace the celibate life without reservations only after the Blessed Virgin appeared to him in a vision and, with a single touch of the hand, blessed him with perpetual flaccidity. And, more generally speaking, Christian history has always had its holy lunatics: ungoverned glossolaliacs, wandering prophets, stylites, flagellants, and so forth; and of course, even today there are snake handlers and Holy Rollers and other practitioners of Christian *vodoun* out there, as well as those deranged Filipinos who have themselves nailed to crosses on Good Friday; and the list could be considerably extended. And, just as we would never allow these extreme and exotic expressions of Christian piety to determine our understanding of the faith as a whole, we should not let the bloodier or more degenerate devotions of ancient religion distract us from the quite sane and luminous faith of many men and women of pagan antiquity, or to blind us to its frequently remarkable familiarity. The same Apuleius who abominates the worshipers of Atargatis ends his book — which for its first ten chapters is just a whimsical, slightly grotesque, and occasionally ribald burlesque — in a state of rapt adoration before Isis, whom he regards as the true source and end of all life: one of the most devout and beautiful expressions of faith in a benevolent and provident divine savior in all of ancient literature, not excepting the Christian texts.

EVEN SO, it is also true — and this is my reason for bringing all this unsavory business up in the first place — that extremes tell us something indispensable about what is ordinary. It is genuinely illuminating to consider how much human beings can torment, torture, and mutilate themselves — physically and psychologically — in pursuit of the divine (however conceived) and how violent they can become in their struggle against all the limitations of their own nature that they imagine separate them from that end. As the old formula has it, *abusus non tollit usum*: the abuse of a thing does not tell against its proper use. But it is also true that the abuse of a thing can reveal a great deal about the true scope of its proper use. Even what we might regard as the ghastliest, most psychotically extravagant deformities of spiritual longing must still in some sense be rooted in the very nature of spiritual longing. They show us, in a somewhat macabre fashion, just how transcendental a longing it is — just how infinite a passion. So deep is the hunger for God or for the Absolute (or whatever) that it can drive many of us to destroy our own flesh, forfeit our posterity, even lay down our lives in the path of this or that Juggernaut. In the grip of this passion, there is no obstruction (not even one's own body) that religious desire is not willing to tear down.

Of course, there are those disposed to see all religious yearning as a psychological disorder, and to them the extreme expressions of such yearning would seem merely to confirm the diagnosis. But this raises a rather troubling question regarding the possibility of a disorder so general and perennial and yet so frequently contrary to the imperative of survival that supposedly motivates all living things. After all, from a thoroughly naturalistic perspective, it requires considerable ingenuity to explain how an organism constructed entirely from "selfish genes" can have evolved an overwhelming longing to be in some sense torn out of the continuum of nature altogether. I know, obviously, that purely Darwinian explanations of religion have been attempted, and that some kind of evolutionary rationale can be devised to explain just about any phenomenon if one is sufficiently inventive. Most such explanations are utterly impressionistic, of course; and, as with most attempts to use Darwinian theory to explain more than it really can, they are largely exercises in making the implausible sound somehow almost kind of likely. Perhaps the most immediately convincing are those that start from some concept of "group selection," and that therefore can avoid dealing too directly with all those particular individuals who consciously forsake their own genetic interests for the sake of supernatural ends. But "group selection" is, as is well known, a profoundly problematic idea in many ways.

Anyway, I am not interested in that argument just at the moment; it would take too long and would prove inconclusive. It is simply part of the intellectual burden of modernity, now that every concept of final and formal causes has been explicitly abandoned, that persons of a rationalist bent have to try to see everything (including, impossibly enough, existence itself) as the effect of blind material or physical causes, even if that means taking a shockingly great number of counterintuitive assertions purely on faith. What does interest me, however, is the irreducible enigma of a passion that is not only a possibility of human nature, but one of its most universal and compelling motives, and yet also one that is so difficult to account for in terms of the narrow economies of material causes. Whether we think it tells us anything about the nature of reality or not, we should at least grant that it tells us something about our own nature that cannot easily be fitted into our "mechanical philosophy."

Just a thought.

# EIGHTEEN

# A Philosopher in the Twilight

In his preface to the *Philosophy of Right*, Hegel rather famously remarks that the owl of Minerva takes flight only as dusk is falling: which is to say that philosophy comes only at the end of an age, far too late in the day to tell us how the world ought to be; it can at most merely ponder what has already come to pass, and so begun to pass away. An epoch yields its secrets to rational reflection grudgingly, only after its profoundest possibilities have already been exhausted in the actuality of history; "when philosophy paints its gray on gray, a form of life has grown old, and cannot be rejuvenated . . . but only understood." It is a winsomely tragic picture of philosophy, but not really a humble one. It may seem to reduce philosophy to an essentially reconstructive, rather than creative, labor; and certainly it implies that philosophers like Kant, who see themselves as harbingers of one or another new dawn, are deluded about their proper roles, like Homerid rhapsodes who have mistaken themselves for Achilles or Hector. But it is also a picture that exquisitely captures philosophy's deep and perilous ambition to be recognized not simply as an intellectual discipline, but as wisdom itself; for true wisdom, as we know, belongs properly to the very old. It also suggests that the greatest philosopher of all would be the one who could plausibly claim to have come most belatedly of all: to have witnessed the very last crepuscular gleam of the dying day and to have learned as no one else now can how the story truly ends. The highest aim of philosophy, then, would be to achieve a kind of transcendent belatedness, an unsurpassable finality lying always further beyond all merely local or episodic philosophies. (Needless to say, Hegel entertained few doubts regarding just who that greatest philosopher might turn out to be.)

It is in the context of this Hegelian mystique of belatedness, I think, that one can best make sense of the later writings of Martin Heidegger (1889–1976), and especially of their sonorously oracular impenetrability (by turns so mesmerizing and so infuriating). In a sense, Hegel's philosophy summoned Heidegger's out of the realm of future possibility. By attempting to devise a grand philosophical narrative that would enclose all other philosophical narratives within its inescapable dialectical logic, Hegel challenged his successors to overcome him — to elude the intricate capaciousness of his logic and thereby to enclose his "final" story in one yet more final. At least, from the period of the "Letter on Humanism" (1947) onward, that is arguably what Heidegger set out to accomplish. Over the last three decades of his life, he sought to go beyond Hegel's heroic feat of "metaphysical closure" by further enclosing the whole history of Western metaphysics (of which Hegel's system is merely the most imposing synthetic expression) within the still larger story of "being" as such, and to tell that story in a language so purged of all inherited conceptual terms and grammars that it could never be enfolded within the language of metaphysics again. Thus, for instance, he even stopped speaking of himself as a philosopher by the end, preferring the seemingly homely title of "thinker." That this postphilosophical language would prove difficult to write was inevitable; that it would prove quite so difficult to read probably was not.

Whatever the case, though, and whatever Heidegger's other motives may have been, his determination to think through what he called "the history of being" — from its remotest origins to its uttermost ending — led him to produce what, for all its eccentricities and deficiencies, remains one of the profoundest meditations on modernity and on the nature and history of modern nihilism written in the last century. It may not ultimately achieve seamless finality, in the Hegelian sense, but then again finality of that sort is one of the metaphysical illusions that Heidegger claims to have left behind. What it does achieve, however, is a vision of Western philosophy and its ambiguously intimate relation to Western cultural history that, if once understood, cannot be easily or confidently dismissed afterward.

Of course, I should add, a more proximate antagonist for Heidegger than Hegel might have been Heidegger himself. We know all too well that his dalliance with the Nazis in the 1930s, while it may have been something less than a marriage, was certainly more than a flirtation. Emmanuel Faye has even tried to argue that somehow the ethos of Nazism subtly pervades all of Heidegger's work. But, in fact, the most mystifying and annoying truth about Heidegger is that just the opposite happens to be the case. His late thought lays out a vision of reality that might be accused of a kind of quietistic fatalism, perhaps, or of moral passivity; but it also describes and denounces the intellectual pathologies that led to the rise of the Nazis with an often haunting power. Whether this indicates some measure of self-knowledge on Heidegger's part, no one can say. In his later days he was so anxious to deny his early complicity with the regime that it is impossible to tell now whether his shame involved any element of contrition. But it may also be the case, perversely enough, that it was the inexpungible stain of his involvement in absolute evil that forced him to contemplate the nihilism of his age with such untiring persistence. After all, if he could show nihilism to be a destiny woven into the very fabric of the West by a long history of intellectual error, as he came to believe it was, then perhaps he could convince himself and others that he was not so much a moral idiot as a victim of fate.

WHO KNOWS, THOUGH? And who cares? In the end, it does not really matter whether Heidegger's late philosophy was a mad labor of craven self-exculpation, or the fruit of genuine moral awakening, or a bit of both. It remains an often brilliant exploration of the ways in which Western humanity has succeeded in creating a world in which all values have become subordinate to the demands of the human will, and in which knowledge and human creativity have become almost entirely confused, conceptually and practically, with the exercise of instrumental reason's mastery over all of reality. Modernity, for Heidegger, is simply the time of realized nihilism, the age in which the will to power has become the ground of all our values; as a consequence, it is all but impossible for humanity to inhabit the world as anything other than its master. As a cultural reality, it is the perilous situation of a people that has thoroughly — one might even say systematically — forgotten the mystery of being, or forgotten (as Heidegger would have it) the mystery of the difference between beings and being as such. Nihilism is a way of seeing the world that acknowledges no truth other than what the human intellect can impose upon things, according to an excruciatingly limited calculus of utility, or of the barest mechanical laws of cause and effect. It is a "rationality" of the narrowest kind, so obsessed with *what* things are and how they might be *used* that it is no longer seized by wonder when it stands in the light of the dazzling truth *that* things are. It is a rationality that no longer knows how to hesitate before this greater mystery, or even to see that it is there, and thus is a rationality that cannot truly *think*.

This much Heidegger took to be obvious. The question to which he continually returned in his late work was not whether this was an accurate portrait of the modern situation, but rather what the history had been that had led Western humanity to this point. Parts of his answer were really somewhat conventional, and similar arguments had already been advanced by various Christian thinkers. Whatever its material causes (about which Heidegger really had nothing to say), the founding ideology of the modern vision of reality was, he thought, easily defined: the triumph of subjectivity in philosophy and of mechanism in science; egoism and technology. A crucial boundary had been *explicitly* crossed, he believed, in the thought of Descartes, who entirely inverted what had hitherto been regarded as the proper relation between the thinker and the being of the world. Whereas almost all earlier philosophers had assumed that the ground of truth lay outside themselves, and so had believed philosophy to be the art of making their concepts and words conform to the many ways in which being bore witness to itself, Descartes's method gave priority to a moment of radical doubt about everything outside the self. Earlier philosophy had generally treated epistemological skepticism as a frivolity to be rejected; Descartes saw it as a problem to be solved.

Hence, rather than beginning from philosophical wonder before the mystery of being (the Platonic and Aristotelian *thaumazein* that is the origin of all philosophy), Descartes began by trying to certify the reality of his perceptions, and upon the foundation of his own irreducible subjectivity as a "thinking substance." And to do this, he was actually first obliged temporarily to blind himself to the witness of being: "I will close my eyes," he says in the third *Meditation*, "stop up my ears . . . avert my senses from their objects . . . erase from my consciousness all images." Only then could he rationally reconstruct the world for himself, upon the *fundamentum inconcussum* of his own certainty *of* himself. Thus, in a way that Heidegger regarded as genuinely "impious," modern philosophy makes the human being — the self — the first principle of reason, and then determines what does or does not count as truth on the basis of what the self is capable of establishing *by itself*. The certitude that Descartes achieved was really of a rather trivial kind, and a poor substitute for the wonder that he had forsaken. Moreover, the world he saw when at last he opened his eyes again and graciously granted it its license to be was no longer the world upon which he had refused to look. It was a fabrication and brute assertion of the human will, an inert thing lying wholly within the power of the reductive intellect. The thinker was no longer answerable to being; being was now subject to him. Under the intellectual and cultural regime announced in Descartes's writings, the mystery of being has simply become invisible to thought. Even the mystery of God is forgotten, says Heidegger; the God of Descartes is a deduction of the ego, serving as a secondary certification of the verity of experience, and defined as a *causa sui* precisely because even divine being must now be certified by modern reason's understanding of causality. God thus is just another kind of thing, the chief function of which is to provide ontological and epistemic surety for all other things. (Heidegger himself, it should be noted, even though he had once insisted that philosophy must be a "methodological atheism," nonetheless refused to foreclose the question of God. In his essay of 1957, "The Onto-Theological Constitution of Metaphysics," he even argued that his own refusal to think of God in received philosophical terms perhaps made room for the truly "divine God" — the God before whom one could sing and dance, to whom one could make offerings and pray — to show himself anew, outside the determinations to which Cartesian rationalism would confine him.)

Anyway, all this said, Descartes is not in any sense the villain of Heidegger's tale. For Heidegger — and here is his truly challenging contention — what becomes explicit in Descartes has been implicit in all of Western philosophy since at least the days of Plato. Like Nietzsche, Heidegger traced the philosophical origins of nihilism back to ancient Athens; but unlike Nietzsche, he did so — or so he believed — without rancor, any impulse to pass judgment, or any lingering trace of metaphysical thinking. For him, the history of being is in a sense the story that being has told of itself down the centuries, over which philosophers have had only small control; and so they cannot be given full credit even for their errors.

HEIDEGGER BELIEVED that Western philosophy was that uniquely privileged tradition in which being, by some strange dispensation, had delivered itself over to human thought, rather than continue to conceal itself behind enticing and forbidding veils of myth. With so great a privilege, though, came great danger as well, because being is not a thing that can be thought about; indeed, to mistake it for any sort of thing that can be found among other things is already to have lost sight of its truest mystery. And yet thought, by its nature, finds it all but impossible not to think in terms of discrete things — discrete beings and substances and principles. Thus, in opening itself to thought, being inevitably also became a source of error. Nevertheless, for Heidegger, there had been a sort of blessed, Edenic moment when the thought of being had not yet gone too far astray. In the pearl-pale dawn of philosophy, in the writings of the pre-Socratics, the mystery of being showed itself with rare immediacy. Hegel had largely dismissed pre-Socratic thought as inchoate and primitive, but Heidegger insisted that just the opposite was true: it was at the beginning, in the first awakening of philosophy, that the Western thought of being was at its uncanniest and mightiest. Precisely because the experience of being had not yet hardened into a system of rigid concepts, reason had not yet attempted to master being as just another finite object of reflection and will. In this essentially prephilosophical philosophy, being revealed itself as the silent, mostly ineffable process by which all things emerge out of the hiddenness of nonbeing, waver for a time in the openness of being, and then pass away into hiddenness again. Or, phrased differently, being was experienced as the passage of all things from future possibility into the nothingness of the past through the narrow juncture of the always disappearing present; and so the thought of being had not yet been separated into a stark opposition between temporality and eternity. The pre-Socratic response to this experience was essentially poetic: not an attempt to devise a hierarchy of categories by which to capture the event in a cage of human concepts, but rather an attempt to name the event of being in its mystery, with an almost childlike innocence, in a language of purest immediacy. For this reason, Heidegger believed, the words those earliest thinkers used, in their original meanings, were still inseparable from the event of being's self-disclosure; for a time, being really manifested itself — which is also to say, retained its impenetrable mystery — in the names that it evoked from those whom it addressed.

Heidegger was fascinated by those names, and liked to descend again and again into their etymological depths, in order to show that, when they were first uttered, they were not the drearily lifeless principles that later philosophy often made them. *Physis*, for instance, before it was reduced to the narrower, largely taxonomic concept of "nature," referred to being as the mysterious upwelling source from which beings inexhaustibly arise and to which they return; it meant something wholly unlike the "physical" forces with which modern reason is acquainted. *Logos*, before it was reduced merely to a "word" conveying facts, or to "reason" in the philosophical sense, or to "principle" or the ground of "logic," referred to being as that power of gathering that brings all things forth into the light of being, holding them together in the unity of the world while also allowing them to shine forth in their separateness. *Aletheia*, before it became "truth" in the limited sense of a correspondence between a proposition and an object of cognition, or of this or that fact about that or this thing, named being as the primordial movement of "unhiddenness," being unveiling itself in beings, the darkness of possibility ever anew pouring forth its secret riches in the fleeting sparks of transient beings. And so on.

The problem with such names, however, is that they cannot be reduced to stable concepts, and so cannot be mastered; and the human intellect craves concepts, and the human will craves mastery. Thought could not dwell forever in the innocent immediacy of being's first advent; and so, inevitably, the almost childlike genius of that primordial apprehension faded away and the mere philosopher replaced the poetic thinker. This is not to say that philosophy would ever completely forget that first awareness of the difference between being and beings; it could not, as the very impulse to philosophy is nothing other than the "forgetful memory" of that difference. But it is to say that philosophy was condemned ever thereafter to a language that was less than a shadow of the language that the first thinkers of being had spoken. Plato was the first great philosopher in this second phase in being's history; it was he who committed the vital apostasy that would lead Western thought down its path of fruitful error. He turned his eyes away from the ungovernable, essentially *inconceivable* flow of time, and so away from the very process by which being shows itself, and looked instead toward a fabulous eternity of changeless essences, the timeless "ideas" or (more literally) "looks" of things; and it was to this latter realm that he accorded the authority of "truth," while consigning everything proper to time to the subphilosophical category of "unlikeness." This, for Heidegger, was the first obvious stirring of the will to power in Western thought, the moment when philosophy first tried to assert its power over the mystery of being, by freezing that mystery in a collection of lifeless, invisible, immutable "principles" perfectly obedient to the philosopher's conceptual powers. Of its nature, such a way of thinking is supremely jealous: it resents the coyness of being in withholding itself from clear and precise ideas; and it resents any form of novelty that might upset its invariable order of essences, anything new — any way of thinking or speaking of being — that might try to come forth into the open.

This is metaphysics in the fullest and, for Heidegger, most problematic sense. It knows no truth that is not immune to the particularities of time. It sees the truth of any sort of object (say an apple) not as that object itself in its strange and lovely transience, passing through its various moments of existence (seed, tree, ripened fruit hanging upon the bough, fruit eaten or moldering away, and so on) but as the unchanging form upon which it is modeled (the apple that never shines forth in the beauty of its own color, that has no flavor or fragrance, that has never lived). This understanding of truth is for Heidegger already nihilistic. It is already an expression of the will to power, though still in a restrained and even self-deluding form. It is at least still pious, it still feels wonder before the mystery of being, even if it has largely forgotten how to name that mystery. But it also inaugurates an entire history of philosophical epochs, one succeeding another — pagan, Christian, secular, it makes no difference — crystallizing into one or another system of abstractions and then dissolving again. This is inevitable, because no system born of the fateful Platonic error can entirely recover any adequate sense of the difference between being and beings. It will always approach being as another kind of thing, another substance or principle. Yet the suppressed awareness of this difference also continues always to drive thought from one inadequate formulation to another. In a sense, it is by their downfall that these systems remind us most poignantly of the mystery that silently abides behind them; but by their failure they also progressively reveal more and more of the will to power that animates them, and more and more they consciously yield to it. At the end of this story, we arrive at a nihilism that no longer hides itself from itself. Having failed to find that ultimate and changeless principle or system of principles that no doubt can corrupt, Western rationality begins to exult ever more in the power it has gained over physical reality during its long pilgrimage through the inconclusiveness of history. For Heidegger, the last metaphysician was Nietzsche, because in Nietzsche's thought the will to power was elevated to a position of ultimate truth; it became the principle of principles. In that moment, metaphysics became somehow perfectly self-aware. It had discovered its deepest essence by having achieved its nihilistic destiny.

It is not entirely clear, I should note, whether Heidegger actually believed that the history of Western philosophy had created the history of Western culture, or whether he held some more vaguely dialectical notion of the relation between the two. What is clear is that he saw his philosophical genealogy of nihilism as also an account of how Western humanity as a whole has arrived at an essentially nihilistic way of living upon the earth. To his mind, our age is simply the age of technology, which is to say that our reasoning is simply a narrow and calculative rationalism that sees the world about us not as the home in which we dwell, where we might keep ourselves near to being's mystery and respond to it; rather the world for us now is mere mechanism, as well as a "standing reserve" of material resources awaiting exploitation in the projects of the human will. The world cannot now speak to us, or we cannot hear it. Being, in its difference from all beings, no longer wakens wonder in us; as it is not a thing we can manipulate, we have forgotten it. Not only do we not try to answer the question of being; we cannot even understand what the question is. The world is now what we can "enframe," whose meaning we alone establish, according to the degree of *usefulness* we find in it. The regime of subjectivity has confined all reality within the limits of our power to propose and dispose. More and more, our culture has become incapable of reverence before the mystery of being, and therefore incapable of reverent hesitation. And it is this pervasive, largely unthinking impiety that underlies most of the special barbarisms of our time.

ONE COULD GO ON indefinitely, really. There is a sort of morose, doom-fraught grandeur about it all that at times becomes positively enthralling. We live, according to Heidegger, in a very deep twilight indeed; ours is the time of the "darkening of the world and the flight of the gods." We are homeless in the world, standing over against it, and it is doubtful we will ever find ourselves at home again, at least if we are forced to rely upon our own meager resources. Now, as Heidegger remarked in a posthumously published interview with *Der Spiegel*, "only a god can save us." To some this darkly prophetic bathos is the most insufferable aspect of Heidegger's later writings. To others it is simply a quaint reminder of the period in which he wrote. In either case, it seems at times painfully absurd when one considers the evils to which he himself had earlier, and for several years, allied himself. And yet, it would be foolish to dismiss his message simply on account of the messenger. It simply cannot be denied that the horrors of the last century were both conceptually and historically inseparable from some of the deepest principles of modernity's founding ideologies. The "final solution" was a kind of consummation of all the evils of European history perhaps, but it was possible as a conscious project only in an age in which humanity itself had first been reduced to a technology (the technology of race). Knowledge of how to split the atom was the inevitable consequence of advances in physics perhaps, but nuclear weapons were also the product of cultures that had reduced all of nature to a morally neutral "technics."

Quite apart from the most acute expressions of modern nihilism, moreover, there is for Heidegger the more chronic reality of a culture in precipitous decline: the degeneration of the arts, the hideousness of our public works, crass consumerism, scabrous popular culture, and so on. For Heidegger, these are perhaps the most telling proofs that all of modernity is a condition of alienation. Humanity's only greatness, he repeatedly insisted, has arisen from an ability to dwell in the world as part of it, at peace with it, nourished and sheltered by its mystery as much as by its bounty. All true art, everything worthy among the works of our hands, comes into being in the space that our intimate closeness to the mystery of being opens before us; our art (especially poetry) is the highest way in which being gives itself to us in any age, showing itself in the creative response it evokes from us, both by its generosity and by its elusiveness. If we are no longer conscious of that mystery, nothing we make will shine with the splendor of the world about us, or draw us nearer to its wonder.

Perhaps the most beguiling moments in Heidegger's late writings are those in which he tries to describe what it means to dwell in the world in a truly human way. They are almost entirely devoid of conceptual content, at least of the sort philosophers tend to like, and at times their language is perhaps overly saturated in a melancholy and somewhat ornamental paganism; but Heidegger had become convinced in his later years that the search for conceptual content is not really the search for truth. So he presented his vision in a series of evocative pictures whose meaning was inexhaustible precisely because it could not be expressed in philosophical categories. The pagan temple, for instance, was one of his favored images (though he also sometimes used the image of a lonely Christian church). The temple, as the center of a people's attention and piety, was the way in which human existence was oriented in space and time and gathered into a unity. It demarcated a boundary between the sacred and profane, and thereby created a sheltered place in which the encounter between human beings and the divine (which is the mystery of being in its most eminent and compelling splendor) could occur. In so doing, it called forth the special artistry and ethos of the age that produced it. In itself it was a central expression of the sometimes antagonistic, sometimes peaceful, but ultimately nuptial union of two realities that Heidegger simply called "earth" and "world." That is, in the elements from which it was made, illuminated under the open sky, it showed forth the hidden riches of the earth, while through the pious craftsmanship of its makers it made manifest the highest powers of a human world.

The most entrancing and obscure of Heidegger's images was the *Geviert* — one of Heidegger's many neologisms, usually translated as the "fourfold" — the "ring dance" of earth and heavens, mortals and gods. This was Heidegger's attempt to provide something like a nonmetaphysical alternative to Aristotle's order of causes, at least in understanding the creations of human culture. It is these four together, he says, in their inseparable but distinct inherence in one another, that create a space that allows human beings to be at home upon the earth, and that allows being to unveil itself in a particular way at a particular moment. This "dance of the four" has, in every age, caused human beings genuinely to create, and to allow being's mystery to shine out from what they create. An object such as, for instance, a silver votive vessel comes into being not only by the interplay between the dark hiddenness of the earth and the radiant openness of the heavens — hidden ores brought up to shine in the light of day — but by the reverently poetic approach of mortals toward the gods, and by the lordly approach of the gods toward mortals out of the hidden realm of the divine, announcing themselves in the powers of nature.

In any event, as I say, this is all only imagery — achingly nostalgic and suggestive imagery — meant only to depict a way of inhabiting the world that Heidegger believed was constitutive of our humanity, but that late modern humanity has forgotten. Beyond that, he had little in the way of recommendations for how we might as a culture recover what we have lost. He did, however, suggest that now that we have reached the end of the metaphysical history of being, we can at least look back over that history and attempt a kind of *Wiederholung*, or "retrieval," of the past, which might allow us to understand nihilism, and perhaps even someday to overcome it. Here is where the twilit Hegelian mystique of belatedness becomes most apparent in Heidegger's thought. It is very late in the day indeed, Heidegger believed, and we are very near the night of total nihilism; but in this the time of highest risk the possibility of healing has opened up as well. Having seen the nihilistic destiny to which our ways of thinking have led, perhaps we can now reflect upon them before it is too late, and learn to put aside the appetite for power, and to cultivate in ourselves instead an attitude that does not repeat the primordial error. This attitude he calls — borrowing the word from Meister Eckhart — *Gelassenheit*: release, letting be, learning not to coerce reality but rather patiently to wait upon it. Simply let the world *be* the world. If we should ever achieve this state of the will, then perhaps the mystery of being might open itself anew to us, God or the gods might return in the glory of true divinity, poets might arise again to speak the names of being. . . . For now, though, this remains a very remote possibility; and the night is rapidly descending.

WHAT IN THE END should we think of Heidegger's genealogy of nihilism? It seems clear to me that we should neither embrace it nor reject it as a whole. The most unfortunately Hegelian element in Heidegger's thought is its drive toward total synopsis. His account of the history of metaphysics is simply too uniform and comprehensive in its claims, and as a result it misrepresents or fails to account for other realities about the history of Western thought that cannot intelligibly be treated as part of a larger history of nihilism. Of course, Heidegger was willing to grant that Western philosophy had never been nihilistic through and through. But he rarely demonstrated any very keen awareness of the ways in which, for instance, Plato's understanding of the Form of the Good, or certain Christian understandings of the analogy between transcendent and created being (and so on), open up paths that certainly cannot terminate in nihilism. And he certainly never considered the possibility that the only way to preserve being's self-disclosure against the human longing for conceptual mastery of reality might be a fully developed metaphysics of transcendent being. That, though, is an argument for another time. What should be said here, however, is that Heidegger's renunciation of metaphysics did not in the end allow him to produce a coherent ontology of his own. His efforts to describe the relation of being to beings in purely immanent terms ultimately added up to very little; certainly they did not provide any convincing answers to such perennial questions as why there are beings at all. At most, all he could do was point to temporality, the ceaseless flow of beings out of nothingness and into nothingness again, and then — in a gesture that often seems as much one of hopelessness as of "piety" — point away toward the mysterious *Ereignis*, the "appropriating event," that somehow brings this about. Because he had left himself no room for any kind of language of analogy, which might have allowed him to say how transcendent being shows itself in immanent existence while still preserving its transcendence; and because moreover he had decided in advance that one cannot speak of being in other than temporal terms; he really could not escape lapsing into a certain fatalism regarding the history he described. Even he had to admit that, if there is no metaphysically "correct" way for being to show itself, perhaps the age of technology really is the next "proper" moment in being's dispensation. If so, all he could do was hope that there might still be a truly human way of inhabiting the world that is coming to pass.

In any event, we are not obliged to make Heidegger's problems our own; and we certainly do not have to accept his story in its entirety to appreciate what is true and troubling in it. It is enough to acknowledge that the possibility of nihilism is indeed part of the entire history of metaphysics, even while insisting that countless ways of avoiding nihilism (even thoroughly metaphysical ways) have also opened up within that history. After all, we could not have arrived where we are purely by chance. And we would be foolish not to take seriously his diagnosis of the special pathologies of modernity. It is good to understand something of the history — and so the historical contingency — of many of our dominant forms of thought, and to see what their more terrible consequences have been and may yet be. And I think we can also appreciate the simple pathos of

Heidegger's disenchantment with philosophy. At times, of course, it is little more than the protest of a weary man, perhaps aware of his own moral and intellectual failures, imploring the voices of philosophy and ideology to cease their babbling. Western humanity has talked its way right to the edge of the abyss — so, please, be silent now. Wait. Listen. Let being speak, let the world be a world again, let the divine show itself to us if it will. But stop talking for a while. It is almost tempting to see Heidegger's history of being as a sort of epic transposition of the private story of a long and disappointing life. It has an air of spiritual fatigue about it, a deep longing for a return to innocence, to immediacy, to childlike wonder and to the child's delight in speaking the names of things: a wise simplicity not yet corrupted by those empty concepts that distance us from the world. It is almost as if he wanted to find a way back again to the experience of the child's first amazement before the mystery of the world, and to linger there forever, speaking a language of pure naming, pure invocation — the language of Adam or of the natural poet. (For the sake of his soul, of course, it would have been good had he understood that the only real return to innocence comes by way of real repentance. But, if he ever did, he gave no evidence to that effect apart from a few phantom hints at the margins of a few enigmatic essays.)

We can also grant, I think, that Heidegger did indeed surpass Hegel as a philosopher of the twilight, and in two senses. In his later years, he liked to speak of the true thinker as a wanderer in the forest, seeking out hidden or forgotten paths, uncertain of his course, but looking for that clearing among the trees where truth might show itself. I do not believe he ever found that clearing, but when I am feeling charitable I am willing to believe he really did seek it. In those moments, I am willing even to indulge his somewhat romanticized view of himself: a figure in the twilight, at the end of a long journey through a large valley and into wooded hills, perhaps pausing on a low ridge that affords him a last narrow glimpse of the paths he has followed, watching the evening descending over the mountains and down toward darkening lakes and fields, trying to fix in memory the shape of a world soon to be lost in night. If nothing else, he certainly did come later in the day than Hegel, and told a story that contained more of evening's wisdom than Hegel's had. And Heidegger was a philosopher of twilight in a more crucial sense too. That is, he understood the vocation of every true thinker to be much the same as the vocation of the true poet, or of any true artist: to bear witness to that haunting and penumbral interval that marks the difference between being and beings, and to attempt to keep it open in our thoughts and our words and our works. He was himself in no sense a morally credible witness, admittedly, but he was an often perceptive one. And he knew that being's mystery, while it is the source of our humanity, never shows itself to us with the undeniable clarity of a distinct thing among other things, but reveals itself only as a kind of intangible shadow at the edges of the things that are. Shadows, however, disappear as darkness falls, so those who can must continue to testify to that difference, to that mystery — because, if it is wholly forgotten, no one can imagine how deep and long the night may be.

# NINETEEN

# The Power of the Sword

This was not the topic I wanted to write about today, but sometimes one gets unexpectedly diverted. So it goes.

Just the day before yesterday, Joe Carter produced a column taking the bishops of Arizona to task for their recent denunciation of capital punishment as incompatible with the gospel, and arguing further not only that capital punishment is permissible from a Christian perspective, but that it is positively required by Scripture. I have never met Mr. Carter, but we have corresponded, and he seems like a decent and morally serious fellow; so it is with some regret that I take exception to his column in public. But I thought he treated a difficult moral issue with an ill-advised excess of confidence, and with a very questionable use of Scripture and theology. I realize, of course, that evangelicals have their own traditions of reading Scripture, and I would have been surprised had Carter treated, say, the story of Noah with quite the bold, broad allegorical brushstrokes one finds in patristic readings. But evangelicals are also required to get the details right, and on this occasion Carter didn't; and certainly evangelicals know, if only from the words of Christ or Paul, that Christians cannot approach the entirety of Scripture as a collection of infallible oracles issuing directly from the lips of God. One really has to consider how Christians are required to read the Bible before proclaiming what Scripture *"requires"* of Christians (the emphasis is Carter's).

This is the substance of my disagreement with Carter, at any rate. He does make a passing reference to the dictates of natural law — at second hand, by way of Edward Feser — but I think that can be largely ignored. To be perfectly frank, most natural law arguments on the matter are hopelessly ad hoc constructions, consisting in prescriptions unconvincingly and willfully attached to endlessly contestable descriptions (but that is an argument for another time). And, even if capital punishment is entirely in keeping with natural justice (and I am more than willing to grant that it is), that has next to no bearing whatsoever on how Christians should understand their moral obligations with regard to it. The gospel, after all, is a terribly disturbing thing when one actually pays attention to its claims. Not only are the law of Christian charity and the workings of divine grace not limited to natural justice; they are often positively subversive of it. There is a kind of apocalyptic indifference to the economy of nature in the New Testament, something altogether unnatural — or, let's just say, supernatural. One can scarcely exaggerate the extravagance of its departures from the equilibrium of normal justice. For instance, not only does it place individual prohibitions on even proportional retribution, it also demands that the Christian compound certain injustices with an *excess* of compliance — surrendering one's coat as well as one's cloak, or more money than is demanded, going a mile farther than one is compelled to do, meeting violent assault by proffering the other cheek, not resisting evil, forgiving one's brother seventy times seven, and so on.

And then there are God's curious dealings with his own "everlasting" promises, freely grafting Gentiles into a covenant on which they have no proper claim, without even the requirements of the law, "contrary to nature" (*para physin*), as Paul says. And, still more shockingly, there is the central mystery of what is said to have happened on Golgotha: not just Christ on the cross asking his Father to forgive those who are murdering him, but the whole drama of God taking the due and *natural* penalty of all human cruelty, violence, selfishness, and sin upon himself, the full "wrath of the law," and then offering forgiveness freely to all, exorbitantly outside the bounds of natural justice — and, at Easter, outside even the bounds of natural causality. None of this may tell us definitively how we should understand a civil government's obligations regarding the preservation of order. It does tell us, however, that in trying to understand the Christian vision of the social good, natural justice can be neither the first nor the final consideration. It is important, but as yet too limited; it still belongs to the "former things" that are passing away. And, to his credit, Carter makes his argument primarily from Scripture and theology. Unfortunately, on both counts, his argument is irreparably defective.

Scripture first.

Carter invokes the Noachide covenant from the ninth chapter of Genesis, and claims that its "everlasting" authority encompasses the commandment that whosoever sheds his brother's blood shall have his blood shed in turn. Now, setting aside the rather profound question of how Christian exegetes are to read the legal prescriptions of the Old Testament, or even the purely historical question of how traditionally they have done so, one should still note that there is something problematic about seeing God's everlasting covenant — his promise — never again to exterminate all life with a flood, and to tie a rainbow around his finger (so to speak) to remind himself of his resolve, as extending to the laws given in the previous verses. Syntactically, it does not. And would Carter contend, then, that the prohibition on eating meat with its blood is eternally binding as well? Has every Liverpudlian who's ever dined on black pudding violated God's everlasting covenant with humanity? And how then should Christians view the Mosaic prescriptions, which are no less "everlasting" in their legitimacy, but which Paul regarded as of no account not only for Gentile Christians, but also for Jewish Christians (hence his rebukes to Peter for keeping the law for appearance's sake)? In any event, Carter's representation of the passage is simply inaccurate. More egregiously unfortunate, however, is his use of Paul's words in the thirteenth chapter of Romans regarding the power of the sword and the authority God has delegated to earthly rulers. It always astonishes me (and I am putting that very weakly) that Christians can find any encouragement in that passage to believe that capital punishment is morally *good*. Certainly Paul says nothing of the sort. He uses the wonderfully vivid image of the one in authority bearing the sword "not in vain," but that is a much vaguer metaphor than Carter grasps. The sword represents the power of coercion, certainly, though not specifically the practice of capital punishment; it has no more prescriptive force than saying, as we might today, "That's why the police carry guns." Even if the "sword" really were clearly meant as a symbol of the power to execute criminals, though, Paul is merely saying that Christians who commit crimes may expect to suffer the wrath of God under the form of civil penalty. He certainly makes no comment on the intrinsic justice or injustice of any particular practice of the state. One assumes, for instance, that he would not necessarily have regarded the Roman habit of crucifying thieves as somehow *intrinsically* just, even if he believed that a Christian who stole something and was caught had brought about his own condign condemnation. More importantly still, this passage says absolutely nothing about what punishments baptized Christians who might come to power — a contingency Paul never envisaged in his wildest imaginings — ought to impose on criminals. The moral content of the entire passage extends only to the actions of individuals under the law; beyond that, it provides no moral instructions for rulers or lawmakers, and there is simply no warrant for claiming that it *requires* Christians to approve of capital punishment. As for Carter's strange *argumentum de silentio* in regard to Christ's words in the fifth chapter of Matthew, it should — like practically all such arguments — be charitably ignored.

The still more significant flaws in Carter's argument, however, are theological. I have to say, I find it strange to see any Christian arguing that the prescriptions and penalties of the law established in the age before Christ make any sort of unambiguous demands upon Christian consciences or putatively Christian societies. (I find it especially strange, for obvious historical reasons, to see a Protestant do it.) For one thing, the Christian who thinks this way seems to have failed to appreciate the special provocations of Christ's own teachings regarding the law. Again and again, Christ "preserves" the law — whether as it concerns the Sabbath or as it concerns the due penalty for adultery — by so radically reinterpreting and reorienting it as practically to invert its consequences. For another, the entire Pauline theology of grace and salvation asserts that the power of the law has been surpassed by the power of God's free gift, and so the concrete prescriptions of the law — and this means not just circumcision and kosher regulations, but its criminal and penal ordinances as well — have now been set aside. The eternal moral truths that the law contains (do not kill, do not commit adultery, and so forth) remain, but the *wrath* of the law has been vanquished in Christ.

I often think that modern Christians would be rather disturbed if they were perfectly aware of Paul's vision of the created order, simply because most of us tend to assume that he was working from premises much like our own. As a result, we rarely grasp how strange and radical his teachings were. For one thing, though we may think in terms of God's providential guidance of nature and history, unlike Paul (and unlike a great many Hellenistic Jews at the time) we do not think of that providence in terms of authority delegated to angelic powers ruling from heavenly courts (*archontes* and *exousiai* and so forth), as the governors or even "gods" of the nations. But, for Paul, the old age — the age of a fallen creation — is one in which these angelic intermediaries, who are the often rebellious or incompetent deputies of God, rule over the various peoples and "elements" (*stoicheia*) of the earth. We, though, tend to read right past Paul's remarks to the Galatians that the old law was imperfect because it came not directly from God, but from his angel (the angel who reigned over Israel and who appeared to Moses) and was passed through a human mediator (Moses himself). The promise of the new age, by contrast, is that now all these heavenly powers have been subdued again, under the foot of Christ, and in the age to come

Christ himself will rule over all creation directly. The book of Romans, of course, provides a deeper and more "nuanced" appreciation of the law of Israel, and that is why Romans provides the most stinging rebukes to triumphalist supersessionists. But, even in Romans, the theological vision is constant. All peoples now belong to Christ as a single body; the partitions of law and custom — even good law and honorable custom — have been broken down; and the wrath of the law has been swallowed up in infinite charity. All had once been bound in disobedience (Jew and Gentile alike), that God might now show mercy on all. And all who belong to Christ have entered already into that new creation, and are forbidden now to retreat again to the "elemental" order of the old.

What, then, does this mean with regard to Christian thinking on capital punishment? For myself, the only compellingly convincing answer is that Christians can have no recourse to it, ever; but I will not go so far as to state that I know that this is what Scripture positively *requires* — and certainly not in those portentously dictatorial italics. What I will say is that, if the gospel is in any measure true, then its challenge is far more radical than is allowed by the sort of argument Mr. Carter makes. In Christ — in the historical event of Christ — so profound a reorientation of moral and metaphysical perspectives has been introduced into history that all our understandings of nature, of holy law, and of moral obligation have been shaken to their foundations. One must first dwell in the sheer wonder of that event before one then tries to make sense of what it demands of us. Where this will lead, I cannot say with perfect conviction. But, when trying to think of capital punishment in light of that event, I suggest we begin by contemplating the only two episodes in the New Testament that seem to have any direct bearing on the issue, and that involve any clear dominical or divine pronouncements. The one is the story of the woman taken in adultery, justly condemned to death under the law, whom Jesus nevertheless refuses to condemn, and sends away only with the injunction to sin no more. The other is the story of Christ's own condemnation at the hands of duly appointed legal authority, for offenses against public order (the cleansing of the temple, after all, was a fairly provocative and, surely in Roman eyes, dangerous act). And that verdict was, of course, overturned by God, and the penalty annulled. Taken together, these two stories may not lay out an exhaustive table of laws before us, but they certainly afford us a glimpse of the moral and spiritual order of the kingdom. And, for Christians, it is the law of the kingdom that is absolute.

# TWENTY

## The Trouble with Ayn Rand

It is one of the most indelibly memorable scenes, and certainly the best twist ending, to have come out of the cinema of the 1960s: Charlton Heston riding his horse along the beach, Linda Harrison mounted behind him with her arms wrapped around his waist, both quite fetching in their late Pleistocene dishabille, until they come upon some gigantic object, visible to the viewer at first only from behind, and just fragmentarily familiar from the ruinous silhouette of its torch and spiked coronal. Heston dismounts, an expression of dawning understanding on his face. The surf breaks about his feet. "Oh, my God!" he exclaims and falls to his knees. "They finally, really did it!" Beating the sand with his fist, he cries out, "You maniacs! Damn you! God damn you all to hell!" The white foam swirls about him again. Only then does the camera draw back, now from the opposite angle, to reveal the shattered remains of the Statue of Liberty. The screen goes dark, but the sound of waves can still be heard.

I do not really want to talk about *The Planet of the Apes* just now. I mention the scene only because, quite unintentionally, I found myself reenacting it only a few days ago, uttering the same lines almost verbatim, sinking to the earth under the same burden of world-darkening despair. Oh, there was no bleak, blinding prospect of the gray and silver sea stretching out toward an impossibly distant horizon, there were no waves breaking with a desolate sigh on the barren strand, there was no horse, no fallen copper colossus, and certainly no beautiful, scantily clad woman nearby. There was, however, the same frantic look of terrible recognition in my eyes, the same pitch of hopeless horror in my voice, the same sense of doom. I had just discovered that some malevolent wretch had done it at last: had made a film of *Atlas Shrugged*. No, worse: the first of what will ultimately be three films, one for each of the novel's three parts. The trailer had been unveiled, someone told me, at this year's CPAC (Conservative Political Action Conference) convention, and it had had all the libertarian livestock jubilantly braying in their stalls. It took only a moment to find it on the web. Then I knew, just as Charlton Heston knew on that beach, that Western civilization was at its end. For decades, this monstrous project had haunted the boardrooms of Hollywood studios and the lofts of emotionally arrested screenwriters; the possibility had been dangled like the sword of Damocles over the head of a defenseless world. But, until now, some merciful power had kept the tragic denouement in abeyance.

I suppose I should have seen it coming. It's the fashion of the moment. Ayn Rand and her idiotic "objectivism" are enjoying a, well, I will not call it a renaissance, so let us say a *recrudescence.* Suddenly she is everywhere. In the stock television footage of Tea Party rallies — there she always is on at least one upraised poster, her grim gray features looming over the crowd like the granitic countenance of some cruel heathen deity glutted on human blood. So it goes. At least it answers one question for me. Civilization is always a fragile accommodation at best, precariously poised between barbarism on one side and decadence on the other, and as a civilization dissolves it begins to oscillate between them, ever more spasmodically, until the final collapse comes. Call it morbid curiosity on my part, but I often wonder where the debris of our civilization will ultimately be heaped; and, if this film portends what I fear, now I may know the answer. Rand was definitely on the side of barbarism.

All right, all right — perhaps I'm being just a little spiteful. I may even be overreacting. The world survived the filming of *The Fountainhead* (if only by the skin of its teeth), and it may yet survive this. And Ayn Rand always provokes a rather extravagant reaction from me, and probably for purely ideological reasons. For instance, I like the Sermon on the Mount. She regarded its prescriptions as among the vilest ever uttered. I suspect that charity really is the only way to avoid wasting one's life in a desert of sterile egoism. She regarded Christian morality as a poison that had polluted the will of Western man with its ethos of parasitism and orgiastic self-oblation. And, simply said, I cannot find much common ground with someone who believed that the principal source of human woe over the last twenty centuries has been a tragic shortage of selfishness. Still, I like to think my detestation of Rand's novels follows from more than a mere disagreement over differing visions of the universe. What's a universe here or there, after all? I prefer to think it's a matter of good taste. For what really puts both *Atlas Shrugged* and *The Fountainhead* in a class of their own is how sublimely awful they are. I know one shouldn't expect much from a writer who thought Mickey Spillane a greater artist than Shakespeare. Even so, the cardboard characters, the ludicrous dialogue, the cretinous perorations, the predictable plotting, the lunatic repetitiousness and ba-nality, the shockingly syrupy romance — it all goes to create a uniquely nauseous effect: at once mephitic and cloying, at once sulfur and cotton candy.

Remember, the chief reason that *The Fountainhead* is among the most hilariously bad films ever made is that it is so slavishly faithful to the novel and to Rand's screenplay. The result is hypnotically ghastly. Dialogue that had been merely stilted on the page became almost surreal in its lousiness when spoken aloud. The only way the actors could deliver the lines was with a cold mechanical exactitude and at a bizarrely cantering pace, as if trying to get them out before they could do any permanent damage to the mouth. For most of the movie, the three leads — Gary Cooper, Patricia Neal, and Raymond Massey — seem to be trying to outdo one another in emotional and facial paralysis. Of course, Cooper never could act; but it is positively painful to watch Neal and Massey struggling to achieve some semblance of dramatic plausibility. The film's defining moment for me is probably the first meeting between Dominique Francon (Neal) and How-ard Roark (Cooper) at the gala opening of a house the latter has designed. "I admire your work, more than anything I've ever seen," Dominique an-nounces without wasting any words on small talk about the weather or the hors d'oeuvres. "You may realize that this is not a tie, but a gulf, between us. . . . I wish I had never seen your building. It's the things we admire or want that enslave us and I'm not easy to bring into submission." (The flir-tatious little gamine.) Really, one has to see the scene quite to appreciate its full idiocy. But, then again, there's also the conversation between the same two characters later that night: "They hate you for the greatness of your achievement," Dominique tells Roark in a tone that oddly seems to combine erotic agitation with profound catatonia. "They hate you for your integrity. They hate you because they know they can neither corrupt nor ruin you." (Bloody *they* — I never could stand those swine.) By the way, in the context of the film, this is actually a kind of foreplay. The whole time she's speaking, Dominique is gazing at Roark longingly, with an inviting come-hither-and-rape-me look in her eyes (which is just what the gal-lant Roark does a little later on). Who can say what the most ridiculous moment really is, though? There's hardly a scene without a rich vein of unintentional comedy. Perhaps it's Roark's imbecile address to the jury at his trial: "The creator stands on his own judgment. The parasite follows the opinions of others. The creator thinks. The parasite copies. The creator produces. The parasite loots. The creator's concern is the conquest of nature. The parasite's concern is the conquest of men." And so on. There, of course, one has the essential oafishness of Rand's view of reality. For her, the world really was starkly divided between creators and parasites, and the vast majority of humanity belonged to the ranks of the latter. "I came here to say I do not recognize anyone's right to one minute of my life," Roark continues, "nor to any part of my energy, nor to any achievement of mine." Rand really imagined that there could ever be a man whose best achievements were simply and solely the products of his own unfettered and unaided will. She had no concept of grace, even of the ordinary kind: the grace of an existence we do not give ourselves, of natural powers with which we could never have endowed ourselves, and of all those other persons upon whom even the strongest among us are dependent. She lacked any ennobling sense that what lies most deeply within us also comes from impossibly far beyond us, as an unmerited gift. She liked to talk about "virtue" a great deal — meaning primarily strength of will and the value that one creates out of one's own native resources — but for her the only important question regarding the relation between the individual and society was who has a right to what. That is, admittedly, a question that must be asked at various times, but it is never the question that true virtue — true strength — asks of itself.

But I suppose I have circled back on myself. Where Rand's fiction is concerned, I suppose aesthetic and ideological revulsion are not really separable. What made her novels not just risibly clumsy, but truly shrill and hideous, was the exorbitantly trashy philosophy behind them. Taken solely as a storyteller, she had many of the skills of the proficient pulp writer. Her overwrought plots, her comically patent villains, her panting, fiery, fierce yet quiescent heroines — all of that would be quite at home in lushly bad romance fiction. Had she not mistaken herself for a deep thinker, she might have done well enough, producing books that filled out that vital niche between *Forever Amber* and *Valley of the Dolls*. Sadly, though, her ambitions would not let her rest there.

And, really, what can one say about objectivism? It isn't so much a philosophy as what someone who has never actually encountered philosophy imagines a philosophy might look like: good, hard, axiomatic absolutes; a bluff attitude of intellectual superiority; lots of simple atomic premises supposedly immune to doubt; immense and inflexible conclusions; and plenty of assertions about what is "rational" or "objective" or "real." Oh, and of course, an imposing brand name ending with an "-ism." Rand was so eerily ignorant of all the interesting problems of ontology, epistemology, or logic that she believed she could construct an irrefutable system around a collection of simple maxims like "existence is identity" and "consciousness is identification," all gathered from the damp fenlands between vacuous tautology and catastrophic category error. She was simply unaware that there were any genuine philosophical problems that could not be summarily solved by flatly proclaiming that *this* is objectivity, *this* is rational, *this* is scientific, in the peremptory tones of an *Obersturmführer* drilling his commandos.

Anyway, I have wandered far from the beach where I began. Let me end with a heartfelt supplication.

Not long after seeing the trailer for *Atlas Shrugged*, I came across the trailer for quite a different kind of film: Terrence Malick's *The Tree of Life*. Malick is the world's greatest living filmmaker, and this project has been with him for years. The two minutes or so of clips that have been released are far more beautiful, moving, and profound than anything associated with the name of Ayn Rand could ever be. "There are two ways through life," a woman's voice announces as the trailer opens: "the way of nature and the way of grace. We have to choose which one to follow." That is arguably the great theme of all of Malick's finest work; and I suspect that the deeper question the film poses is whether these two ways can become one. If what little I have heard about the film is right, moreover, the answer will have something to do with a love capable of embracing all things, and of both granting and receiving forgiveness. But we shall see. Whatever the case, this is my plea: Do not go to see *Atlas Shrugged*. Do not encourage those people. Go instead to *The Tree of Life*, which — whether it should prove a triumph or a failure — will be the work of a remarkable artist who really does have something to tell us about both nature and grace (two things about which Rand knew absolutely nothing). So make the wise cinematic choice here, for the good of your own soul, but also for the sake of a rapidly foundering civilization.

# TWENTY-ONE

# Great-Uncle Aloysius

In one of my columns last January, I mentioned that there had been no practicing pagans in my family since the death of my great-uncle Aloysius Bentley (1895–1987), who liked to welcome in the New Year by sacrificing a goat or a pair of woodcocks to Janus and Dionysus on the small marble altar he kept in his garden (carved for him by a sculptor who specialized in funerary monuments). It was only a passing reference, and one I did not expect would attract much notice; but apparently some readers found the story somewhat outlandish, even to the point of doubting its veracity. I suppose I understand their suspicions. After all, how many men are really named Aloysius? I should point out, however, that in all things onomastic my great-uncle's parents were given to exotic turns: they called his older sister Fiammetta Celesta, his younger brother Antoninus Impius, and their favorite Great Dane Apollonius Maior. Actually, his full personal name was Aloysius Gaius Stilicho, but most people knew him simply as Al, while his wife and a few other of his particular intimates called him Wishus; by the time I came to know him, when he was in his seventies, he had legally added Philostratus to his collection of gaudy appellations and had taken to signing all official documents and correspondences "Phil."

Of course, I imagine some skeptical readers were reacting more to his religious predilections than to his name. This too, I suppose, I understand. He was not raised pagan, however. The Bentleys were Quakers for the most part, and that was the tradition in which he was reared. He was always grateful for his early religious formation, he would say in later years, because it taught him an abhorrence of dogmatic formulations and because, once he had discovered his true spiritual path, it required only a short, elegant jeté on his part to cross the distance between the Friends' attendance upon the indwelling light of Christ and the later Platonists' mystical contemplation of the inner light of *nous*. He was also glad he had never been baptized, he said, as it meant that his conversion did not amount to actual apostasy; as far as he was concerned, he had never really been a Christian in the full sense. He deeply disliked the prejudice against Christianity that he found among so many of his fellow Maryland pagans, and it would have grieved him to say that he had in any sense rejected the church. Rather, his was the view of Symmachus: that there cannot be only one path to the great mystery of God. All that said, though, I imagine his choice of creed marks him as a man of peculiar temperament.

He was, it is true, something of an eccentric. As a boy, he had received so rigorous and exhaustive a classical education from his father that he never really knew how to live on cordial terms with the modern world. He refused to learn to drive. He believed that mechanical watches were an offense against nature and the "divine cyclophoria" of the heavens. He was an avid sailor, but would not allow an outboard motor to be attached to his boat (a converted skipjack), even for emergencies; his piety dictated, he said, that he submit himself entirely to the will of Poseidon and Aeolus. And, in general, his tastes in all things were irregular. For instance, he came to believe that Sacheverell Sitwell was the greatest writer in the history of English letters, and privately published a monograph on the subject entitled *Whom Shakespeare Might Envy*. But he was a sincere and thoughtful man, and he was anything but a wanton syncretist of the New Age variety. He detested the factitious neopaganisms of his time; groups like the Hermetic Order of the Golden Dawn, with their occult fixations, he regarded as sordid fairground frauds; he called Margaret Murray a charlatan and a demoness; and in general he saw neopaganism as a garish and graceless mockery of true religion. Only an authentic and genuine restoration of the old ways, he said, would lure the gods back from that hidden place to which they had retreated some centuries before.

Consequently, the liturgies he constructed for his garden rites were drawn from sources of (in his words) "uncorrupted antiquity." Admittedly, in his twenties, just after his conversion, he dabbled a bit in Iamblichan theurgy and relied overly much on the Chaldean Oracles and Julian's hymn to Lord Helios for his devotions; but he soon began to favor older and (as he would have it) more "rustic" observances, feeling they were closer to the authentic soil of Peloponnesian religion, and he began drawing instead on the *Homeric Hymns* and the *Sibylline Oracles*. I have fond memories of that walled garden behind his dilapidated townhouse in Towson, with its riot of ungoverned flora, and its quaint little statues of satyrs and nymphs peering out from under tangles of vines or the shadows of hedges. Often we would dine there, when the weather allowed, and it took only a few glasses of wine to render my great-uncle buoyantly loquacious. He would hold forth on his metaphysical speculations, the two or three rapturous visions of Apollo that had been granted him in his thirties, his hopes for finding funding for a Vestal college in Glen Burnie or La Plata, and his admiration for Algernon Swinburne (whose entire corpus of verse he seemed to have committed to memory). The food was always delicious. His wife was called Polly, originally because her Christian name was Mary, and later because she had had her name changed to Polyhymnia. The two were exquisitely well matched, and the tenderness of their affection for one another was resplendently evident even when they were well into their eighties. They had met in 1922, at a Saint Trifon's Day parade in Baltimore's Little Bulgaria, and within a few weeks were engaged; within two months, they were married. She was a great beauty in her youth, and was still a woman of striking aspect and bright eyes when I knew her.

For the most part, nothing in my great-uncle's religion made him any more unusual than the average Presbyterian or Freemason. There were a few embarrassing incidents — the time a neighbor caught a glimpse from an attic window of him and his wife dancing naked around their garden altar, or the time I visited him during the Dionysia and he came to the door wearing a ritual ornament that, divorced from its religious context, seemed rather lewd. But in general he cut a rather ordinary figure in the neighborhood. His funeral rites were probably a little on the illegal side, but we executed his wishes to the letter. He was not much interested in northern European paganism while he lived, but he keenly wanted to punctuate his life with a kind of Viking envoi. The director of the crematorium had been his friend, and had attended the same temple in Catonsville, and so he helped arrange for the pyre and the cortege of sails that processed down into the broad southern expanse of the Chesapeake Bay. The sight of my great-uncle's boat, the *Zeus of Salamis*, burning on the waves — a golden and tremulous blossom of flame against the amethyst dusk, undulously reflected on the darkening blue and silver waters — was one of the most stirring spectacles I have ever been privileged to witness.

What became of Great-Uncle Aloysius thereafter I cannot hope to know in this life. I rarely think about such things. Perhaps his ghost was sent wafting off blissfully among the asphodel of the Elysian Fields, or was granted a berth in the Limbo of the Virtuous Pagans (even if Dante believed it a place reserved only for those born before the Christian dispensation). But who can say? All I know is that I have met few men more devout than he, and that his faith — unlike a great many forms of American Christianity — had some actual basis in history and tradition. And surely an indulgent providence might take that into account in determining his final abode.

# TWENTY-TWO

# Seven Characters in Search of a Nihil Obstat

The muses are gaily capricious in the favors they bestow upon us, but humorlessly imperious in the demands they make of us. One never knows when inspiration may strike; one knows only that, when it comes, it must not be resisted. In my case, the occasion was an idle afternoon this past week, as I was irascibly considering the reaction of a few conservative Catholic critics to Terrence Malick's strange, beautiful, perhaps slightly mad, and deeply Christian film *The Tree of Life*. One review even described the sensibility of the film as "New Age," a judgment bizarrely inapposite to Malick's often dark, often radiant, emotionally austere, and deeply contemplative art. The film, in fact, is brilliant, mesmerizingly lovely, and almost alarmingly biblical. Even if one is not enchanted (as I most definitely am) by Malick's signature cinematic mannerisms, or by the fleeting hints of his more recondite intellectual preoccupations (Heidegger? Gnosticism? Buddhism? Russian Sophiology, perhaps?), surely one ought to recognize the ingenious subtlety of the scriptural allegories around which the film is built, and of the film's meditations on the mystery of God's silence and eloquence, and on innocence and transgression, and on the divine glory that shines out from all things.

Or so I was thinking as I drowsed there, warming my pelt in a pool of sunlight. Then, however, it occurred to me that perhaps, after all, these critics did have a kind of point. Oh, yes, *The Tree of Life* is profoundly, if mysteriously, *scriptural* — with its images of Eden, Cain and Abel, God speaking out of the whirlwind, divine Wisdom dancing at the heart of creation, Christ the man of sorrows, and so on — but is that sufficient to make it a truly *Catholic* film, at least of the sort these earnest critics so obviously crave? And I realized that probably it is not: it contains no pericopes from the catechism, no triumphant affirmations of papal primacy, no satisfying deathbed conversions, no heartwarming tableaux of the happy Catholic family warm in the embrace of Mother Church, no nuns, no Bing Crosby, no Italians . . .

And that was when Melpomene pounced (the frolicsome wanton). In an instant it came to me, like a flash of lightning: the plot of the perfect Catholic film. Not simply *a* Catholic film, mind you, but that film than which none more Catholic can be thought. I shall not describe to you the instantaneous thrill of elation that seized me — that intoxicating sense of mingled fear and bliss, so like a giddy bride's exquisite apprehensions on her hymeneal night — but I will say that I leapt up from my window seat and immediately began sketching out the scenario. I have thought of little else since then, and have applied myself assiduously to the mighty task. It's slow going, admittedly — nothing truly great emerges quickly from the blazing crucible of poetic transport — but I'm getting there. Here is what I have so far (I'm sure you'll keep it to yourself):

## Scenario for *Prey of the Hound of Heaven*

1952. Long shot of an old but handsome house in a respectable middle-class neighborhood of some eastern American city. Close-up of a garden statuette of the Blessed Virgin, standing in a bed of white lilies. A distant murmur of solemn voices. The voices suddenly become fully audible; cut to interior panning shot: white plaster walls, a crucifix, a fading photograph of a young man in military uniform (World War I) bordered by black funerary ribbon, another photograph of a very similar young man in a priest's collar, and finally an attractive woman in her forties kneeling alongside her three children (two girls and one boy, all around ten years old), praying the rosary.

Close-up of one girl, Mary Catherine: a bored and sullen expression, warily darting eyes, lips barely moving; she is not really praying; she idly fingers the beads of her mother-of-pearl rosary. Close-up of the boy, Danny [or Anthony], who smiles knowingly [or scowls uncertainly] at his sister as he prays in a clear voice.

Cut to dinner table that same night. Father — an imposing yet dapper figure in a high collar and necktie — is saying grace. Passing of plates, distribution of food, close-ups of enigmatic expressions [or barely suppressed laughs] on the children's faces. Father tells of labor agitations down at the docks [factory, garment district, corn exchange] where he works. "In hard

times," he declares at one point, "men will turn to anything, even a godless
socialism."

[Perhaps we had better make the year 1932 instead of 1952.]

Mention is made of Grandfather, who has lived a reprobate's life for
some years in a foreign city [Berlin? Singapore?] and is no longer in regular contact with the family. Mother announces that a letter has arrived
from Uncle Ben. Mary Catherine asks why Uncle Ben does not return
home from [name of some South or Central American nation where there
may have been a communist insurgency or anticlerical government in
1932 or 1952]. Mother patiently reminds her that, after Uncle Edward was
killed in the Great [or Spanish-American] War, Uncle Ben took holy orders and devoted his life to the Indians [or peasants] of [the nation mentioned above], who need him now more than ever. Danny [or Anthony]
asks why God does not make everything all right for the Indians [or peas-
ants] and bring Uncle Ben home. Mother explains that sometimes grace
must crush us utterly ("Like dust on the heels of God") in order to make
us whole ("That's how we know it's grace"). Close-up of Mary Catherine,
who is not listening.

Cut to Uncle Ben, unshaven, unkempt, superbly seedy, seated at a
plain wooden table in some hovel without any glass in its windows. His
clerical collar has become detached at one side and hovers limply over the
open top buttons of his sweat-soaked black shirt. He is staring at a faded
and wrinkled photograph (of his family, taken in his childhood), next to
which stands a nearly empty bottle of mescal; he picks up the bottle with
a violently trembling hand and places it to his lips. At that moment a stun-
ningly lovely young Indian maiden [or peasant girl] rushes in and tells
him [Spanish with subtitles] that the *Federales* [or rebels or "soldiers"] are
coming and that he must flee to the forest with the tribe [or village]. Ben
looks at her with an expression of infinite fatigue. She enjoins him again
to follow her, now with greater urgency: "Who will pray for us if you don't
come? Who will give us the body of Christ or hear confession when we are
dying?" Ben sighs, rises wearily and somewhat unsteadily, and says, "Sí,
sí, entiendo. Vendré."

Cut to the band of refugees, now deep in the jungle, kneeling before a
makeshift altar — two rotting boards supported on piles of rocks — where
Ben is saying Mass. Many close-ups of haggard but reverent Indian [or
peasant] faces. [This scene should be unnecessarily prolonged.] Cut to Ben,
later, sitting on a boulder by a running stream. He draws the mescal bottle from his knapsack, finds it empty, and flings it morosely away. Enter
Pedro, one of the tribal [or village] elders, who tells Ben that everyone is

relying on his faith. "Faith?" says Ben bitterly as he stares at the water from incarnadined eyes. "Do I even know what that means anymore?"

Cut to interior of a church back in the States. Mother, Father, and the three children are kneeling in their pew; the priest is at the altar (Latin Mass, plenty of incense); golden light streams down from a high window. Close-up of a statue of the Blessed Virgin, tenderly cradling the infant Christ in her arms. Close-up of Mary Catherine, not praying but instead staring covetously at the magnificent earrings of the lady in the pew in front of her. Close-up of Danny [or Anthony] gazing with precociously haunted eyes at the crucifix above the high altar.

Cut to the end of the service, the priest shaking the hands of his parishioners as they are departing. He asks after Mother's father; she grimly reports that they have had no word for some time. The priest assures her that her father will always find a warm welcome in the parish.

From this point on, I have not yet worked out the exact order of scenes, but I have a general idea of the plot. The action in North America will leap forward twenty years to 1972 or 1952, but will continue to be intercut with scenes of Uncle Ben in 1952 or 1932.

Father is now dead, having perished in a Typhus epidemic eight years earlier. Mary Catherine has become estranged from her family, having been debauched by a laodicean Protestant, then having lapsed into a life of frivolous materialism, and finally having become infatuated with a communist named Rod who has taught her to scorn her faith. When she tells Rod she is carrying his child, he merely laughs at the conventions of monogamy and the bourgeois family and tells her that she is only one of the women with whom he shares his bed.

Meanwhile, Danny [or Anthony] has begun to sink into despair, no longer certain what he believes. Philosophy has corrupted him. His childhood friend Tony [or Donnie] has become involved with a local crime boss, running numbers [or drugs]. There are some plot complications [to be determined later], in consequence of which Tony [or Donnie] is shot by a member of a rival gang and dies in the rain, late at night, on the pavement outside a Catholic church, with Danny [or Anthony] bent over him weeping and cursing heaven.

Later we see an angry Danny [or Anthony] talking to his priest, asking how a good God could let his friend die like that — or, for that matter, permit "what happened to Uncle Ben." The priest explains the necessity of suffering in a fallen world and then holds forth on purgatory for five minutes or so, explaining the concepts both of sanctification and of temporal punishment. When Danny [or Anthony] says he finds it all so hard to believe, the priest assumes an avuncular tone and remarks that the truth is often incredible. Later Danny [or Anthony] visits his mother, who tells him that, but for our sufferings, we could know nothing of the love that heals. "Think of Uncle Ben," she says.

Uncle Ben's story resumes *in medias res:* soldiers have surrounded the refugees in the jungle and are methodically massacring them; Uncle Ben is screaming "No!" over and over again as two Indians [or peasants or soldiers] hold him back. Later, he and the surviving refugees are marched through the jungle and imprisoned at a compound governed by the dreaded and elegantly mustachioed Comandante "El Monstruo" Rodriguez [or by the dreaded and coarsely bearded rebel leader known only as "El Toro del Bosque"]. Executions are to commence at dawn and to continue until the surviving Indians [or peasants] reveal the whereabouts [of something — maybe a gold crucifix from their church].

Among the prisoners is a dissolute old ruffian called Carlos who mocks Ben for believing in God in this world where only force rules, and who curses the nuns who taught him the same lies when he was a boy in the mission school. Ben merely says, "Perhaps you're right," and goes on caring for the wounded among his fellow prisoners. We see him administer last rites to the same lovely young woman who persuaded him to flee in the first place; he does not shed any tears.

At some point Ben is interrogated by El Monstruo [or El Toro], a surprisingly urbane if darkly cynical soul, who asks Ben what has become of his God — "The God who left these wretches you love to die in the forest" — and who reveals that he was raised in a devout household and even briefly studied for the priesthood, before learning that the universe is nothing but a cold chaos of violence. At the end of his strength, Ben admits that he does not know if he has any faith left: "Is God there? Why is he so silent? Does he care? I don't know if I know how to believe anymore, but that silence is all I have now. I have to cling to that silence, and hope to find God within it . . . somewhere."

The next morning, as executions are about to begin, Ben asks to take the place of [someone — details to be worked out later] before the firing squad. As Ben is led away, Carlos kneels to receive his benediction. Poignant strains of movingly discordant Indian songs [or plangently sad peasant melodies] accompany him as he departs into the light shining in through the dungeon doorway. Later, we see El Monstruo [or El Toro] alone in his office; he opens his desk drawer and removes a small crucifix from beneath some files; "Madre . . . mi madre . . . ," he mutters. He instructs his lieutenant to release the prisoners.

Back in the States, in 1972 or 1952, Mother has received word from Grandfather. He is near death and longs to see her. Mother, Danny [or Anthony], and [name of third child] journey to Grandfather's vast stately home in England. The old man is failing fast. Carla — his mistress in years past, now merely his constant companion — has summoned a priest on several occasions, but Grandfather will not receive him. The priest, a garrulous and cheerful old Irishman, assures Mother that, in the end, the nets of grace can catch even the most elusive fish. At the hour of Grandfather's death, with his loved ones kneeling all about him and the priest bending over him, unctuous cotton swab in hand, and with Danny [or Anthony] praying for some clear sign, the old man feebly crosses himself and promptly expires in the odor of sanctity. A cloud passes from before the face of the sun and the room is filled with golden light. Danny [or Anthony] has found his faith again.

Mary Catherine is now a whore living in a dismal single room above a cheap dive whose neon light flashes through her window all night long. She has left her baby in the care of the nuns at a foundling home "over on the east side." Danny [or Anthony] finds her, after months of searching. She does not want to see him, but he forces his way in. He begs her to come home, but she merely tells him to leave.

Before going, however, he draws something wrapped in a pink handkerchief from his pocket and gives it to her; "This is from Mother," he says. Mary Catherine unwraps it; it is her mother-of-pearl rosary. She begins weeping uncontrollably and sinks to the floor. Her brother crouches beside her, holds her close, and tells her that love — the love of God and of her family — will never let her go. Thereafter, brother and sister retrieve the baby from the orphanage and return home, where Mother embraces her daughter and takes the baby in her arms. Mary Catherine gazes rapturously at her child. We see the garden statuette of the Blessed Virgin again, somewhat more weathered, but still standing.

The last scene is of Indian [or peasant] girls laying flowers on Uncle Ben's grave, marked by a humble wooden cross, now obviously many years old. Long shot of sunset over the jungle; reprise of the poignant Indian [or peasant] music from Uncle Ben's death scene.

Cut to credits. Allegri's *Miserere* [or the *Misa Criolla*].

# TWENTY-THREE

# A Splendid Wickedness

The literature of Spain's "Golden Age" produced two figures — Don Quixote de La Mancha and Don Juan Tenorio — who quickly escaped the confines of the works that gave them birth and took up exalted but previously unoccupied stations in the Western imagination. Each soon became as much an archetype as an invention, somehow existing beyond his written story. In either case, moreover, the result was rather curious, since neither figure in his final form was so much a mythic aggrandizement of the literary model as an almost total inversion. The mythic Quixote — the paladin of the impossible, the heroic dreamer, the holy fool whom Unamuno regarded as a kind of "saint" and "Christ" — is not really the Quixote of Miguel de Cervantes. The old "knight of La Mancha" was intended by his creator principally as an object of mirth. By the same token, the mythic Juan — the irresistible seducer, the apostle of lighthearted satyriasis, the proud rebel against society and heaven, whom Kierkegaard saw as the perfect personification of sensuousness and Camus saw as a hero of the absurd — is not really the Juan created by Tirso de Molina in *El Burlador de Sevilla y convidado di pietra*. Tirso's character is definitely a roué, but hardly a virtuoso of the boudoir. His appetites are lavish, but his methods are generally jejune, and his conquests are the results not of personal magnetism, but of cunning opportunism. True, he bravely defies the laws of God and society, but not as a philosophical rebel; rather as a moral oaf.

Why it should have been precisely *these* two figures who were together wafted up to the zenith of Spain's literary zodiac is a fascinating question; it is hard not to think that so perfect a juxtaposition of contraries must express some kind of transcendental cultural logic. But, just at the moment, the more interesting question is why one of them — Don Juan — should have so precipitously disappeared from Western cultural consciousness sometime in the early decades of the twentieth century. Both figures, of course, have withdrawn to a considerable degree from popular awareness, especially outside the Spanish-speaking world; but Quixote's myth still retains a concrete shape, and something of his story remains fixed in our minds. Juan, by contrast, has disappeared almost entirely, or been replaced by a vague and insipid popular portrait of some primped and purring amorist who bears no real resemblance to him at all. And yet, until less than a century ago, his story was by far the better known, more influential, and more vital of the two. For three centuries, playwrights, poets, and essayists returned to him not only regularly, but almost obsessively. And then, all of a sudden, he was gone. What became of him?

There is an immediately tempting answer. Quixote has survived the ravages of time chiefly because he is of his nature timeless; he enchants us with his absolute exorbitance, his ability to inhabit a parallel reality of his own, corresponding wholly to his own poetic and moral creed. Hence, he floats high up above any age as a kind of shimmering antithesis, perennially impossible, beautiful, and moving; indeed, he is more attractive the more implausible his values come to seem. Perhaps, then, we might assume just the reverse in the case of Juan: perhaps today we live in an age of such pervasive "Donjuanism" (understood simply as insouciant sensualism) that the original has lost his power to scandalize, surprise, or even interest us. I think, though, that this answer rests upon an irreparably flawed premise. I would, in fact, argue the opposite: that Juan is not familiar to us at all today, and that the reason our cultural imagination no longer has much room for him — and would certainly be incapable of producing another figure like him — is that he, far more than the buoyantly eternal Quixote, is a figure fixed in a particular cultural moment. He is not timeless, but only epochal. He personifies a long but circumscribed historical episode, apart from whose ambiguities and energies he is unintelligible: that twilight interval stretching between the late Renaissance and contemporary secular modernity. Juan was the greatest immoralist of European literature precisely because he served as the negative image of the moral convictions and capacities of his time and place, the exemplary contradiction of an entire and coherent vision of the good, whose story magically combined a certain nostalgia for fading cultural certitudes with a certain cynicism in regard to them. So, when the values of his time disappeared, he dissolved with them. I would also argue that if he could speak to us again today as clearly as he did to earlier generations, it would not be in the amiable tones of someone we know and understand, and who would understand us in turn, but in a distant, almost prophetic tone, full of ironic moral reproach. He would tell us not of ourselves — of either our virtues or our vices — not even satirically. Rather, his story would remind us of a vanished magnificence, inseparable from a now largely abandoned conception of what it is to be human.

I SHOULD NOT GET too far ahead of my argument, however. My claim makes sense only in relation to a very specific definition of who Don Juan really is, and that is a difficult matter. Unlike Don Quixote, who made his debut in a work of genuine literary genius, Don Juan has always somehow exceeded the occasion of his first appearance. In fact, we are not even sure when he really did first appear. Tirso de Molina (the *nom de guerre* of Gabriel Téllez, a monk in his day job) wrote most of his plays between 1605 and 1625; but he did not include *El Burlador de Sevilla* in any collection of his works, so we do not know when — or perhaps even if — he wrote it. More to the point, as entertaining as Tirso's play is, it is neither an extraordinary literary achievement nor even necessarily the most authoritative version of the tale. Its chief importance lies in its having initiated a theme that for three centuries of European letters seemed nearly inexhaustible, and for having established the canonical pattern of Juan's tale as it was told in most subsequent renderings up to the time of Mozart's *Don Giovanni*. In the end, therefore, "Juan as such" is an abstraction, derived from a positively oceanic literary history, of which any distillate is necessarily only very partial. He has no single, wholly solid form, but comes to us in a series of shifting translucencies.

Certain essential elements of the character are there from the very beginning, however, if only in an inchoate way, and endure throughout his literary career. The most important, and by far the most *attractive* (literarily speaking), is his proud impenitence. This in itself is odd. Tirso intended his protagonist as a cautionary example of the vicious and debased state to which unrestrained appetite reduces a soul; his Juan, far from being meant to engage our sympathy, is for the most part rather uninteresting: an ordinary profligate, cad, and sexual predator of noble extraction, with sufficient means to pursue his desires, and without any discernible sign of a conscience to impede the pursuit. When he comes to a bad end, we are supposed to recognize it as divine justice, and to concur with the verdict. But that is not quite what happened. Inadvertently, Tirso endowed his character with a faint but invincible glamor. A man so recklessly devoted to his own passions that he can careen knowingly into the very embrace of hell, without wavering from the course his own character steers him on, is intrinsically interesting. However repellant we may find his deeds, we cannot help but feel a certain exhilaration at, and even envy of, his unconquerable exuberance. And this, more than anything else, accounts for the figure's profuse longevity in European letters. It was Juan's insane inflexibility of will that almost all later versions of the tale, even when they were not intended to do so, seemed to celebrate.

One only has to review the action of Tirso's play (which established the canonical Juan narrative) to see that it is essentially a morality drama. It begins late at night in the royal palace of Naples, where Juan has gone disguised as one Duke Octavio so that he can bed the Duke's fiancée, the Duchess Isabela. She discovers the imposture too late to save her honor (such as it is), but before Juan can elude the guard; he does eventually escape, though, his true identity still undiscovered, and flees the city. Isabela, to save face, allows Octavio to bear the blame. En route to Seville, Juan and his servant Catalinón ("coward") are shipwrecked, but manage to swim to shore, where Juan promptly seduces, enjoys, and abandons the fisherman's daughter who comes to his aid. In Seville, Juan finds that report of his Neapolitan adventure has reached the court of Castile, as has Duke Octavio, but fortunately the duke still does not know who cuckolded him. The king, however, guesses easily and commands Juan to marry Isabela — whom he has summoned from Naples — and grants the duke the hand of a certain Doña Ana as a consolation. But Ana loves a marquis, and Juan, knowing this, disguises himself as her paramour and attempts a nocturnal assault on her virtue, of the sort that had succeeded with Isabela. Ana is not fooled, however, and calls for help. When her father Don Gonzalo, commander of the Order of Caltrava, comes to her rescue, Juan kills the old man and flees. The marquis is arraigned for the murder. Later, passing through the countryside, Juan happens upon a peasant wedding feast, seduces the new bride with promises of marriage, deflowers her, and then slips away back to Seville. There, however, forces are gathering against him: Isabela, Octavio, the fisherman's daughter, the marquis, the peasant bride, and even Juan's own father, Don Diego. Meeting Juan in a church, Catalinón warns his master of the danger, but Juan is unimpressed. He comes upon a statue of the murdered commander in a side chapel and, mockingly pulling its beard, invites it to dinner. When, surprisingly, the statue appears for his meal, Juan betrays only momentary consternation, and then plays host with all the panache one expects of a true hidalgo. He even takes the statue's proffered hand and accepts its invitation to dine the following night in Don Gonzalo's chapel. Juan confesses to himself that the stone had burned his hand, and that he had felt fear, but he quickly shrugs that off as something unmanly. The next night, he goes to dinner as appointed, dragging Catalinón along; there, after the amenities have been observed (a dish of vipers, a cup of gall), the statue takes Juan again by the hand and draws him down to hell. Juan cries out in pain, and even asks to be shriven by a priest, but otherwise meets his end bravely. In the final scene, Don Diego's honor is restored, Octavio is reunited with Isabela, and the marquis is returned to Ana.

Anyone familiar with most of the notable versions of the tale from the seventeenth and eighteenth centuries will recognize almost all the standard elements here, however much names and details may shift about in various tellings. Only a few additional features needed to be added by Tirso's successors. In the anonymous *Il Convitato di Pietra*, from the 1650s, Juan's servant (now called Passarino) for the first time both produces the famous list of his master's conquests and cries out in despair for his wages when his master is taken to hell. And, in the various versions that became part of the repertoires of the *Commedia dell' Arte*, the elevation of the story's comic aspects over the tragic became more pronounced. The French playwright Dorimon penned a version in which Juan treats his own father so callously that the old man dies from emotional shock, and this may be how the element of parricide entered the standard narrative. The most original seventeenth-century treatment of the story is, without question, Molière's *Dom Juan ou Le Festin de pierre* (1665), which, even if it is not a work of genius, is the work of *a* genius, and is the first treatment of Juan of genuine literary interest. Still, it has all the appearances of a work Molière might have concocted over a few wine-drenched afternoons. It is written in prose, its structure is sprawlingly haphazard, and the abrupt finale is as nonchalant a piece of *deus ex machina* as any hack might have flung in the face of his audience. But the dialogue is hilarious, the characters have real dimensions, and the language is frequently splendid. Molière gave the world the French Juan: acerbic, coolly proud, skeptical, nonchalantly raffish, earnestly frivolous, naturally polygamous, a bad but not particularly abusive son, a duelist but not a murderer. The most arresting seventeenth-century version, however, is certainly Thomas Shadwell's lurid and lunatic extravaganza, *The Libertine* (1676), whose "Don John" is not merely a *burlador* or rake, but something like Satan's less reputable twin brother. The antinomian monster at the center of this play is a prolific murderer and rapist, who has murdered his own father and is laying plans to rape several nuns; he is also a thief, a blasphemer, and — almost as bad — a philosopher. As he and three equally evil boon companions rampage across the stage, committing one atrocity after another with delirious gaiety, they also spin out elaborate but perfectly cogent rational justifications for their actions, of an almost proto-Nietzschean kind. And, even on the brink of damnation, amid a roiling phantasmagoria — ghosts of his victims, devils, the living statue, hell's fire — he expresses neither fear nor remorse, but goes to his perdition proudly affirming his unshakable loyalty to himself, with a courage so insane it almost deprives hell of any significance. When the curtain falls, one is left wondering whether the devil is ready to receive him, or might be too shocked at his morals. Molière's and Shadwell's renderings were aberrations, however. In the almost countless versions that appeared between Tirso's play and Da Ponte's libretto for *Don Giovanni* (1787), Juan remained very much the villain Tirso had made him: a violent, rapacious, unreflective, and unrepentant seducer whose fate is both just and satisfying. So he remained in *Don Giovanni*. And so, but for shifting cultural fashions, he might have remained indefinitely: a perennially popular theatrical motif, but not yet a fully fledged myth.

SOMETHING UNANTICIPATED, however, happened to Juan as he moved into the third century of his literary existence. The tacit sympathy he had perhaps always enjoyed among the patrons of the theater began to reshape his narrative explicitly. In the Romantic Age, he became more glamorous, was invested with deeper pathos, and was finally burdened with profundity. He remained a seducer, but now one to whom women were naturally drawn; and his desire for women, which had formerly been simple animal appetite, now took on the character of heroic "striving," an insatiable longing for the perfection of love or deification of the passions. The Romantic Juan actually *loved* women, or at least loved "woman" as an ideal, and in despair of finding the ideal embodied fled from one woman to another. So said E. T. A. Hoffman in 1814. In 1830, in *The Stone Guest*, Alexander Pushkin depicted Juan as a womanizer, but one who can unexpectedly lose his young, impetuous heart to Anna. Byron's Juan (who really little resembles the Juan of the classic narrative) has a soul of almost infinite romantic vulnerability. In a poem of 1844, Nikolas Lenau portrayed Juan as a disillusioned erotic idealist, embittered and defeated by his own passions. Juan became, in short, a symbol of the rebellion of sentiment against society or heaven, and thus a tragic lover whose soul was worth contending for. Now his damnation, rather than being merely the condign consummation of a rogue's career, became the tale's crucial moment of philosophical truth. Some playwrights went so far as to rescind the sentence in the final moments. Others sent Juan to hell, but almost in triumph. Hell seemed merely to endow him — his defiance, his virility, his freedom of will —

with a dark Miltonic grandeur. This tendency reached a quiet climax in Baudelaire's poem "Don Juan aux enfers," which shows Juan being ferried across the waters of death by Charon, surrounded by the specters of all his victims, while remaining utterly, contemptuously impassive:

> Mais le calme héros, courbé sur sa rapière,
> Regardait le sillage et ne daignait rien voir.

> (But the hero, unperturbed, leaning upon his rapier,
> Gazed at the wake and deigned to see nothing.)

When Yeats, in 1914, described the eunuchs in hell's street gazing enviously at mighty Juan riding by, he was making use of what by then was a literary commonplace.

The Romantic eye was particularly suited to see something in Don Juan more interesting than had been noticed in the past: some deeper significance lurking behind all that romping, glittering, ravenous exuberance — some secret sadness or divine discontent. But the more the Romantics encumbered his story with "meaning," by converting his unreflective sybaritism into a Promethean defiance of the gods, the more they deprived him of his few engaging qualities: mirth, frivolity, childish pride, thoughtless wickedness. Most egregious in this respect were those poets and playwrights who saw some sort of deep analogy between Don Juan and Dr. Faust — on the grounds that both go to hell, or nearly do, and that both are *striving* after something, whether absolute knowledge or absolute sensuousness. Nicolas Vogt actually conflated the two figures in his immense, ludicrous, mercifully unfinished *Gesamtkunstwerk* from 1809, *Der Färberhof*. Christian Dietrich Grabbe, in 1829, produced *Don Juan und Faust*, a vast, seething swamp of large ideas, exaggerated passions, incoherent action, crushing monologues, demented lyricism, and adolescent moral nihilism, which is somehow made even more unbearable by its numerous moments of poetic brilliance. In this play, Faust and Juan — each magnified or reduced to a symbol of a certain kind of spiritual temperament — vie for the love of Anna, whom Faust ends up killing. Both go to hell — Faust in remorse, Juan in defiance — but only in order to prove that Satan is more powerful than either. And it was not only Germans who brought the two figures together. Some French authors did it as well, with (needless to say) a lighter touch: Eugène Robin in 1836, in his poem "Livia," and Théophile Gautier in 1838, in his poem "La Comédie de la mort." And various later versions of Juan's story were influenced by

Goethe's *Faust* even when the good doctor made no personal appearance on stage. Alexei Tolstoy's 1860 poem *Don Juan* even includes a prologue in heaven and a final redemption scene. And the denouement of José Zorilla's glutinously pious (and still popular) 1844 play *Don Juan Tenorio* — in which Juan is saved from hell at the last moment by the pure spirit of the one woman he truly loved — is a particularly unfortunate encore on the part of Goethe's Eternal Feminine.

By the end of the nineteenth century, I think it fair to say, the myth was fully formed. None of the twentieth-century revisions of the story made any actual contributions to the legend. The best of them — Shaw's *Man and Superman*, Rostand's underrated and somewhat savage *La Dernière nuit de Don Juan*, Frisch's *Don Juan oder die Liebe zur Geometrie* — were sardonic commentaries on a legend already fully formed. Each starts from the presupposition that we already know who Don Juan is and what he represents, and that we will therefore be able to appreciate the playwright's comic or caustic variations on the story. And then, around about midcentury, his story ceased altogether to generate any significant works of literature. A few philosophers continued to write about him, a few psychologists — perhaps a fate worse than hell — seized on him as a pathology or a psychological type. And then he more or less receded permanently to unvisited library shelves, a superannuated archetype.

AGAIN, WHY IS THIS SO? And, again, the obvious but inadequate answer would be that Juan's ability to fascinate, exhilarate, and alarm has been lost in our age of unrestrained sensuality, voluntarism, glandular liberation, and relaxed consciences. Not that such an answer is wholly false: certainly the more picaresque side of Juan's adventures — the veil of night, the cloaked figure stealing over balconies and through windows, the sordid *incognito* — seems only quaint in light of today's morbidly austere and functionalist venereal aesthetics. Contemporary erotic etiquette, even among the young, has so drained physical love of its enticingly forbidden and urgent quality, and so dispelled its atmosphere of rapturous risk, moral uncertainty, tantalizing mystery, and irresistible yearning, that the actual quantum of pleasure in the transaction has been largely diminished to a very transitory set of neural agitations. One should speak a reverent word or two for the aphrodisiac virtues of emotional innocence and cultural inhibition. Fruit stolen after midnight from a walled and moonlit garden has a sweetness that the riper fruit purchased at midday in the market lacks.

All of that being granted, however, there is more to the mystery of Juan's disappearance than that. For one thing, his was never just the story of a self-indulgent hedonist on the prowl; it always possessed a larger metaphysical significance. No matter how great Juan's metamorphosis had been in his translation from baroque to Romantic literature, his legend continued throughout to speak of transgression, of the power of unrestrained desire, and of the spiritual paradox of free will. Behind the tale's winsome glitter or lurid glare, there was always the shadow of a sacred or demonic drama, however the sympathies of the poets may have shifted one way or another over time. Moreover, if one looks back over all the figure's variations — the Latin or Teutonic Juan, the baroque or Romantic Juan, Juan the pure voluptuary immune to disenchantment or Juan the shattered idealist of love — one sees that two crucial elements remain fairly constant: first, he is indeed a true sensualist, delighting not only in sex but also in food, wine, poetry, and song; and, second, he is truly courageous to the last, going to his doom gladly rather than attempting a repentance incongruous with his nature. These are obvious points, of course, but they should be understood in very particular ways. To say he is a sensualist is to say he is both servant and master of the senses, in all their elemental power. And to speak of his courage is to speak not of his spiritual rebellion or cosmic despair, but only of his exultant indifference to anything but the inalienable power of his own will. And, on both of these points, Don Juan is a figure curiously alien to modern sensibilities.

That may seem an odd assertion, admittedly. We tend to think ours is a hedonistic age, and individual liberty is certainly its highest value. But distinctions should be drawn. For one thing, though there are no doubt many sensualists among us, ours is by no means a sensualist *culture*. Genuine sensualism requires a fairly healthy sense of natural goodness, and some developed capacity for discrimination. Late Western modernity, especially in its purest (that is, most American) form, certainly values the available and the plentiful, but not necessarily the intrinsically pleasing. As far as the actual *senses* are concerned, ours is in many ways a culture of peculiar poverty, evident even — perhaps especially — in its excesses. The diet produced by mass production and mass marketing, our civic and commercial architecture, our consumer goods, our style of dress, our popular entertainments, and so forth — it all seems to have a kind of premeditated aesthetic squalor about it, an almost militant indifference to the distinction between quantity and quality. There has always been, of course, a division between popular and high culture, but usually also some continuity in kind between them. Today it often seems as if truly aesthetic values have been moved out of the social realm altogether, into ever smaller private preserves. Certainly they are not central to our concept or experience of the common good, even though we may occasionally make a public pretense of caring about such things. Our culture, with its almost absolute emphasis on the power of acquisition, trains us to be beguiled by the bright and the shrill rather than the lovely and the subtle. That, after all, is the transcendental logic of late modern capitalism: the fabrication of innumerable artificial appetites, not the refinement of the few that are natural to us. Late modernity's defining art, advertising, is nothing but a piercingly relentless tutelage in desire for the intrinsically undesirable. True sensualism, by contrast, is a longing for real intimacy with the world of sensible things. What Juan desires is desirable of itself, and his appetency is a real expression — however corrupt — of the dignity and loveliness of incarnate life. He is a thoroughly unethical soul, but his way of life is still an ethos, not simply a state of unremitting distraction. When he pursues or embraces the phenomenal aspect of what he desires, he at least seeks some kind of communion with the thing in itself, some capture of the whole nuptial totality of form and matter. Late modernity prepares us to live far more contentedly in their divorce: material goods without formal beauty, phenomenal diversions without material depth, nervous stimulation without sensuous enrichment. If our style of life is a materialism, it is of an oddly disembodied kind, and does more to shield us from the senses than to liberate them.

By the same token, Juan's pride and willfulness are more than mere bourgeois self-indulgence or late modern narcissism. His self-love is destructive, even demonic, but it certainly is not petty. Frivolous as he is, his tale is cast against a backdrop of cosmic significance, because he still inhabits a coherent moral universe. He knows the rules that govern it, and by the end certainly understands the consequences of violating them; but he rejects the moral order nonetheless. Even setting aside all those Romantic exaggerations about Juan's Promethean or Luciferian defiance of God, one can still say that his unwillingness to repent and his insistence upon accepting that final dreadful invitation actually affirm both the existence of divine law and the godlike power of the soul to choose its own destruction. In the end — and this is the principal reason his myth has lost its power for us — his tale is a volatile combination of the most exalted idealisms and the coarsest cynicisms of an age of radical change. He was born in the waning light of the last epoch of triumphal Christian humanism, the inverted double of the Renaissance man, and his story was a satire in the full Attic sense: a satyr-play concluding a glorious but exhausted drama, at once mocking and celebrating the cycle it brought to a close. Hence his long progress from worthless rogue to champion of the passions to psychological cliché to obsolescence perfectly symbolizes the transition from the premodern to the postmodern cultural imagination, moral and aesthetic: from faith to disenchantment to resigned equanimity. He could not have been invented earlier than he was, and he could not have endured any longer than he did. His proper element was that long cultural gloaming in which the old moral metaphysics retained its formal authority, but not its credibility. In just a few brief centuries, all the old paradigms would be entirely recast: the mechanical philosophy would transform nature from a living theophany into a spiritless machine; secularization would subordinate all human associations to the bare dialectic of state and individual; the ideology of market economics would reduce human community to the impersonal algorithms of private interests; Darwinian biology (both as science and as a metaphysics) would absorb human nature into the mechanistic narrative; and so on. In the end, modernity would have achieved its inevitable revision of our understanding of ourselves and our world, and the mythic Juan — personifying the irresoluble tension between what was passing away and what was coming into being — would at the last quietly melt away. His myth vanished because it was essentially a myth of withdrawal; his odyssey through European letters was, from the first, a single long recessional.

So I return to where I began. The figure of Don Juan is an imaginative impossibility in our time because he comes from a period in which the human being was understood not merely as a biological machine, generated randomly out of the incessant flux of an aleatory universe, but as a radiant and terrible enigma, dangerously and daringly poised between beast and angel, hell and heaven, the elemental abyss and the infinite God: a period in which it was still just possible to believe that human freedom was not merely the all but illusory residue of a random confluence of mindless physical forces and organic mechanisms, but a glimpse of the transcendent within the world of matter. Juan's wickedness, by its sheer garish or stylish flamboyance, still reflected an exalted — and not merely sentimental — sense of human dignity. Even his sexual esurience was not just brute impulse, but the darkly distorted image of an angelic liberty. This cannot be the case for us. Our culture is not subject to the torments of immutable moral laws or to the allure of the transcendent good; the terror and the ecstasy of the absolute are not the deep flowing springs of our shared conscience. In such an age, there can be no such thing as splendid wickedness, simply because, if we do not see ourselves in the light of the Good beyond being, nothing in our nature can be cast in sufficiently striking relief. And now that so many of the acts that once seemed to place our souls in the balance have become matters of moral indifference, most of the choices we make are by definition unimportant, and the heroism or antiheroism of moral choice is all but impossible. This is simply the modern condition; perhaps it is a blessing. It means, however, that not only our virtues, but also our vices, have been robbed of their poetic resonances. Individual writers will, of course, always be able to dream up deplorable but charismatic rogues with enormous appetites, like George MacDonald Frasier's Flashman or Roald Dahl's Uncle Oswald; more ambitious artists may produce the occasional picaresque amoralist with a gift for momentarily transforming the bleak absurdity of existence into a rude carnival, like Alvaro Mutis's Maqroll the Gaviero. But, beyond that, our shared cultural imagination has no real place for a moral and metaphysical drama like Juan's.

As I have said, the figure of Quixote abides because he is borne aloft by his beautiful and mysterious timelessness. But Juan was never timeless: he was weighed down from the beginning by a whole history of cultural dissolution; and now, in his majestic frivolity and obdurate impenitence, he is beyond our ken. If we could grant him once again a little of the attention he can no longer command, however, he might remind us of a world in which the moral meaning of the universe could be read in a single soul, because a sublime and integral sympathy united them, as macrocosm and microcosm, totality and epitome. And still, whether we are conscious of it or not, the heroic scope of his negations rebukes us with the image of a human grandeur perhaps no more unattainable than in the past, but certainly far more unimaginable. Any modern attempt at the invention of a Don Juan, or of any similar archetype of animal vitality or spiritual revolt, would fail almost inevitably. The figure we would produce would have no meaning now: no depth, no height, neither deformity nor beauty. Compared to Juan, whoever might emerge from our common cultural imagination to take his place would simply be too damned boring — or, more precisely, too boring to be damned.

# TWENTY-FOUR

## *Aloysius Bentley's "Melancholy"*

Certain readers have requested in various ways (pseudonymous e-mails, menacing telegrams delivered in the dead of night, and so on) that I supply a few more details from the biography of my great-uncle Aloysius Bentley (1895–1987). As you may recall, he was the last practicing pagan in my extended family; once his obsequies had been performed, and the last flickering embers of his funeral bark had disappeared beneath the waves of the Chesapeake, the old faith had no remaining votaries in the clan. I am not sure, however, that I have much to tell — at least, not without excessive preliminary explanation. It occurred to me, however, that I might say something about a particularly significant episode from his life, and provide a few specimens from his own poetic record of those days. You see, Aloysius Bentley was a poet of sorts, and I am (by default) his literary executor. His verse, of which he published only a few samples in his lifetime, was of a fairly traditional and formalist kind. Most of it was written in heroic couplets, probably because of his special devotion to Pope ("The only Pope to whom I would bend my knee," he would quip in his rare fractiously sectarian moments). By far, the longest poem he ever produced was his immense, unfinished discursive epic (about 38,000 lines, as it stands) *Theophaneia*, whose title was a reference to the yearly unveiling of the sacred images in the inner sanctuary of the Apolloneion at Delphi, to celebrate the god's return at the end of winter. He wrote most of it in the summer of 1920, when a fit of deep depression had driven him into retreat at the Bentley summer home in Dorchester County, out on the Eastern Shore. I know I have said that his conversion to paganism from Quakerism was, in his eyes, a natural and largely uneventful transition; but he did mention now and then that his complete commitment to "the way of the gods" was occasioned by a brief "passage through dejection."

He was twenty-five, and he was suffering from an acute abhorrence of what he saw as the special evils of modernity: the disenchantment of nature, the reduction of the world to a soulless machine, the hideousness of modern architecture, the decline of the arts, the rise of a crass materialism. His mood had been exacerbated, moreover, by any number of recent events: the Great War, the Spanish influenza pandemic, passing of the Volstead Act, and so on. And he had come to believe that the pathologies of modern society could not be healed by what remained of "cultural Christianity," which he saw as a paradox that had always been imperiled, from its inception, by internal forces of dissolution. Only if the old gods returned, he concluded, would the world speak to Western humanity again. But an intellectual conviction is not yet faith. When he arrived on the Eastern Shore, he was a pagan merely by disposition; by the time he left, he was a pagan in his heart; and his poem describes how he emerged from doubt and despondency into that condition of radiant cheerfulness that characterized him throughout his later life.

Unfortunately, only the roughly 1,400 lines of the poem's prelude in three cantos, entitled "Melancholy," are written out in a final fair copy. The rest of the chapters exist as a tumult of variant texts, festooned with revisions and often illegible marginal notations. To extract something like an authoritative text from those pages will require a slow and laborious process that I have not yet had the time or courage to undertake. But the "Melancholy" section is a rather wonderful portrayal of the state of mind that carried my great-uncle across the bay, as well as of the first faint glimpses of that "heathen grace" that he believed was beckoning him out of his despair. It is worth quoting at some length.

Part One is called "The Fall of Night," and begins by setting the scene:

The lambent sapphire of the sky of day
In trembling streams has melted quite away;
The West now dons crepuscular attire
And wraps himself in gold and crimson fire;
The chaste moon through the turquoise twilight pours
Her pearl-pale light upon our lustrous shores,
And by her glassy essence opaline
Makes strand and surf with iridescence shine;
Now silver stars, cold, fair, and wanly bright,
Are scattered on the sable cope of night.

Eternal order rules despotic time:
The sky is beautiful, the sea sublime —
On high, the *primum mobile* rotates,
In my great clock the moment pendulates —
And ever down the scale of nature flow
Sidereal magics, guiding earth below.
    The westward wind is fragrant with fresh brine
And perfumes from the swaying groves of pine;
Here on the Eastern Shore of Maryland,
Where mighty trees above flat acreage stand,
The stridulations of the insects make
A music full of bliss and ardent ache;
Gold fireflies glisten on the wine-dark night,
And float, and burn: small gems of ghostly light.
I take up — hearing ocean's surge afar —
My ruddy wine, my dusky sweet cigar;
My great bay windows open lie — I gaze
Out over fields dissolving in a haze,
And silhouetted on night's blue I see
The stern colossus of my black gum tree;
The rarest airborne orchid of the night,
A Luna moth, floats by, jade-green and white.
All should be peace within, the fretful heart
Should rest in idle calm, and fears depart —
And yet it is not so: my thoughts are grave;
I find that I am melancholy's slave.

The poet now ponders the causes of his disaffection, but can find no diagnosis in the books he consults ("Hermetic manuals, treatises on sin . . ."). Then he considers what cures he might attempt, quickly dismissing pharmacology, psychiatry (which he calls "a romp of charlatans"), and "positive thinking"; he lingers over the possibility of contemplative prayer, but ultimately concludes that he is not equal to its demands:

So many demons vex the mystic's night —
Pride, sadness, wrath, the worm of appetite,
The noonday devil (*akedia*), desire,
And visions of the everlasting fire —
Were I to contend with that chthonian host,
Ingloriously the field would soon be lost.

And so he resigns himself to a state that today, I suppose, we might call "bipolar":

> I am a ship adrift on passion's seas,
> My every want I'm eager to appease:
> I am a roisterer, a sybarite,
> Orgiastic Bacchus, drunken, all delight . . .
>> And then Prometheus, torn by eagle's claws,
> Not knowing my transgression, or God's laws. . . .

Finally he begins to fall asleep:

> Tobacco's opiate, abetted by drink,
> Makes me vertiginous, my senses sink;
> Fatigued, lulled by dark nepenthes, I feel
> A languid Ixion on a sluggish wheel.

There follows a long allegorical dream that concludes with a vision of the old gods departing into a hidden realm ("From the barren earth, through the empty heavens").

Part Two, "Late Morning," resumes the narrative the next day, in a voice that seems a little, so to speak, hung over:

> Drunk with the torpor of midsummer light,
> I should be free from demons of the night —
> The throbbing bombinations of the bees,
> The treetops swaying in the humid breeze,
> As woodbine's balm comes dropping through the air —
> A day too heavy for such heavy care. . . .
>> Yet still the shadow lurks within and tells
> My secret mind of all its million hells.

This section is the poem's longest, and contains a remarkably exhaustive survey of my great-uncle's indictments of the modern world's morals, arts, and politics, including a now rather dated critique of Spengler's recently published *Der Untergang des Abendlandes*. At the end of this elegant rant, the poet grows calm by looking at the beauty of the countryside around his house:

> . . . I require no device
> Of art to praise this earthly paradise.

Just now a citron-blazoned swallowtail
Across my garden flutters, starts to sail,
Then vanishes amid rose-haunted shadows,
To float off to his honey-colored meadows.

Part Three, "Late Afternoon," merely recounts a long walk the poet
takes to clear his thoughts:

Nearby the Lesser Choptank's currents roll —
There still is time for a riparian stroll.
I'll amble with the pilgrim's barest goods
Between the river and the skirting woods —
A good cigar, a flask of scotch, and thou —
And pen my verse below the black gum bough;
I'll walk to where the low slope of the land
Before the waters melts in splendent sand. . . .
    Occasionally I see the dryads flit
From bole to bole, or in high branches sit. . . .

From this point on, the poem continually wavers back and forth between
frank examinations of the poet's state of mind and fleeting reveries. In one
of the more charming passages, the poet imagines the nearby woods as a
mythic forest and himself as Actaeon on the hunt:

The flush, the quickened, then the slackened pace,
And all the sweet elations of the chase:
Dew-silvered woods, the mist-gray light of dawn,
The violet shade, the grazing doe and fawn —
Then morning's sky puts off its somber hue
And through the branches breaks a fiery blue —
The mournful belling of the stag, the bays
Of loping hounds, the sun's green-golden rays,
The plash of ferns, the splash of blood, the gleam
Of dancing daylight in a stony stream,
The arrow loosed, the dreadful wound, the horn
Whose echoed note grows ever more forlorn,
Until at last the quarry's flight is stayed,
And silence fills the green sun-dappled glade. . . .

He adds that, could he be vouchsafed a glimpse of Artemis, he would hap-

pily then submit to her wrath, to be "rent asunder by the hounds of love."
It ends with the poet arriving at the shore's edge (actually the shore of
the Choptank, an estuary of the bay, but here he takes a few geographic
liberties):

> Continuing on, I see the sprawling ocean,
> The surge of its eternal massive motion.
> From here, sky's blue looks richer on the waters,
> Like the Aegean, where sport Poseidon's daughters;
> Upon its pearled horizon billows coil
> And glimmer in the sun like silver foil;
> The nymphs sing sweetly in their limestone caves,
> While ceaseless thunders roll across the waves;
> I see beyond a gauzy mist of rain
> A rainbow's gleam, a sky like cymophane. . . .

At this moment, the poet confesses, he cannot tell if he is on the edge
of madness or at the threshold of some transforming revelation. After a
short, probably ill-advised discourse on the delightful cuisine of the bay
region ("The fair rockfish whose flesh could not be moister, / The succu-
lent blue crab, the mollid oyster . . ."), he leaves the reader with an image
of himself standing upon the shore:

> A melancholic, but not lame or halt . . .
> The air is sharp with the cruel tang of salt . . .
> How fierce my demon when he vaunts and raves . . .
> How wild the joyous sparkling of the waves . . .
> I shall be well, if I can only sleep . . .
> A crystal swell unfolds the azure deep. . . .

Anyway, for what it may be worth, I hope some day to have time to
produce a proper edition of as much of the poem as Great-Uncle Aloysius
completed. I was very fond of him, whatever doubts I may have entertained regarding the cogency of his personal philosophy, and so I hope the
poem's appearance might constitute something of a literary event.

# TWENTY-FIVE

# *Graysteil*

A mong the more curious relics of my family past is the bronzed left thumb of my agnate ancestor Graysteil Bentley, who lived from 1789 to 1850 and who was the sole proprietor of a small merchant shipping fleet of (at the time of his death) eleven vessels. It is a somewhat ghastly object, principally because the bronzing was so expertly done that every line of the middle joint and the cuticles is perspicuously visible (though, happily, its severed lower knuckle is discreetly concealed in a cap of filigreed silver). It rests under glass on a bed of crimson velvet in a small ebony case, to which is affixed a minute brass plate whose now barely legible inscription reads "Varium et Mutabile Semper Femina." As a child, I was fascinated and appalled by this macabre vestige of a man long since reduced to dust, but did not think to inquire into the story behind it until I was about fifteen. It was my uncle Robert-the-Bruce Bentley who told me the tale.

At the time of Graysteil's birth in Baltimore, his family had already made its fortune in shipping. His father's forebears had settled in St. Mary's City in 1634, at the founding of Cecilius Calvert's Maryland colony. His mother was a Scot (hence his rather recherché "Christian" name). Graysteil was, it seems, a precocious and promising lad. He was an avid reader, a lover of poetry, fluent from an early age in French and Spanish (both taught to him by his nurse, a Creole woman from Louisiana), a musician whose virtuosity on the spinet was a great source of pride to his mother, and largely indifferent to the family's mercantile concerns. His father was occasionally vexed at the boy's dreamy temperament, but was too indulgent to attempt to alter it. The family business suffered during the War of 1812, when the entire Bentley fleet was commandeered by the United States government and six ships were lost. But by 1817 the Bentley

Line was thriving again and Graysteil's father, seeking to forge an alliance with a larger shipping firm in Louisiana, sent his son to New Orleans as his liaison. To his delight, Graysteil not only easily ingratiated himself to the firm's chief proprietor, but within a few months had embarked upon a romance with the latter's daughter, Lucinde. She was a great beauty, by all accounts, as well as being heiress to a great fortune, and at nineteen never wanted for suitors. She was also a lover of the arts, especially poetry. Graysteil was entirely smitten. In his journals, according to my uncle, he rhapsodized about Lucinde's "sapphire eyes" and "hair of sable silk" and "alabaster skin," but was even more ecstatic in his praise of her refinement of nature, the delicacy of her sentiments, and the charm of her conversation. She showed every sign, moreover, of welcoming Graysteil's attentions. He had a rival for her affections, however, a wealthy plantation owner bearing the ominous name of Maximillian Ganellon. He was tall, handsome, and rumored to be something of a cad ("Max le malfaisant" he was sometimes called). Unlike Graysteil, he had no interest whatsoever in "higher things": music and poetry bored him, his conversation rarely strayed away from the secure redoubts of hunting and money, his chief occupation was gambling and his chief diversion (allegedly) women of low degree, and his only conspicuous virtues were his prognathous jaw and broad shoulders. It was inconceivable to Graysteil that the woman who had seized the citadel of his soul could possibly prefer this lissome brute to him. And yet she continued to admit Ganellon into her presence, with every bit as much effervescent gaiety as she accorded Graysteil's visits.

Relations between the two men were poor from the moment of their first meeting, and the sullen suspicion with which each viewed the other soon degenerated into open hostility. Graysteil was somewhat impetuous, it seems, in both his affections and his aversions, while Max Ganellon was a proud and possessive man jealous of everything he considered his by right. Finally, in circumstances of which no precise record remains, one of the men called the other out, and a duel was fought one warm misty dawn just outside the quiet purlieus of New Orleans. Each assumed the correctly oblique posture, confronting the other with as narrow a target as possible; but Graysteil, while holding his left arm folded close against his back, seems to have left his thumb extended behind him. When shots were exchanged, Ganellon missed Graysteil's chest, but his ball quite by chance amputated Graysteil's thumb at its base. Graysteil's shot went entirely wide. The doctor in attendance immediately demanded the duel's cessation, and all present — antagonists and seconds alike — agreed that honor had been satisfied. Before departing, one of Graysteil's seconds retrieved his thumb, thinking it a rather indecent object to leave lying in the dust. With his wound cleaned and dressed by the doctor, faint from pain and shock, and wishing to recover himself properly before venturing out from his rooms again, Graysteil took to his bed for the rest of the day. As he lay there, he resolved to approach Lucinde's father and seek his consent for their marriage. Surely he had proved the depth of his devotion beyond any doubt. Early in the evening, however, a letter arrived from Lucinde informing him that, having only just learned of the duel late in the morning, she had realized all at once that, while she had felt terrific anxiety for both the combatants, it was the thought of any harm coming to "dear Max" that had pierced her to her core. She knew then that it was he whom she truly loved and that he alone, having won her heart, had any just claim upon her hand. When the doctor arrived next morning to check in upon his patient, he brought the severed thumb with him, washed in spirits and sealed in a green glass phial, not wishing to dispose of it on his own. Graysteil stared at it without words for several moments, and then asked if the doctor knew of any bronze smiths in the city.

Graysteil soon returned to Baltimore, where he began to take a more active role in the running of the Bentley Line. A loss of dexterity in the remaining digits of his left hand caused him to eschew the spinet ever after, and his passion for poetry seems to have cooled considerably. His father died in 1818 and his mother (unexpectedly) in 1821; soon thereafter he appointed his cousin as his agent for running the line and made preparations for a voyage. It was his intention, he said, to immolate himself in the "pyre of the sun." In fact, he sailed on one of his own ships to the Azores, where he had purchased a house and lands on Pico Island. There he remained for the better part of the next quarter century, pursuing the twin interests of botany (foliate morphology in particular) and seashells. A bit of pernicious family gossip credited him with siring an indeterminate number of illegitimate children by Portuguese women during those years, but no evidence was ever produced to support it. In 1845, he returned permanently to Baltimore where, within only a few months, he contracted a marriage with a respectable woman more than thirty years his junior who presented him with three healthy sons in four years. He would never see them grow to manhood. One day in June of 1850, while making some kind of an inspection of one of his ships for insurance purposes, he suddenly announced that he intended to scale the rigging. He had never been a sailor, and was hardly a young man, but no one could dissuade him. When he was twenty feet or so aloft, a slight pitching of the ship caused him to lose his footing; and, while his right hand was able to support his weight for a moment, his left could get no grip, and he plummeted to the deck below. Two days later, as he lay dying in his bed, he told his cousin that but for the missing thumb he would not have fallen, and that it was only appropriate that Lucinde's betrayal would ultimately be the cause of his death.

Anyway, I am not entirely sure what to make of the story of Graysteil's shattered heart and hand, or of the special significance he attached to the grisly memento that he kept with him to his death, and that he directed be passed on as an inalienable part of his estate as an "admonition to fools who vest their hopes in the fickle heart of woman." I married young and my twenty-fifth wedding anniversary is rapidly approaching, and the association has left me spiritually content and anatomically intact. Good Confucian that I am, I try to heed the wisdom of my ancestors. But I think that, where *les affaires du cœur* were concerned, Graysteil Bentley's perspective was somewhat distorted. Losing both one's thumb and the love of one's life on a single fateful day can do that to one, I would imagine.

# TWENTY-SIX

# Lupinity, Felinity, and the Limits of Method

Sometimes, late at night, when the branches of the large pine outside my window are swaying in a hot breeze and brushing with a sinister whisper against my window panes, and sleep seems to loom far above me like some inaccessible peak floating in the cerulean depths of the Himalayan sky, I find myself worrying obsessively about the thylacine and the fossa. What accounts for them? Are they perhaps signs of some cosmic mystery that the sciences will ultimately prove impotent to penetrate? Are they quadrupedal portents of the transcendent? Or are they signs of a physical determinism so absolute as to be indistinguishable from fate?

If you are not given to similar anxieties, however, you may not know what I am talking about. So maybe I should try to explain what I mean.

The great danger that bedevils any powerful heuristic or interpretive discipline is the tendency to mistake method for ontology, and so to mistake a partial perspective on particular truths for a comprehensive vision of truth as such. In the modern world, this is an especially pronounced danger in the sciences, largely because of the exaggerated reverence scientists enjoy in the popular imagination, and also largely because of the incapacity of many in the scientific establishment to distinguish between scientific rigor and materialist ideology (or, better, materialist metaphysics). This has two disagreeable results (well, actually, far more than two, but two that are relevant here): the lunatic self-assurance with which some scientists imagine that their training in, say, physics or zoology has somehow equipped them to address philosophical questions whose terms they have never even begun to master; and the inability of many scientists to recognize realities — even very obvious realities — that lie logically outside the reach of the methods their disciplines employ. The best example of the latter, I suppose, would be the inability of certain contemporary champions of "naturalism" to grasp that the question of existence is qualitatively infinitely distinct from the question of how one physical reality arises from another (for, inasmuch as physics can explore only the physical, and the physical by definition already exists, then existence as such is always "metaphysical," or even "hyperphysical" — which is to say, "supernatural").

But that is all matter for another time. Here I do not want to argue about being. I have, rather, a very simple worry to confess about the competence of method — any method — to recognize its own boundaries. All method, after all, as the etymology of the word exquisitely shows, is an elective practice of cleaving to a particular path (*met'-hodos*), a labor of limiting oneself to a particular approach to a problem in order to achieve as precise an understanding of that problem as may be achieved from one perspective. But that means that method always remains *only* a perspective, however powerful it may be: a willful blindness to many things for the sake of seeing a few things with a special clarity. A man peering into a microscope has been vouchsafed a glimpse into realities that the naked eye could never see, but he may also fail to notice the large fire that has just started on the far side of his laboratory, near the only exit. Modern experimental science began to coalesce into a general method with the rise of the mechanical philosophy and the shattering of the old Aristotelian fourfold structure of causality. That may be only an accident of history, in long retrospect; but, whatever the case, the magnificent force and fecundity of modern scientific method are in part the consequence of a conscious decision to eschew any explanation for any physical phenomenon that requires the invocation of final or formal causes. By thus prescinding from teleology and causative morphology, experimental science was allowed to devote itself unwaveringly to those material and efficient processes at work within any physical event (though here "material" and "efficient" no longer have the meaning they had in Aristotelian thought). In Daniel Dennett's language, science learned to think in terms of "cranes" only, and entirely to discount the possibility of "skyhooks."

Even so, it would be worse than naïve to imagine that the sciences have thereby proved the nonexistence of final and formal causes. In fact, by bracketing such causes out of consideration, scientific method also rendered itself incapable of pronouncing upon any reality such causes might or might not explain. Now, of course, the typical reply to this observation (from the aforementioned Daniel Dennett, for instance) is to say, with some indignation, that modern science *has* in fact demonstrated the utter superfluity of final and formal causal explanations, because the sciences have shown that they do not need finality or formality to understand the processes they investigate. That, however, is an empty tautology: of course modern scientific method discovers the kind of reality it is specifically designed to discover; and even in cases where it finds its explanatory reserves overly taxed, it must presume that in future some sort of "mechanical" cause will be found to restore the balance, and so issue itself a promissory note to that effect. But, again, this may mean that it must also overlook realities that actually lie very near at hand, either quite open to investigation if another method could be found, or so obviously beyond investigation as to mark out the limits of scientific method with particular clarity.

Which brings me to the thylacine and the fossa.

The thylacine, if you do not know, was an apex predator once found in Australia, Tasmania, and New Guinea, of which some old film footage still exists, but which was rendered extinct sometime last century. It was, for want of a better term, a marsupial wolf. Though only, at most, very distantly related, by very remote extraction, to some of the same ancestors as the placental mammalian canines of other lands, its skeletal shape, its behaviors, its movements, and so on were remarkably lupine. The fossa is another predator, happily not extinct — not yet, at any rate — and is an inhabitant of Madagascar. It is a viverrid (probably), a distant cousin of the mongoose, but it has a large number of felid traits; that is, it moves, hunts, and to a large degree looks like a cat, inside and out. Now, I have heard evolutionary biologists speak about both animals on more than one occasion, and the usual explanations adduced for either animal's morphological resemblance to species far removed from its own are drawn, to varying degrees, from genetics and convergent evolutionary theory. There are similar codes embedded deep in the labyrinths of the genetic material that thylacines and wolves, or fossas and cats, inherited from some amazingly ancient common ancestors. Or similar environmental pressures were exerted on the evolutionary processes of all the creatures involved, resulting in some very similar morphologies. Or both, really.

I am not qualified to pronounce on these things, though I have two melancholic molecular biologist friends who become vague and evasive when I raise the issue with them. One worries that, as the "classical conception of the gene" has begun to fall apart in recent decades, and the idea of genetics as a science of information flow, analogous to the reading of software programs, has been challenged by a more indeterministic view of genetic material, it is not exactly clear how genetic coding could prove so cohesive and unidirectional over such vast epochs. Organisms, he tells me, as systems, use genetic material in such various ways that "there is no such thing as a 'gene for' this or that." So it would take some considerable run of improbable coincidences for two complex systems to evolve separately while employing the same material in such similar fashion. The other approvingly quotes Gould's famous assertion that, if the tape of life were wound back again to the time of the Burgess Shale and allowed to play forward again, it would arrive at totally different results. The notion that there is evolutionary convergence in certain details of physical development across species divisions — the shape of a wing, the mechanism of a cameral eye — makes good sense to him, but the independent full development of close morphological analogues like the timber wolf and the thylacine seems to strain his credulity. If evolution is a sort of "algorithmic" process of chance mutations, incredibly numerous and rare and unpredictable, selected by adventitious environmental conditions, and is a process moreover whose course is cumulative but not accumulative — progressive but not directed — then it is certainly surprising that genetic variation over millions of years under varying conditions in different regions could actually produce such similar results in such complex organic structures. Not that either man suggests that the working theories are wrong. And I, for what it is worth, have no opinion in the matter whatsoever. I am not qualified to have an opinion. It simply strikes me as pleasing to imagine supplementing (or even underpinning) the genetic and the convergent explanations with the Platonic or Aristotelian suggestion that, perhaps, there is such a thing as the form of the wolf or the form of the cat — lupinity or felinity as such — that impresses itself upon the somewhat intractable material substrate according to the prevailing conditions in a given time or place. Then the existence of both a placental mammalian wolf and a marsupial wolf, born at the end of evolutionary genealogies separated by oceans for millions of years, seems hardly surprising at all. If nothing else, this notion is not much more incredible than the idea that there is, say, a sort of cat-shaped niche out there in certain ecosystems that environmental forces will inevitably cause to be filled. (Then again, maybe it all has something to do with the Great Chain of Being.)

That, however, is also not my point. I have no doubt that evolutionary biology has much to say, and will continue to find more to say, regarding these strange symmetries across discontinuities in the lineages of living things. My question really is one regarding method. If there were a case in which modern biological method came up against a reality that seemed to point toward orders of causality it could not logically investigate without altering its working premises radically, would it be able to recognize that it had reached its limit? Could it admit as much to itself, or tell us about it? It is an imprecise question, so open as perhaps to be vacuous, but I raise it just the same; because, only when a method is conscious of what it cannot explain, can it maintain a clear distinction between the knowledge it secures and the ideology it obeys.

# TWENTY-SEVEN

# America and the Angels of Sacré-Coeur

*I will pour out my spirit upon all flesh; and your sons and your daughters shall prophesy, your old men shall dream dreams, your young men shall see visions.*

— Joel 2:28

From the outside, Montmartre's Sacré-Cœur Basilica presents something of an aesthetic problem. It is a striking edifice, needless to say, soaring up as it does at the very summit of Paris, a bright white riot of demi-ovate domes and cupolas, elongated arches, and intrepidly clashing decorative motifs. But it is also very much a product of its time, with a little too much fin de siècle preciosity about it. If one views its alleged fusion of Romanesque and Byzantine styles at a sardonic slant, it can look suspiciously like a meretricious pastiche, full of late Romantic medievalist and orientalist clichés. Contemplated at a distance, under the Parisian sky, it all sometimes seems not so much an organic expression of the spiritual aspirations of French culture as a patently synthetic memorial to them, concocted from equal parts morbid nostalgia and sugary fantasy.

On the inside, however, it is very different: more austere, more a matter of softly golden stone and muted sunlight. There is, admittedly, that huge, hideous mosaic from the 1920s in the apse (a titanic Christ with a gilded heart, flanked by the lesser colossi of the Blessed Virgin and Saint Michael, all three towering over a scampering horde of mitered and haloed imps), but otherwise the interior is genuinely, if somberly, beautiful. And one feature of the vault can produce an effect that is truly sublime. There are four large stone angels with outspread wings, carved in relief, one each, in the pendentives below the central dome. When one enters the basilica out of bright daylight, however, they are not immediately visible, but remain hidden in the shadows below the ring of windows at the dome's base. It is only as one's eyes adjust to the dimness that they emerge, all at once, from the darkness. If one is unprepared for it, it is a startling experience, even slightly terrifying; for just a few seconds, one senses the advent — and the gaze — of immense and numinous presences. At that moment, any lingering aesthetic reservations can be set aside. However dubious certain features of its design may be, there can be no doubt just then that Sacré-Cœur does authentically express something of the genius of French Christian tradition. You see, it is all a question of causality. Obviously, those angels looming so magnificently overhead are there as a result of the material and efficient causes that went into the building's planning and construction: travertine limestone, bricks, sculptors, Paul Abadie, money, the political tensions of the Third Republic, and so on. But, in another sense, it was the angels who summoned the basilica into being; they provided the final and formal causes that raised it up out of the substrate of mere unformed matter. Were it not for the transcendent longings they embodied, or for the ecstatic creativity those longings once evoked, there would be no church there at all. And one knows this, however fleetingly, in the instant of their apparition.

After all — and this is a truth so certain that only the most doctrinaire Marxist or lumpen British atheist could deny it — the structure of culture is essentially an idealist one, and a living culture is a spiritual dispensation. A civilization's values, symbols, ideals, and imaginative capacities flow down from above, from the most exalted objects of its transcendental desires, and a people's greatest collective achievements are always in some sense attempts to translate eternal into temporal order. This will always be especially obvious in places of worship. To wax vaguely Heideggerian, temples are built to summon the gods, but only because the gods have first called out to mortals. There are invisible powers (whether truly divine powers or only powers of the imagination) that seek to become manifest, to emerge from their invisibility; and they can do this only by inspiring human beings to wrest beautiful forms out of intractable elements. They disclose their unseen world by transforming this world into its concrete image, allegory, or reflection, in a few privileged places where divine and human gazes briefly meet. Such places, moreover, are only the most concentrated crystallizations of a culture's highest visions of the good, true, and beautiful; they are not isolated retreats, set apart from the society around them, but are in fact the most intense expressions of that society's guiding rationality and creativity. It is under the shelter of the heavens made visible in such places that all of a people's laws and institutions, admirable or defective, take shape, as well as all their arts, civic or private, sacred or profane, festal or ordinary. This is a claim not about private beliefs, or about the particular motives that may have led to any particular law or work of art, but about the conceptual and aesthetic resources that any culture can possess or impart; and those are determined by religious traditions — by shared pictures of eternity, shared stories of the absolute. That is why the very concept of a secular civilization is nearly meaningless. This is also to say, incidentally, that a culture's greatest source of strength is a source of considerable fragility as well. When the momentary thrill induced by the angels of Sacré-Cœur subsides, what remains is merely a certain poignancy: the realization that the emotional power of those figures, insofar as it cannot be accounted for merely by a trick of the light, emanates entirely from the past. It has nothing to do with the future. Given the late date of the basilica's construction, and given the realities of modern France, it is impossible not to see that splendidly overwhelming but very temporary act of disclosure as a valedictory performance, a last epiphany before a final departure, at the end of a cultural history that now shows no capacity for renewing itself. Civilization is a spiritual labor, an openness to revelation, a venture of faith, subsisting to a great degree on things no more substantial than myths and visions and prophetic dreams; thus it can be destroyed not only by invading armies or economic collapse, but also by simple disenchantment.

All of which brings me to my topic: the uncertainties of the American future and the possible role religion may or may not play in that future. If it seems I have taken a rather roundabout approach to the issue, my earnest defense is that, to this point, I have been talking all along about America; I have simply been doing so *sub contrario*. American religious life, in all its native expressions, is so odd and paradoxical that it is often most easily approached indirectly, stealthily, from behind, as it were; and, to my mind, one of the best ways of doing this is to begin one's approach from France. The contrast is so edifyingly stark. So much of what historically made France a great nation is all but entirely absent from America, while so much of what has made America a great nation is all but entirely alien to France; and it may be the case that many of the principal weaknesses of each are among the other's principal strengths. This is not, of course, a comparison between two distinct civilizations — at least, not if one uses that word in its grandest, most inflexible, and haughtiest sense. America's chief originality lies in the political, social, and economic experiment that it undertook at its founding; but it is a very young nation, and delightfully diverse, and its culture is largely a blended distillation of other cultures. Often blamelessly derivative, but also often shamefully forgetful of even the recent past, it is a nation that floats lightly upon the depths of human history, with sometimes too pronounced a sense of its own novelty. So, obviously, there is no American equivalent of Sacré-Cœur: some consecrated space haunted by the glories and failures of a deep past, ennobled and burdened by antique hopes and fantasies, emblematic of an ancient people's whole spiritual story, but also eloquent of spiritual disappointment and the waning of faith. There are places of local memory, so to speak, especially in the South, but their scope is rather severely circumscribed. America's churches, when they are not merely serviceable clapboard meetinghouses or tents of steel and glass, are mostly just imitations of European originals: imported, transplanted, always somewhat out of place. They tell us practically nothing about America itself, and even less about whatever numinous presences might be hovering overhead.

And yet those presences are there. There may not be a distinctive American civilization in the fullest sense, but there definitely is a distinctly American Christianity. It is something protean, scattered, fragmentary, and fissile, often either mildly or exorbitantly heretical, and sometimes only vestigially Christian; but it can nevertheless justly be called the American religion — and it is a powerful religion. It is, however, a style of faith remarkably lacking in beautiful material forms or coherent institutional structures, not by accident, but essentially. Its civic inexpressiveness is a consequence not simply of cultural privation, or of frontier simplicity, or of modern utilitarianism, or even of some lingering Puritan reserve toward ecclesial rank and architectural ostentation, but also of a profound and radical resistance to outward forms. It is a religion of the book or of private revelation, of oracular wisdom and foolish rapture, but not one of tradition, hierarchy, or public creeds. Even where it creates intricate institutions of its own, and erects its own large temples, it tends to do so entirely on its own terms, in a void, in a cultural and (ideally) physical desert, at a fantastic remove from all traditional sources of authority, historical "validity," or good taste (Mormonism is an expression of this tendency at its boldest, most original, and most deliriously effervescent). What America shares with, say, France is the general Western heritage of Christian belief, with all its confessional variations; what it has never had any real part in, however, is Christendom.

In one sense, this is not at all surprising. America was born in flight from the Old World's thrones and altars, the corrupt accommodations between spiritual authority and earthly power, the old confusion of reverence for God with servility before princes; and, as a political project in its own right, the United States was the first Western nation explicitly founded upon principles requiring no official alliance between religious confession and secular government. Even if this had not been so, the ever-greater religious heterogeneity of America over the course of its history would surely, sooner or later, have made such an alliance absurdly impractical. And so, in fact, America was established as the first truly modern nation, the first Western society consciously to dissociate its constitutional order from the political mythologies of a long disintegrating Christendom, and the first predominantly Christian country to place itself under, at most, God's general providential supervision, but not under the command of any of his officially recognized lieutenants. The nation began, one could argue, from a place at which the other nations of the West had not yet arrived. In another sense, however, when one considers the result, it is all rather astonishing. America may have arisen out of the end of Christendom, and as the first fully constituted political alternative to Christendom, but it somehow avoided the religious and cultural fate of the rest of the modern West. Far from blazing a trail into the post-Christian future that awaited other nations, America went quite a different way, down paths that no other Western society would ever tread, or even know how to find. Whereas European society — moving with varying speed but in a fairly uniform direction — experienced the end of Christendom simultaneously as the decline of faith, in America just the opposite happened. Here, the paucity of institutional and "civilizing" mediations between the transcendent and the immanent went hand in hand with a general, largely formless, and yet utterly irrepressible intensification of faith: rather than the exhaustion of religious longing, its revival; rather than a long nocturnal descent into disenchantment, a new dawning of early Christianity's elated expectation of the kingdom.

Now, admittedly, I should avoid excessive generalization on this matter. Just about every living religion has found some kind of home here, bringing along whatever institutional supports it could fit into its luggage. Many such creeds have even managed to preserve the better part of their integrity. Still, I would argue (maybe with a little temerity), such communities exist here as displaced fragments of other spiritual worlds, embassies from more homogeneous religious cultures, and it is from those cultures that they derive whatever cogency they possess. They are beneficiaries of the hospitable and capacious indeterminacy of American spirituality, but not direct expressions of it. The form of Christianity most truly *indigenous* to America is one that is simultaneously peculiarly disembodied and indomitably vigorous, and its unity is one of temperament rather than confession. The angels of America have remained, for the most part, unseen presences, unable or unwilling to emerge from their hiddenness into the open visibility of a shared material or intellectual culture; and yet, perhaps for this very reason, they have also retained the sort of terrible force that their Old World counterparts lost some time ago. They may, therefore, be very clever angels. Never coming out of the shadows in great national churches, or dancing attendance on kings, or lending much of a hand in civil government, they also never risked being weighed down by human political history. Because they never revealed themselves too carelessly to the eyes of faith, they also never exposed themselves to the scornful gaze of disbelief. France's angels, by contrast, had for centuries been perceived as complicit in the injustices of the *ancien régime,* and so could hardly claim immunity when the old order fell, or escape the resentments and skepticisms that that order had bred. But America's angels have kept their mysterious transcendence intact to this day, and with it their power to inspire spiritual longings, even of the most extravagant kind.

None of this is to say, however, that American society has somehow really succeeded in erecting a partition between its religious and its civic identities. Cult and culture are never separable, even if their relation does not involve any explicit union between a particular religious body and the power of the state. American spirituality may be particularly rich in those kinds of devotion that are most elusive of stable institutional form: enthusiasm and ecstasy, apocalyptic mysticism and gnostic individualism, dreams and visions. But, even so, America is — as much as any nation has ever been — its religion; and its greatest cultural virtues and defects are all bound up with the kinds of faith that flourish here. Years ago, as an aid to teaching undergraduates and a partial remedy to the boredom of the lecture hall, I devised a needlessly florid typology for describing the various shapes taken by modern Western nations in Christendom's aftermath, and of the various ways in which Western societies have gathered up the fragments of the old concords between church and state. As a mnemonic device for my students, it was a ghastly failure; but, as a useful oversimplification, it was a spectacular triumph (which makes it baffling that, with the exception of a partial reference to it in an article in the *New Criterion* some years back, I have never thought to put it in print till now). I told my students to think of modern Western nations, and of their various attitudes toward the social and political remains of the old Christian order, under three figures: pseudomorphs, exuviae, and poltergeists; and

I proposed, as an example of each type, respectively, the Soviet Union, France, and the United States.

Pseudomorphism — for those who have not recently leafed through manuals of crystallography or volumes of Spengler — is that process by which one crystal assumes the alien shape of another, through chemical or molecular substitution, or by being forced into the space evacuated by its predecessor. It seemed to me an elegant metaphor for the way that, for instance, Soviet political culture had supplanted the late Russian version of Byzantine caesaropapism not by just dissolving the latter's basic forms, but by trying to colonize them from within: in place of the old authoritarianism, a new absolutism, with a more comprehensive state apparatus and a more fanatical intolerance of heresy; in place of Eastern Orthodoxy's emphasis upon eternity within time and the light of the kingdom amid history's darkness, the Soviet faith in the providential sovereignty of material dialectic and the ineluctability of the socialist utopia; in place of the ethereal gold and temperas of Byzantine iconography, the shrill vermilion and lifeless opacity of Soviet realist portraiture; in place of the relics of incorruptible saints, Lenin's pickled cadaver in a glass box; and so on.

Exuviation, on the other hand, is the shedding of skins or shells, and exuviae are what are sloughed off. The image works especially well if one thinks of those translucent integumental husks that cicadas leave behind them, clinging tenaciously to the bark of trees. It is an apt metaphor for all those enchanting vestiges of religious tradition found in societies that, like France, have lost the faith so thoroughly that even the passion of revolutionary impiety has long since subsided. There the remains of the old order are reduced to ornamental souvenirs, the lovely traces of vanished dreamworlds; they just linger on, quietly, in old buildings, museums, tastes, customs, the calendar, turns of phrase, shared stories, a few legal traditions, a few moral premises, a few imperturbable pillars of cultural sensibility; but everything that once inhabited, shaped, and animated them is gone. They are exquisitely dead. They can excite indifference, tender memories, casual contempt, but rarely love or belief. They have become elements of a general aesthetic and moral atmosphere, and nothing more.

As for poltergeists, there the image is less obscure. Everything I have already said about American religion explains the metaphor: a force capable of moving material realities about, often unpredictably and even alarmingly, and yet possessing no proper, stable material form of its own. American religion lacks the imposing structures of culture, law, and public worship that Christendom evolved over the centuries, but its energy is almost impossible to contain. It has no particular social place, and yet it is everywhere.

If this typology, however, seems a little too dainty or a little too neat, it might be better simply to talk in terms of the relative vitality of (excuse the postmodern fillip here) "force and structure" in a nation's religion. Soviet society, by grotesquely inverting rather than destroying the religious grammar of Russian culture, showed that both the spiritual and the institutional aspects of Russian Christendom, however diminished at the time of the revolution, still had a little life in them. The serene urbanity of today's French secularism, the pragmatic laicism of French republicanism, and the relaxed anticlericalism of French society as a whole testify to French Christendom's absolute dormancy in all its aspects. In the case of either nation, though, religious force and structure persisted or declined more or less together. In America, by contrast, as happened nowhere else, they suffered a schism, fairly early on, whose result — or, at any rate, sequel — was that religion's public structure was shattered, but the force contained within it was released. One might have expected that a spirituality without the tangible support of civic religion would disperse over time; but perhaps the passion of faith often thrives best when it is largely unaccommodated, roaming on its own in wild places. After all, when one considers the first three centuries of Christian history, when the faith had no such support, it may make perfect sense that, in the wake of Christendom's collapse, the forms of Christianity that proved most lively would be those that possess something analogous to the apocalyptic consciousness of the earliest Christian communities: their sense of having emerged from history into the immediacy of a unique redemptive event, their triumphant contempt for antique cult and culture, their experience of emancipation from the bondage of the law, their aloofness from structures of civil power, and their indifference to the historical future (for the present things are passing away). There may even be some advantage in the absence of strong institutional organization, at least in certain circumstances. It may well be that the translation of Christianity's original apocalyptic ferment into a cultural logic and social order produced a powerful but necessarily volatile alloy. For all the good that this transformation produced in the shaping of Western civilization (which no sane person could deny), it also encumbered the faith with a weight of historical and cultural expectation wholly incompatible with the gospel it proclaimed. Certainly Christian culture has excelled, as no other ever has, at incubating militant atheisms and even self-conscious nihilisms, and this may have something to do with its own innate tension between spiritual rebellion and social piety. Perhaps the concrescence of Christianity into Christendom necessarily led in Europe, over the course of centuries, to its gradual mortification, its slow attrition through internal stress, and finally its dissipation into the inconclusiveness of human history and the ephemerality of political orders. The relation between force and structure had become so hardened at the end that the one could not escape the fate of the other.

Whatever the case, the American religion somehow slipped free from this story before it reached its denouement, and so it is not inextricably entangled in the tragic contradictions of historical memory. At its purest, in fact, it is free of almost all memory, and so of all anxiety: it strives toward a state of almost perfect timelessness, seeking a place set apart from the currents of human affairs, where God and the soul can meet and, so to speak, affirm one another. For a faith so thoroughly divorced from history, there is no set limit to the future it may possess. And if, as I have said, culture is always shaped by spiritual aspirations, this all has a very great bearing on what kind of future America might possess. History is not created by historical consciousness, after all; the greatest historical movements are typically inspired by visions of an eternal truth that has somehow overtaken history. This is simply because a people's very capacity for a future, at least one of any duration or consequence (good or bad), requires a certain obliviousness in regard to time's death-bound banality, a certain imaginative levity, a certain faith. The future is often the gift of the eternal.

I have gone some distance, I suppose, without offering some specific example of this "American religion" I keep referring to. This is because I really do understand it as something intrinsically impalpable and shapeless: a diffuse and pervasive spiritual temper rather than a particular creed. But, for clarity's sake, I may as well admit that I regard American evangelicalism, in all its varieties — fundamentalist, Pentecostal, blandly therapeutic — as the most pristine expression of this temper. I say this not because of evangelicalism's remarkable demographic range, its dominance in certain large regions of the country, or its extraordinary missionary success in Latin America and elsewhere, but simply because I am convinced of its autochthony: it is a form of spiritual life that no other nation could have produced, and the one most perfectly in accord with the special genius and idiocy, virtue and vice, of American culture. Whatever one's view of evangelicalism, only bigotry could prevent one from recognizing its many admirable features: the dignity, decency, and probity it inspires in individuals, families, and communities; the moral seriousness it nourishes in countless consciences; its frequent and generous commitment to alleviating the sufferings of the indigent and ill; its capacity for binding diverse peoples together in a shared spiritual resolve; its power to alter character profoundly for the better; the joy it confers; and so on. But, conversely, only a deep ignorance of Christian history could blind one to its equally numerous eccentricities: the odd individualism of its understanding of salvation, its bizarre talk of Christ as one's "personal Lord and Savior," its fantastic scriptural literalism, the crass sentimentality of some of its more popular forms of worship, its occasional tendency to confuse piety with patriotism, and so on. I am frequently tempted to describe it as a kind of "Christian bhakti," a pure ecstatic devotionalism, as opposed to those more "Vedic" forms of Christianity that ground themselves in ancient traditions. In fact, American evangelicalism not only lacks any sense of tradition, but is blithely hostile to tradition on principle: What is tradition, after all, other than man-made history, and what is history other than exile from paradise? What need does one have of tradition when one has the Bible, that eternal love letter from Jesus to the soul, inerrant, unambiguous, uncorrupted by the vicissitudes of human affairs? In some of its most extreme forms, it is a religion of total and unsullied reverie, the pure present of the child's world, in which ingenuous outcries and happy gestures and urgent conjurations instantly bring forth succor and substance. And, at its most intensely fundamentalist, so precipitous is its flight from the gravity of history into Edenic and eschatological rapture that it reduces all of cosmic history to a few thousand years of terrestrial existence and the whole of the present to a collection of signs urgently pointing to the world's imminent ending.

Now, I know I am describing only a few extreme variants of only one variant of Protestant Christianity in America. I might point out, however, that I am also describing acute forms of a spirituality whose chronic forms can be found liberally distributed throughout America's religious communities, even in certain circles within American Catholicism, Judaism, mainstream Protestantism, and so on. That, though, is of only passing interest. My central claim is that what one sees with particular clarity in evangelical piety is a deep spiritual orientation that both informs and expresses the American mythos: that grand narrative, going back to colonial times, of a people that has fled the evils of an Old World sunk in corruption, has cast off the burden of an intolerable past, and has been "born again" as a new nation, redeemed from the violence and falsehood of the former things. It is not difficult, of course, to enumerate the weaknesses of a culture shaped by such a spiritual logic. It is a spirituality that, for example, makes very little contribution to the aesthetic surface of American life. This is no small matter. The American religion does almost nothing to create a shared high culture, to enrich the lives of ordinary persons with the loveliness of sacred public spaces, to erect a few enduring bulwarks against the cretinous barbarity of late modern popular culture, or to enliven the physical order with intimations of transcendent beauty. With its nearly absolute separation between inward conviction and outward form, it is largely content to surrender the surrounding world to utilitarian severities. It could not do otherwise even if the nation's constitution were not formally so secular. It would not have the imaginative resources. It is a religion of feeling, not of sensibility; it might be able to express itself in great scale, but not as a rule in good taste. It is, however, a religious temperament wonderfully free of cynicism or moral doubt, and so it may have a singular capacity for surviving historical disappointment and the fluctuations of national fortune. Its immunity to disenchantment seems very real, at any rate. It may, in fact, grow only stronger if the coming decades should bring about a decline in America's preeminence, power, international influence, or even solvency. Whatever the case, it is unlikely to lapse very easily into a decline of its own, or vanish into some American equivalent of the spiritual exhaustion and moral lassitude of post-Christian Europe.

For myself, I should confess that I approach the relation between America's cultural and religious futures with an insoluble ambivalence. This is, in part, because I have no emotional investment in America's preeminence among modern powers. Our geopolitical ascendancy during the latter half of the twentieth century was very much an accident, however inevitable it may have been. It was the result of the country being dragged back into a history of which it had taken leave centuries before, and into the psychotic savagery of midcentury European affairs, and into a global ideological struggle for the future. It would not be any great tragedy if all of that should now prove to have been a very transient episode. In relative terms, American prosperity and power will remain formidable enough for some time, and I cannot see why anyone should fret over anything as intrinsically worthless as global "leadership." The question that should concern us, it seems to me, is whether in years ahead America will produce a society that has any particular right to a future. By this, I mean nothing more elaborate than this: How charitable and just a society will it be, how conscious will it be of those truths that transcend the drearier economies of finite existence, and will it produce much good art? And all of that will be determined, inevitably, by spiritual forces. It is not obvious, however, what those forces will be, or what they can do. It is very much an open and troubling question whether American religiosity has the resources to help sustain a culture *as* a culture — whether, that is, it can create a meaningful future, or whether it can only prepare for the end times. Is the American religious temperament so apocalyptic as to be incapable of culture in any but the most local and ephemeral sense? Does it know of any city other than Babylon the Great or the New Jerusalem? For all the moral will it engenders in persons and communities, can it cultivate the kind of moral intelligence necessary to live in eternity and in historical time simultaneously, without contradiction? Will its lack of any coherent institutional structure ultimately condemn it to haunting rather than vivifying its culture, or make it too susceptible to exploitation by alien interests, or render it incapable of bearing any sufficiently plausible or even interesting witness to the transcendent . . . ? And so on and so on. There is much to admire in the indigenous American religious sensibility, without question, but also much to deplore, and there is plenteous cause for doubt here.

Still, the worst fate that could befall America, one far grimmer than the mere loss of some of its fiscal or political supremacy in the world, would be the final triumph of a true cultural secularism. I know that there are those, on both the left and the right, who still believe in the project of an "enlightened" secular society; some — curiously ignorant of premodern and modern history alike — actually cling to the delusion that secular society on the whole is a kinder, fairer, and freer arrangement than any known to earlier ages. And, then again, one does not need to be quite that credulous to be profoundly grateful (as I am, for instance) for the dissolution of the old alliance between religious orthodoxies and the mechanisms of political power. Nevertheless, whatever one may say in favor of secularism's more agreeable political expressions, its record to this point, as an ideology or a material history, has been mixed at best: monstrous warfare, totalitarian regimes, genocides, the inexorable expansion of the power and province of the state, the gradual decline of the arts and of civic aesthetics . . . It can scarcely be taken very seriously as the model of what a society ideally ought to be. Even when it is not breeding great projects for the rectification of human nature or human society — not building death camps or gulags, not preaching eugenics or the workers' paradise — the secularist impulse can create nothing of enduring value. It corrupts the will and the imagination with the deadening boredom of an ultimate pointlessness; weakens the hunger for the good, true, and beautiful; makes the pursuit of diversion life's most pressing need; and gives death the final word. A secular people — by which I mean not simply a people with a secular constitution, but one that really no longer believes in any reality beyond the physical realm — is a dying people, both culturally and demographically. Civilization, or even posterity, is no longer worth the effort. And, in our case, it would not even be a particularly dignified death. European Christendom has at least left a singularly presentable corpse behind. If the American religion were to evaporate tomorrow, it would leave behind little more than the brutal banality of late modernity.

In the end, though, on the matter of religion and the American future, I am certain of very little. I know only how unprecedented and hence unpredictable our historical situation is. The angels of Sacré-Cœur are now, for the most part, sublime symbols of an absence; once images of a seemingly inexhaustible supernatural source of cultural possibility, they have become little more than ironic evocations of a final cultural impotence. They were raised aloft in the fading twilight of a long, magnificent, and terrible epoch, during which a glorious vision of eternal splendor was given profuse and enduring concrete form; but they were not the harbingers of a cultural renewal. America, by contrast, has never known either that glory or that failure. Our angels continue to move in their inaccessible heavens, apparently still calling out to mortals, still able to provoke our sons and daughters to prophesy, our old men to dream dreams, our young men to see visions. Who knows, then? Perhaps the quieter strengths they impart to our culture — its deeper reserves of charity and moral community, the earnestness of its spiritual longings, its occasional poetic madness — will persist for a long while yet, and with them the possibility of cultural accomplishments far more important than mere geopolitical preeminence. There is, at least, some room for hope.

# TWENTY-EIGHT

# Mediocrity's Tribute

Along the coast, it was the sort of morning one can describe only as "Homeric." You know: rhododactylic Dawn rising from her loom to spread her shimmering gossamers over the shadowy mountains and echoing sea, dark-prowed fishing barks drawn up on the milky strand and caressed by the golden foam, the distant thunders of ennosigaean Poseidon and argikeraunic Zeus vying above the wine-dark waves, and so on. Or so I imagine. I was actually a few hundred miles inland, in a montane grove of loblolly pines and mixed deciduous trees, awash in flickering sunlight, drinking coffee and reading a newspaper. But I had Homer on my mind just then, for various reasons, and so was in a somewhat epic mood: overflowing with an unwonted sense of animal vitality, the world about me all joy and power, terror and fluent beauty, I was Diomedes upon his day of glory . . .

Such moods are fleeting, alas. As Chōmei knew, even the remotest mountain retreat cannot keep the pains of transience at bay. My eyes alighted upon a report that Roland Emmerich (director of such cinematic masterworks as *Independence Day* and *2012*) had just made *Anonymous*, a movie all about how the works of Shakespeare were really written by Edward de Vere, a very minor poet and the seventeenth Earl of Oxford. All at once, the world had lost its glowing vigor; rosy-fingered Dawn was now a scowling crone with withered talons, laboriously carding the coarse wool of the dreary clouds; the sea had turned to molten lead; Poseidon and Zeus had long ago retired to a managed care facility. I set my coffee aside and went to fetch the gin from the cupboard.

If you are unacquainted with the "Oxfordian hypothesis," count yourself blessed. It was born in 1920, in a book by a demented English Comtean

whom Fate, with her unerring sense of poetic justice, had given the name
J. Thomas Looney — a man whose ignorance was so profound it verged
on a kind of genius. Looney offered no actual proof for his claim; instead,
he attempted to divine the private philosophy of the author of the Shakespearean corpus and then sought out a highborn Elizabethan gentleman
who seemed to fit the portrait he had drawn. He also asserted that Oxford
was the true author of the works of John Lyly, Anthony Munday, and Arthur Golding (an incoherent farrago of disparate styles, true, but — hey
— in for a penny, in for a pound). Patently worthless as it was, Looney's
book inaugurated yet another conspiracy theory concerning the nonexistent mystery of the "true identity" of the author of Shakespeare's plays;
and, since then, the Oxfordians have elbowed themselves to the front of
the "anti-Stratfordian" mob. What is fascinating about the theory itself,
in a purely morbid way, is not only that it lacks even a shadow of a scrap of
documentary evidence, but that in fact all the real documentary evidence,
which is quite substantial, shows it to be incontestably false (and, indeed,
leaves no room for rational doubt that the true author of Shakespeare's
plays was Mr. William Shakespeare of Stratford).

Now, to say that the Oxfordians have no evidence for their beliefs is
not to say they have no arguments. The devout Looneyite can produce a
900-page tome in defense of his delusion at the drop of a lavender-scented
handkerchief. But to venture into one of those unwholesome volumes (say,
Charlton Ogburn's psychedelic rhapsody *The Mysterious William Shakespeare* or the ghastly Joseph Sobran's *Alias Shakespeare*) is to wade into a
swamp of misstatements, insinuations, suppressions, confusions, historical blunders, and quasi-occult cryptology. Even so, the sheer weight of all
that claptrap has the power to sway the credulous, even among persons
otherwise competent in their own fields (actors, journalists, statisticians,
Supreme Court justices, and so on) who simply lack enough knowledge to
sift the truth from the nonsense. Oxfordianism is to Shakespearean studies what *The Chariots of the Gods* is to archaeology or *The Da Vinci Code* is
to Christian history, and genuine scholars of Elizabethan and Jacobean
literature routinely publish unanswerable demolitions of its claims. But,
in a media-addled age, mere scrupulous scholarship is rarely a match for
shameless intellectual dishonesty or emotional derangement. Really, the
most hilarious aspect of Looneyism is probably its choice of protagonist.
I say this not just because Oxford died about a decade too early to cover
Shakespeare's career (and Oxfordian attempts to redate the plays accord-
ingly fail dismally); nor because "stylometric" computer analysis (which
is frighteningly accurate) repeatedly reckons the odds against Oxford be-

ing the "true" Shakespeare as roughly infinite; nor because the conspiracy would have required the complicity of an absurdly large range of Shakespeare's associates, friends, and collaborators, as well as lawyers and Masters of the Revels and so on; nor because Oxford was a vicious, pompous, inane fop; nor because . . . (well, the list is endless). I say it principally because Edward de Vere was almost sublimely devoid of talent. At least the Baconian and Marlovian factions in the anti-Stratfordian cult champion men who actually possessed literary gifts. Looney chose a man who was, if anything, the anti-Shakespeare of his age. But Oxford was an aristocrat, and Looney believed fanatically in class distinction and purity of blood. A few lesser critics had been claiming for decades that Shakespeare's plays were written by some widely traveled man with a classical education and an intimate knowledge of the inner workings of Elizabeth's court, rather than by some tradesman's son, educated at a grammar school. Nothing could have been further from the truth, actually — unlike the plays of, say, Ben Jonson or the "University Wits," Shakespeare's show no signs of excessive classical or cosmopolitan culture — but Looney did not know that, having little education himself, and the idea of a Shakespeare with aristocratic pedigrees suited his social philosophy perfectly.

I suppose I should not really care. Oxfordianism is annoying and silly, granted, but in time will subside in popularity. But I find the whole phenomenon morally troubling. I cannot prove it (which should not bother the Looneyites), but I suspect that the most fervent Oxfordians are motivated principally by resentment: the capon's envy of the cock, so to speak. Persons of mediocre talent, consigned to a middling rung on nature's scale, but who imagine themselves tremendously gifted, often take violent offense at real greatness. And Shakespeare's genius is so exorbitant, and the fecundity of his literary imagination so monstrous: the thought that such prodigious art was produced just by nature, unassisted by special advantages and attainments, must seem intolerable to a certain sort of person. Ah, but if in fact the "real" writer was a child of privilege, forged in the crucible of social eminence, possessed of secret inner knowledge — why, then, his genius is somehow more explicable. And that in turn makes more explicable the conspiracy theorist's own lack of achievement, for this too can be ascribed to a conspiracy — a conspiracy of circumstance, the connivance of fate, a cosmic miscarriage of justice.

Who knows, though? The real issue is one of common decency. When we talk about, say, the authorship of Homer, we know that the attribution is irreducibly uncertain: part legend, part conjecture, and part (but what part?) truth. In the case of Shakespeare, however — one of the few literary figures who can plausibly be said to be greater than Homer — we know exactly who he was, when he lived, how he earned his bread and reputation. To attempt to rob him of his posterity out of envy, foolishness, or callous indifference to the truth is rather pernicious. There is no mystery about Shakespeare other than the perennial mystery of genius, which is at once prodigal and parsimonious: distributed regardless of social station or just deserts, but to only a very few. This truth may be excruciatingly galling to some, but to persons of good will and healthy mind it should simply elicit grateful admiration and ungrudging recognition. And, anyway, if this lot really wants to make their conspiracy theory interesting, they need to fill in the cracks better. No Oxfordian has yet convincingly responded to the "stylometry" problem, for instance. If they were really on their game, however, they would argue that this merely exposes another conspiracy hitherto unsuspected, and that the works commonly attributed to Oxford are clearly products of another hand. I propose Francis Bacon. As for the inevitable discovery of similar incompatibilities between Bacon's style and "Oxford's," one need only argue that, of course, "Bacon's" works were really written by someone else altogether. As for who this might have been, the answer seems obvious: William Shakespeare of Avon, who it turns out was a far more cunning and mysterious figure than any of us ever suspected . . .

# TWENTY-NINE

# The Priceless Steven Pinker

I sometimes find it hard to believe that Steven Pinker really believes what he believes; surely, I think, some occult agency in his mind is forcing his conscious intellect to accept premises and conclusions that it ought to reject as utterly fantastic. I suppose, though, that that is one's normal reaction to ardent expressions of a faith one does not share; at its worst, it is just a reflex of supercilious fastidiousness, like feeling only an annoyed consternation at having to step over someone in the throes of mystical ecstasy in order to retrieve one's umbrella from the closet. A healthier sentiment would be generous and patient curiosity, a desire to learn whether the believer has in fact — guided by a rare purity of heart — glimpsed truths to which one's own cynicism or coarseness has blinded one.

Not, of course, that Pinker would care for that way of putting the matter. He detests religion and thinks of himself as a champion of something he blandly calls "reason" (that is the most enchantingly guileless aspect of his creed). In his latest book, *The Better Angels of Our Nature: Why Violence Has Declined*, he devotes over seven hundred pages to arguing the case that modernity, contrary to the common impression, has seen a steep decrease in every kind of violence — domestic, political, criminal, and martial — as a result of a variety of causes, but principally because of the triumph of "Enlightenment" ideas. It is a simple narrative, and at many points a painfully simplistic one, but it is clear and bracing and probably merits some sympathetic consideration. Whether Pinker himself does the tale justice, however, is debatable. He occasionally attempts evenhandedness, but subtlety is not one of his strengths, especially where objections to his claims are stronger than he is willing to grant. He is definitely not an adept historian; his view of the past — particularly of the Middle Ages, which he tends to treat as a single historical, geographical, and cultural moment — is often not merely crude but almost cartoonish (of course, he is a professed admirer of Norbert Elias). He even adduces two edited images from *Das Mittelalterliche Hausbuch* as illustrations of "the everyday texture of life in medieval Europe," without noting that they come from a set of astrological allegories about planetary influences, from which he has chosen those for Saturn and Mars rather than, say, Venus or Jupiter (think what a collection of Saturnine or Martial pictures he might have gathered from more recent history). It is perfectly fair for Pinker to call attention to the many brutal features of much of medieval life, but one would have more confidence in his probity if he acknowledged at least a few of the moral goods that medieval society achieved despite its material privations. He says nothing of almshouses, free hospitals, municipal physicians, hospices, the decline of chattel slavery, the *Pax Dei* and *Treuga Dei*, and so on. Of the more admirable cultural, intellectual, legal, spiritual, scientific, and social movements of the High Middle Ages, he appears to know nothing. And his understanding of early modernity is little better. His vague remarks on the long-misnamed "Wars of Religion" are tantalizing intimations of a fairly large ignorance.

Perhaps such complaints miss the point, though. Pinker's is a story not of continuous moral evolution, but of an irruptive redemptive event. It would not serve his purpose to admit that, in addition to the gradual development of the material conditions that led to modernity, there might also have been the persistent pressure of moral ideas and values that reached back to antique or medieval sources, or that there might have been occasional institutional adumbrations of modern "progress" in the Middle Ages, albeit in a religious guise. He certainly would not want to grant that many of his own moral beliefs are inherited contingencies of a long cultural history rather than discoveries recently made by the application of disinterested "reason." For him, modern culture's moral advances were born from the sudden and fortuitous advent of the "Age of Reason," which — aided by the printing press — produced a "coherent philosophy" called *"Enlightenment humanism,"* distilled from the ideas of "Hobbes, Spinoza, Descartes, Locke, David Hume, Mary Astell, Kant, Beccaria, Smith, Mary Wollstonecraft, Madison, Jefferson, Hamilton and John Stuart Mill." (Make what you will of that bizarre gallimaufry, but we know what he means: not the dark side of the "Enlightenment" and the printing press — "scientific racism," state absolutism, Jacobinism, the rise of murderous ideologies, and so on — but the *nice* Enlightenment of "perpetual peace," the "rights of man," and so on.)

Well, each to his or her own tribalism, I suppose. It is pleasant to believe one's society is more "enlightened" or "rational" than all others, and Pinker has every right to try to prove the point. He would be more convincing, though, if only the central claim of his book were not so entirely dependent upon a statistical fiction. That is to say, yes, of course modern societies have reduced certain kinds of brutality, cruelty, and injustice. Modern technology makes it far easier to control crime. We have weapons both too terrifying to use in open combat and so precise that we can kill at great distances, without great armies, out of sight and mind. We have succeeded at reforming our own nations internally in ways that make them ever more comfortable, less threatening, and more complacent. Our prison system is barbaric, but not overtly sadistic, and our more draconian laws rarely inconvenience the affluent among us. We have learned to exploit the labor and resources of poorer peoples not by enslaving them, but merely by making them "beneficiaries" of globalization. The violence we commit is more hygienic, subtler, and less inconvenient than that committed by our forebears. Even so, the numbers do not add up. Pinker's method for assessing the relative ferocity of different centuries is to calculate the total of violent deaths not as an absolute quantity, but as a percentage of global population. But statistical comparisons like that are notoriously vacuous. Population sample sizes can vary by billions, but a single life remains a static sum, so the smaller the sample the larger the percentage each life represents. Obviously, though, a remote Inuit village of one hundred souls where someone gets killed in a fistfight is not twice as violent as a nation of two hundred million that exterminates one million of its citizens. And even where the orders of magnitude are not quite so divergent, comparison on a global scale is useless, especially since over the past century modern medicine has reduced infant mortality and radically extended life spans nearly everywhere (for one thing, there are now far more persons too young or too old for fighting). So Pinker's assertion that a person would be thirty-five times more likely to be murdered in the Middle Ages than now is empirically meaningless.

In the end, what Pinker calls a "decline of violence" in modernity has actually been, in real body counts, a continual and extravagant increase in violence that has been outstripped by an even more exorbitant demographic explosion. Well, not to put too fine a point on it: So bloody what? What on earth can he truly imagine that tells us about "progress" or "Enlightenment" — or about the past, the present, or the future? By all means, praise the modern world for what is good about it, but spare us the mythology. And yet, oddly enough, I like Pinker's book. At one level, perhaps, it is all terrific nonsense: historically superficial, philosophically platitudinous, occasionally threatening to degenerate into the dulcet bleating of a contented bourgeois. But there is also something exhilarating about this fideist who thinks he is a rationalist. Over the past few decades, so much of secularist discourse has been drearily clouded by irony, realist disenchantment, spiritual fatigue, self-lacerating sophistication: a postmodern sense of failure, an appetite for caustic cultural genealogies, a meek surrender of all "metanarrative" ambitions. Pinker's is an older, more buoyant, more hopeful commitment to the "Enlightenment" — and I would not wake him from his dogmatic slumber for all the tea in China. In his book, one encounters the ecstatic innocence of a faith unsullied by prudent doubt. For me, it reaffirms the human spirit's lunatic and heroic capacity to believe a beautiful falsehood, not only in excess of the facts, but in resolute defiance of them.

# THIRTY

# Death the Stranger

Damian Michael Bentley (1834–1897) was the first cousin of one of my great-grandfathers (if I were patient enough, I would work out what that makes my relation to him). He was also, according to my surveys of the archives, the only confirmed metaphysical materialist dangling from any branch of my family tree. Then again, I would not know of his convictions at all had not both he and his daughter Norah been such punctilious diarists; so who knows what curious fruits might have ripened unremarked on obscurer boughs? Whatever the case, in the religiously kaleidoscopic chronicles of my extended family, he is the only avowed atheist to leave any indited trace. He claimed, in fact, to have cast off faith in God when he was only eight — or, as he phrased it in a poem he wrote when he was twenty-three, "Though still a lad of tender years, unfledged, / With manly strokes I breasted ev'ry wave, / 'Til out the icy seas of childish faith, / I reached the blessed shore of unbelief." (Mercifully, he abandoned poetry not long after that.) And he clung fast to his atheism right up to his final days, and perhaps — though the record is unclear on this — to the grave. There is nothing particularly extraordinary in any of that, at least not in the context of the middle or late nineteenth century; but what made Damian's atheism somewhat odd was its firm alliance to a rather macabre fascination with death.

If there is one great theme running through his literary remains, such as they are, it is an almost romantic fixation upon death as "our dearest friend, how often cruelly spurned" (another of his youthful forays into verse). It was to this strangely tender passion that he attributed his lifelong interest in taxidermy, which he described as a "palpation and contemplation of the mysterious essence of life, which is but inert matter accidentally arranged into organic machines, now reduced to its original and true lifelessness." For many years, he considered becoming a mortician, before finally following his father into dentistry. In 1876, he founded what he called the "Maryland chapter" (though there was only the one) of the Society of Death Our Friend, an organization dedicated to weaning men and women from their fear of death, and teaching them to love it instead as "the balm and nectar of oblivion," a "sweet release from carnal torments," and the "healing sleep of eternity." At its apogee, the society boasted six members.

It is perhaps not entirely surprising, then, that during the last four weeks or so of his life, as he lay abed cosseting his failing heart, Damian came to believe that he was being visited daily by death personified. There was nothing else alarming about his state of mind: he showed no signs of dementia, ran no fevers, and was fully conscious while the sun was up. He merely insisted that each day, between breakfast and lunch, Death dropped by for a brief conversation, usually seated in a cushioned window seat, listlessly swinging a foot back and forth above the carpet. He appeared not in the form of the tall, cowled, skeletal specter of lore, scythe in hand, but as a dapper, unimposing, slightly plump man of pallid complexion "with hints of olive about the eyes," always dressed in a charcoal-gray morning suit. As reported by Norah (who, to her father's dismay, remained faithful to her mother's high church Episcopalianism), the conversations were anything but enlightening. Far from revealing anything of moment to Damian, Death generally liked to chat about such matters as the weather, or recipes for oyster pie, or recent advances in dental technology. Not only would he not confirm for Damian that consciousness dies with the body, he tended to deflect all such questions with a slightly stertorous sigh of boredom. In the end, Damian found his visitor anything but amiable. "Father spoke to Death again today," Norah wrote on the eve of Damian's demise. "He says he feels no real kinship with the fellow and now doubts whether he really knows Death at all. He declares himself much disappointed."

THOUGHTS OF DAMIAN came to me as I was reviewing Lucien Lévy-Bruhl's classic 1922 study, *La Mentalité primitive*, which I think was the first anthropological treatise to note that "primitive" societies often find it impossible to conceive of death as a natural phenomenon. Since then, many anthropologists have written about tribal societies scattered throughout the world that genuinely believe that death is always unnatural, and that were it not for the operations of various malevolent unseen agencies, employing poisons or magic or some other discreet weaponry, some lives might continue on indefinitely. In those societies, every death is assumed to be a kind of murder. When I used to tell this to my students, they often responded with indulgent mirth: What, after all, can one expect from peoples who know nothing about modern physics or organic chemistry? I tried, however, to discourage the reaction. In fact, I did my best to convince them that this supposedly "primitive" intuition is, in a very profound sense, quite correct, and follows from an insight into the conditions of human experience far subtler than our culture (whose most taxing spiritual labor is watching television) could possibly generate. Death can never be truly "natural" for us, precisely because we are conscious of it, and so — quite unnaturally — it has a meaning for us, even if we think that meaning to be simply the end of all meaning. True, we are as subject as any other animal to the circle of natural existence: the rise and fall of generations, the cycle of birth and death. But, as we are rational beings, endowed with reflective consciousness, our existence is not simply circular or organic, but also prospective and creative. To be human is to be open to the future, to a horizon of possibilities that cannot be contained within the limits of nature. We form plans, harbor expectations and ambitions, obey desires that far exceed the present moment; we are capable of novelty, imagination, resolve. When death comes, therefore, even late in life, it comes as the interruption of a story that might otherwise have continued to unfold — an anticipated guest, perhaps, but always arriving out of season. Death confirms us in our animal nature, but contradicts something essential to our humanity.

Now, obviously, one could just as well say that death "belongs" to our nature in a way that it cannot for any other animal, that only our consciousness of our finitude makes us capable of having stories to interrupt, that we alone enjoy the "privilege" of approaching our deaths with wills reconciled to its inevitability and expectations shaped by the limit it sets, and that our terrible knowledge of mortality gives shape and purpose to our lives. All of this, however, amounts only to another way of describing the same predicament: our consciousness of death constitutes an absolute alienation from the rest of the natural world. Death torments us with the possibility of ultimate nothingness, and so awaits us as that final crisis that makes all life questionable. If not for this openness to the future that at once makes us conscious of our deaths and makes death an interruption of our lives, we would not be subject to either hope or despair, and would not exist in exile from the natural cycle of life and death. We might even be at peace. Surely this is a very significant part of the explanation for the presence of sacrificial cult — of the classic *do ut des* variety — throughout most of human religious history. Contrary to the rather fatuous notion that "primitive" religion sprang from a pathetic need to pretend that death is not real, most ancient religions offered no comfort at all regarding life's end; of death's finality there was little doubt. What sacrifice accomplishes, however, is a reconciliation with death, a transformation of death into an occasion for overcoming that abnormality that estranges us from nature's perennial cycles and burdens us with fear and grief. It allows human beings to participate directly in that endless round of feeding that sustains the cosmos. The Aztec priest feeding the sun with human blood, the Vedic priest feeding the ancestors with the sweet smoke of his oblations, and all sacrifices of this basic "alimentary" kind open a ritual path back into the circle of natural creation and destruction, and allow human beings consciously to embrace death as part of a sacred mystery to which they too belong, and so to find temporary respite from their awareness of death as the ultimate contradiction.

Needless to say, it is in the end an impossible resolution to our dilemma. For us, there is no return to the savage peace of natural life and death; we would not be human if not for our spiritual exile from that sublime, interminable recurrence. No matter how tempting it may be to succumb to the "naturalistic" fallacy of believing otherwise, and no matter what "common sense" might tell us, a deeper spiritual wisdom within us knows who our last and most *unnatural* enemy is. As Damian learned to his chagrin, we mortals can never forge a true friendship with the eternal stranger.

# THIRTY-ONE

# Through a Gloss, Darkly

In French and English, the Latin verb *traducere* — "to transfer," "to convert," "to lead across," but also "to expose to shame," "to defame," "to disgrace in public" — diverged into two very different derivatives, each reflecting only one aspect of the etymon. The principal meaning of the French *traduire* is "to translate"; that of the English "traduce" is "to malign," "to demean," or "to slander." Now, as it happens, I like to think that some invisible intelligence is at work behind the ramifying furcations and mutations of linguistic evolution, composing an ingenious polyphony of echoes and ironies out of what we hear only as the tumult of Babel; but, even if one believes these things are all only a matter of chance, one should be able to appreciate the artful aptness here. All translations of texts, not only the inaccurate or slovenly ones, are slanders of the originals, at least to some degree. The very worst translators are not necessarily those who are most awkward or inept — the intelligent reader can often make an intuitive vault over mere stylistic deficiencies — but those who let their own sensibilities intrude too ostentatiously between the reader and the original text, thus subordinating the idiom of the original authors to their own. But even the scrupulous, competent, and self-effacing translator is engaged in a kind of well-intentioned treachery. This is true even in those rare fortunate cases when great works find translators whose gifts are comparable (or superior) to those of the original authors: Thomas Urquhart's Rabelais, for example, or John Florio's Montaigne, or Tobias Smollett's Cervantes; or even in those still rarer cases when an author is improved by conversion into another tongue. (The reason the French labor under the bizarre misapprehension that Edgar Allan Poe was a great poet, for instance, is that so much of his work was translated by Baudelaire.) What even a translator of genius can never give us, however, is the original author's true likeness. Even the best translation is a darkened mirror, in which one glimpses only a partial figure moving among shadows. At times the mirror becomes very obscure indeed, at others delightfully bright; but at no time can any translator permit us to meet the artist face-to-face.

The problems of translation have been in my thoughts a great deal lately, for a variety of reasons. The most trivial of these is that I have been dipping into foreign versions of some of my own books, as well as I can, and sighing at the frequent accidental deformations of meaning. It is not that I feel myself greatly aggrieved by the mistakes I find; the texts in question are not exactly deathless masterpieces to be dithered over reverentially by their poor translators. I have, however, begun to wonder whether such distortions of meaning are not inevitable. If nothing else, seeing what has become of my own words at the other end of the linguistic alembic has begun to make me doubt the profit in the whole enterprise of translation, even as I grant the necessity of that enterprise. In my last book but one, for example, there is a passage in which I cast scorn on Christopher Hitchens's claim that religion poisons "everything" simply by flinging out a smirking succession of interrogatory sentence fragments. I ask, for example, whether Hitchens's accusation applies: "To the music of Palestrina and Bach, Michelangelo's Pietà, 'ah! bright wings,' San Marco's mosaics, the Bible of Amiens, and all that gorgeous blue stained glass at Chartres?" In the Polish version of the book, however, that line reads: "Do muzyki Palestriy i Bacha, do *Piety* Michala Aniola, wierszy G. M. Hopkins, mosaik w bazylice San Marco, *Biblii z Amiens* Ruskina i wspanialych blekitnych witrazy w Chartres?" Now, there are three problems here, of which perhaps only one could have been avoided. I suppose I cannot complain about that somewhat leaden phrase "the verse of G. M. Hopkins," since few Polish readers could be expected to recognize the flash of those wings. I would rather my un-italicized reference to the Cathedral of Amiens — Picardy's "Bible de pierre" — had not been turned into a reference to Ruskin's splendid book *The Bible of Amiens*. In fact, though, it is only the part about Chartres that causes me real concern, even though I cannot hold the translator to account. What is missing from the translated version is simply the particular and, I imagine, untranslatable intonation of the original: the wry and maybe slightly effete waspishness of the "all that" and the "gorgeous," and the faint hint of mockery they are meant to convey.

But, then again, this stubborn autochthony of tone is an old story. "Poetry is what gets lost in translation," says Robert Frost. No poem has ever really been translated, though occasionally a new poem has been successfully hung upon the frame of the old. Vladimir Nabokov was probably right, in his edition of *Eugene Onegin*, to produce an exactingly literal line-by-line gloss, polished but drab, and to inform his Anglophone readers that the actual experience of Pushkin's poetry was closed to anyone not fluent in Russian. It is everything that cannot be captured in the glass of a gloss that gives a poem life, or that endows even a mildly lively sentence with whatever vigor it may possess. My quandary just at the moment, however — and this is the principal reason I have been pondering these matters — concerns not the elusive subtleties of poetry, but the polysemous mysteries of sacred literature. I have recently agreed to undertake a translation of the entire New Testament, and in making notes on obscure passages have found myself occasionally wondering whether any translation of the text could ever be much more than either a private interpretation or a dogmatic confession. Of course, all ancient scriptures are great archives of words with inexhaustible connotations and associations, coming as they do from the distant past and largely alien cultures, expressing metaphysical and spiritual concepts of their nature irreducible to simple definitions, and (most important) attempting to name realities that lie beyond words. As the opening sentence of the *Tao Te Ching* has it, "Tao k'o tao, fei ch'ang tao": "The Tao (or Way) that can be named is not the eternal Tao." Then again, that translation hardly skims the surface. Quite apart from the vast range of meanings contained in that humble word "tao" — metaphysical, religious, moral, poetic, or what have you — there is the condensed, oracular paradoxicality of the phrasing: of the six ideograms, "tao" appears three times, so that one might almost translate the subject as "The Tao that can be tao'd"; and, in that second instance, the ideogram can mean "uttered" or "talked about," but also "trodden" or "walked." The most mundane rendering of the verse, come to think of it, might be "The eternal Path is not the sort of path you go walking on."

THAT, HOWEVER, is not something I need to worry about just now; at the moment I am wondering how I should deal with the first verse of John's Gospel. Certainly no English term can begin to capture the depths and scope that the term *logos* had acquired in the philosophical and religious cultures of Hellenistic late antiquity; "Word" is so inadequate as to be practically meaningless. And how is one to capture the verse's crucial distinction between the articular and inarticular forms of the word "God" — *ho theos* as opposed to *theos* — which many Christians, Jews, and pagans of the time would have read as a distinction between God Most High and a merely derivative or subordinate manifestation of the divine, but which mysteriously disappears altogether in the twentieth chapter when Thomas addresses the risen Christ as *ho Theos?* And how . . . ?

Well, I shall have to decide later.

I suppose I should take some comfort from the thought that the translator's dilemma is only an acute instance of a chronic condition. The "indeterminacy of translation" (to borrow a phrase from one of my least favorite philosophers) is a universal reality, one that cuts across not only our efforts to make sense of foreign tongues, but even our daily labor to make sense of one another, or even to understand what we ourselves mean when we speak. In fact, our quandary is not even limited to the ambiguities of language: all experience is already an interpreted reality, transmitted through the patient intellect's docile apparatus of perception, composed by the agent intellect's transcendental and formal powers. The *Ding an sich*, the *verum essentiale* of a thing — or what have you — comes to us only through the mediation of senses and concepts, and through the elaborate encodings of culture and language. Thus the soul's primordial appetite for truth in itself, its orientation toward a horizon of perfect understanding and immediacy, has here only shadows — though often golden shadows — to feed upon. I suppose that is why perhaps the loveliest and most absorbing promise in Paul's letters is that one day we will not only peer into a glass, darkly, but see face-to-face: the original author, having translated himself into a human idiom, will translate us into the idiom of the divine, without loss, confusion, or separation, and the restless human desire always to understand yet more (of which the imperfect art of translation is one small manifestation) will at last achieve satiety, because we will at last understand even as we are understood.

Not that this gives me any better idea what to do with the word *logos*.

# THIRTY-TWO

# God and the Mad Hatter

Materialism, being a fairly coarse superstition, tends to render its adherents susceptible to a great many utterly fantastic notions. All that is needed to make even the most outlandish theory seem plausible to the truly doctrinaire materialist is that it come wrapped in the appurtenances of empirical science. This is not particularly blameworthy. True believers in any creed are usually eager to be persuaded that there is better evidence supporting their convictions than there really is. But there is a special kind of pleasure to be extracted from the credulity of materialists, if only because they are more prone than most other fanatics to mistake their metaphysical presuppositions for purely rational conclusions drawn from dispassionate reasoning.

Consider, for instance, the recent and curious episode of the "God Helmet." If you have not heard of it before, this was a device that for a time was believed to have the power to induce "religious" experiences in those who wore it, simply by stimulating the temporal lobes of the brain with weak magnetic field emissions. Its inventor was the cognitive neuroscientist Michael Persinger, who began studying religious mental states as early as the 1970s, and who eventually hit upon the theory that all such experiences have something to do with the structure of the bicameral brain. Perhaps, he speculated, a man who finds himself seized by a mystical sense of an unseen presence — God, an angel, an extraterrestrial, a ghost, a fairy, what have you — is merely experiencing a transient excitation of neurons that causes his brain's left hemisphere to become indirectly aware of the distinct and usually tacit "alternate self" of the right hemisphere. Whether or not that could be proved, however, he was sure that the full spectrum of transcendental experiences, from out-of-body episodes to alien abductions to contemplative bliss, could be reduced to the neurological effect of certain electromagnetic events. To prove his hypothesis, he constructed a helmet that would allow him to apply small sustained magnetic pulses to one or both of the temperoparietal regions of a person's brain. He hoped in this way to reproduce the entire diapason of extraordinary conscious states, from the vaguely numinous to the vividly visionary; and in 2002 he and his collaborator Faye Healey published results of laboratory studies allegedly proving that the helmet worked. Whereas two-thirds of those who had worn it and been exposed to doses of magnetism had supposedly reported a sense of some sort of presence (with varying degrees of intensity), only a third of those who had worn an electrically inert version of the device reported similar feelings.

Those sounded like substantial results, and the next logical step would have been yet more rigorous investigations. What immediately followed, however, was nothing so jejune as a series of clinical studies or critical explorations of Persinger's and Healey's claims, but rather an effervescent season of celebrity. Excitable print and broadcast journalists, thinking that the source of human religion had actually been discovered in the cerebral cortex, made Persinger's device briefly famous. At once, it was transformed from an unwieldy item of laboratory equipment into an indispensable fashion accessory of the materialist vogue. Metaphysical skeptics arrived from every quarter, donned Persinger's bizarre millinery, and waited for the doors of perception to fly open. The results were varied. The British psychologist Susan Blackmore, whose grasp of reality is so tenuous that she believes in "memes," claimed to have been carried through a succession of almost unbearable emotions and intuitions and phantom sensations. Richard Dawkins, whose grasp of reality is so tenuous that he invented the idea of "memes," found himself entirely unaffected (apart from a minor spell of dizziness), and pronounced himself disappointed. Others reported elaborate hallucinations of a vaguely spiritual kind, or fleeting images, or reveries about pretty girls, or indistinct impressions of unseen presences, or nothing at all. Persinger had a number of explanations for the differences in the reactions his device prompted, none of which could be tested. For instance, he suggested that Dawkins's immunity to the helmet's power was due to a peculiar temperoparietal insensitivity. Since his studies had involved no neural imaging or any other mechanism for identifying the specific part of the temporal lobes supposedly affected by magnetic fields, the assertion was quite meaningless. So were most of his claims regarding his findings. But no one seemed disposed to ask awkward questions. God had been found out to be a transient electrochemical agitation of a cluster or two of neurons. The BBC was satisfied. What else matters?

Alas, it was all nonsense. To this day, there are obdurate materialists who believe in the God Helmet, but it has been discredited in every significant way. It turned out that the protocols Persinger employed for choosing his test subjects and controls, without divulging the purposes of his experiments, were almost comically inadequate. Moreover, after the results of the initial studies had been published, everyone who came seeking an encounter with the gods or spirits nestled in their cerebral cortices did so with clear expectations, and responded to Persinger's device in whatever ways their personal suggestibility determined. Then, however, scientists at Sweden's Uppsala University attempted to reproduce the results reported by Persinger and Healey, under a rigorous regime of proper experimental controls. They consulted with Persinger, and employed methods and technology identical to his own, but conducted their study as a proper "double-blind" experiment. In 2004, the results appeared: none of the significant phenomena described by Persinger and Healey could be duplicated. Magnetic fields had no observable power to induce intimations of unseen presences in the test subjects, let alone extraordinary transcendental states of consciousness, and the Swedish researchers convincingly demonstrated that the effects reported by wearers of the God Helmet were largely products of their own imaginations.

Now, in fact, there really would have been no great problem for believers in the supernatural had Persinger's device really worked, or had the theory behind it been true. Even if it had turned out that religious states of consciousness have their physiological concomitants in a particular part of the brain, which could be stimulated artificially by magnetic fields, that would have had no religious implications at all. After all, practically no one is so thoroughgoing an idealist or dualist as to imagine that the human mind is not an embodied reality that operates through a physical brain. It may well be the case that there are certain brain events necessarily associated with experiences of the spiritual world; but, then again, there are certain brain events associated with hearing the music of a piano, or seeing an open lotus blossom, or tasting wine. So what? In the case of the God Helmet, however, such considerations scarcely matter, because the one thing that none of the researchers or journalists who made that ludicrous device famous ever thought to ask was whether the experiences described in the original studies actually resembled real religious experiences at all. Nothing so strikingly demonstrates the sheer intellectual slovenliness with which these experiments were initially approached than the utter absence of hermeneutical scrutiny brought to bear on the phenomena supposedly disclosed by Persinger's magic electrical hat. In all the great religions and metaphysical philosophies of the world there exists a rich and compendious spiritual literature, which describes the full range of spiritual experience — from the devotional to the contemplative to the mystically unitive — in remarkable depth and detail, and with a very large degree of unanimity on several "phenomenological" matters. Anyone familiar with that literature knows that the experiences supposedly induced by the God Helmet were quite unlike real religious experiences (with the possible exception of certain sorts of mantic states at the margins of cultic practices). One thing common to almost all great contemplative literature is an insistence upon the lucidity, clarity, and continuity of spiritual experience. For the most part, such experience does not involve visions; even when it does, however, they are nothing like the convulsive emotional fluctuations, hallucinations, and mildly psychotic episodes described by many of the users of Persinger's device. Even mystic ecstasies have a quality of transparency and cogency wholly different from the delirious dissociations into which certain of the believers in the helmet's power worked themselves up.

All of this should have been obvious from the start: the clinical incompetence of the original studies, the extravagance of the conjectures surrounding them, the sheer absurdity of the device itself, and the religious illiteracy of those who took it all seriously. And indeed, it would have been had Persinger's theories not appealed so deeply to the materialist imagination, and had they not seemed for a brief exciting moment to confirm certain materialist dogmas. Most of us tend to see what we wish to see, and to think that it is reality in its unadorned essence. Materialists believe that absolutely everything, even the formal structures of culture and the intentional structures of consciousness, can be reduced without remainder to an ensemble of mechanistic interactions among intrinsically mindless physical elements; and I suppose anyone capable of believing that is capable of believing practically anything.

# THIRTY-THREE

# Jung's Therapeutic Gnosticism

For the better part of a century, Carl Jung and (later) the executors of his estate kept the manuscript of his unfinished *Red Book* — or *Liber Novus*, as he originally entitled it — hidden safely away from public scrutiny. Even Jung's most ardent admirers, making their hopeful pilgrimages to Zurich, were denied so much as a glimpse into its pages, no matter how plangent their entreaties. For a time, the book was even locked away in a Swiss bank vault. The result, inevitably, was that it became something of a legend among Jungians: a secret visionary tome, written in the master's own hand, containing the mystic key to all his thought. Jung himself, after all, had once spoken of the book as the "numinous origin" from which all the work of his later years had flowed. Clearly, many came to believe, the family was jealous of its treasure.

In reality, Jung's son Franz probably kept *The Red Book* hidden only because he regarded it as an embarrassment, or at least as so eccentric a performance that its release could only harm his father's already precarious reputation. His refusal to grant the curious access to the text was reportedly marked by a sternly protective peremptoriness. But after Franz's death in 1996, the Jung estate slowly relented. In 2009, the book at last appeared, in a large, lavish, very expensive English critical edition that included a complete, full-scale, and high-definition photographic reproduction of the original manuscript. It is, if nothing else, an impressive physical object. *The Red Book* is an immense illuminated manuscript, which Jung indited on cream vellum in the private scriptorium of his study over a period of about sixteen years, copiously illustrated with elaborate, vivid, and occasionally ghastly painted panels, and bound in red leather. He was a talented amateur calligrapher, as well as a minor painter with a fairly good sense of color and a modest flair for abstract design. His visual imagination was somewhat vulgar apparently, but occasionally striking. There is something almost kaleidoscopic about the final product of his labors, what with its bright colors and constantly shifting images (narrative and pictorial). Chiefly, however, it is meant to have the appearance of a holy book, because that is precisely what it purports to be: a genuinely revealed text, recording visions imparted to Jung during a period of intense psychological and "parapsychological" struggle. The official story of the book's genesis is that Jung began receiving revelations in 1913, when he was thirty-eight years old, beginning with three premonitory trances in which he twice saw a great flood inundating Europe and once saw something like rivers of blood glowing on the far horizon. He would have dismissed the episodes as symptoms of mental fatigue had not the onset of war the next year convinced him that they had been genuine auguries of the future. So he undertook to lay open his thoughts to whatever other messages his unconscious mind might care to send him, and soon began suffering terrifying and absorbing visions and auditions (and, apparently, the odd paranormal event), which he called his "active imaginings," but which he sometimes feared might be signs of incipient psychosis.

Some of that may be true. Then again, *The Red Book* might really be no more than a mediocre artist's abortive attempt at a great work of art, draped in a veil of apocalyptic mystique to hide its deficiencies. Or the truth may lie somewhere in between. It does not matter, really. Whatever stories Jung may have told *about* the book, the story he tells in its pages is of a perilous odyssey through fantastic interior landscapes — a twilit borderland of the mind, somewhere between dreams and waking, supposedly the haunt of great artists, mystics, and lunatics — where, at the risk of his sanity, our redoubtable hero has gone on a quest to find his lost soul. Along the way, he encounters a succession of allegorical figures who, we are informed, are not merely fictions of his own devising, but real and autonomous powers dwelling in the depths of his psyche. The most important of these is Jung's special spirit-guide, Philemon, an ancient magician with a flowing white beard, a kingfisher's wings, and the horns of a bull. Jung also meets a woman who turns out to be his own soul personified; the hero Siegfried, whom he rather discourteously murders; a bird-girl; a one-eyed tramp dying by the wayside; a jocund rider in red who reveals himself to be the devil (and who helps put Jung in touch with his vegetative side); a heretical Christian anchorite from the Libyan desert; a huge, horned, axe-wielding god named Izdubar (or Gilgamesh) who has been made lame by the "terrible magic" of science and whom Jung reduces to the size of an egg and places in his pocket; the Cabiri (ancient Greek chthonic deities), who are really only subterranean gnomes; the disembodied shade of Christ; and so on. Many of them seem intent on getting Jung to abandon his conventional belief in any real dichotomy between good and evil, and to recognize that God and the devil are just two sides of a single reality; none of them, however, has any great gift for getting to the point. And, needless to say, Jung has many curious adventures in his inner world. He wanders through forests and mountainous wastes, walks beside radiant seas, skulks in caverns beneath the earth, ambles about inside a volcanic crater, and even visits hell a few times. He encounters two enormous snakes, one white and one black, entwined in battle until the latter leaves off and attempts to crush Jung (as he is contemplating a cross). Later, clad in green and wearing a hunting horn, Jung stands guard before a tower until the devil arrives and teaches him that it is far better to cavort in the greenwood as a forest sprite than squander one's days in somber vigilance. In hell, he devours the liver of a little girl (I do not recall why, exactly). He is briefly confined in a madhouse. He plays Parsifal in Klingsor's magic garden. On the orders of a gnome, he severs the "knot" of his own brain with a sword. He is dangled between heaven and earth like the Hanged Man of the Tarot. And so on and so on. (And so on.)

NO NEED to go on rehearsing all of that, though. What is interesting about *The Red Book* is not its "plot," much less whatever special "wisdom" Jungians might have the patience to wring from its pages. I have to admit that I have never been an admirer of Jung's writings, even on those rare occasions when I have fleetingly spied what looked like a glimmer of insight among their caliginous fogs. *The Red Book*, however, makes his other works seem quite tolerable by comparison. It is an essentially silly exercise — sub-Nietzschean, sub-Blakean, sub-Swedenborgian — full of the kinds of garish symbolism and pompous antinomianism one expects only from adolescent minds. To anyone seeking fantastic journeys through strange oneiric realms, I would much more readily recommend Lewis Carroll's Alice books, which are far better written, far better illustrated, and far more profound (Humpty Dumpty's discourse on the meanings of words puts all of Philemon's drearily portentous maunderings to shame). *The Red Book* is fascinating not in itself, but as an extraordinary symptom of a uniquely late modern spiritual paradox, which I can only call the desire for transcendence without transcendence.

The book's religious sensibility, I think it fairly uncontroversial to say, is thoroughly Gnostic, in a number of ways. It is, for one thing, simply saturated in imagery and concepts drawn from the Gnostic systems of late antiquity, and its narrative form — its incontinent mythopoeia, its rococo excesses, its figural syzygies and archons and aeons (or whatever one might call them) — has all the occult grotesquerie of authentic Gnostic myth. More to the point, its entire spiritual logic is one of "gnosis": a saving wisdom vouchsafed through an entirely private revelation; a direct communication from a mysterious source that is also one's own deepest ground, but from which one has become estranged; a truth attained not through the mediations of nature or culture, and certainly not through the moral "law," but solely in the apocalyptic secrecy of the illuminated soul. And yet, it is also almost wholly devoid of the special pathos that is the most enchanting, sympathetic, and human aspect of ancient Gnosticism: the desperate longing for escape, for final liberation, for a return to the God beyond. Jung's scripture is, in the end, a gospel not of salvation, but of therapy — not of deliverance, but of conciliation — and in this sense it truly is a *liber novus*, a newer new testament, a "sacred" book of a kind that only our age could have produced. Like any Gnostic treatise, it offers access to a secret inner knowledge that has the power to release the soul from slavery and delusion; but the liberation it offers is quite unlike anything promised in the literary remains of the various Gnostic schools of late antiquity. To the Gnostics of old — to indulge in a bit of synoptic generalization — this world is an immense prison guarded by malevolent powers on high, a place of exile where the fallen and forgetful divine spark dwelling deep within the *pneumatikos* (the "spiritual man") languishes in ignorance and bondage, passing from life to life in drugged sleep, wrapped in the ethereal garments of the "souls" it acquired in descending through the planetary spheres, and sealed fast within the coarse involucrum of an earthly body. The spiritual experience at the heart of the Gnostic story of salvation was, as Hans Jonas puts it, the "call of the stranger God": a call heard inwardly that awakens the spirit from its obliviousness to its own nature, and that summons it home again from this hostile universe and back again to the divine *pleroma* — the "fullness" — from which it departed in a time before time.

Thus the spiritual temper of Gnosticism is, first, a state of profound suspicion — a persistent paranoia with regard to the whole of apparent reality, a growing conviction that one is the victim of unseen but vigilant adversaries who have trapped one in an illusory existence — and then one of cosmic despair, and lastly a serenity achieved through final detachment from the world and unshakable certitude in the reality of a spiritual home beyond its darkness. The deepest impulse of the gnostic mind is a desire to discover that which has been intentionally hidden, to find out the secret that explains and overcomes all the disaffections and disappointments of the self, and thereby to obtain release. It is a disposition of the soul to which certain individuals are prone in any age, but one that only under special circumstances can become much more than a private inclination. What the specific conditions were in the late antique world that caused the gnostic tendency to crystallize on so large a scale, in so many distinct sects, with such irrepressibly luxuriant myths and doctrines, is hard to say: perhaps the despondency induced by an ever more cosmopolitan and ever less hospitable imperial civilization, the dissolution of local cultures and cults amid the fluid diversity of changing populations and beliefs, a growing remoteness from the indigenous deities in whose presence more settled peoples were accustomed to dwell, a pervasive sense of religious rootlessness . . . all these things and more. Whatever the case, there are periods when the human longing for transcendence can find so little to nourish it in this world that it begins to seek for another reality altogether, of which this world is not even a shadow.

ON A NUMBER of occasions, Jung wrote about the ancient Gnostics in a somewhat more analytic key than *The Red Book* permitted; and those works provide a wonderfully illuminating picture of the odd ways in which he at once adopted but subverted Gnostic themes in his thought. As far as he was concerned, the Gnostics of old should be understood as his own distant, if naïve, precursors: they had, he believed, dimly intuited many of his own "discoveries" regarding the psyche, but had then ineptly translated them into mythic cosmologies and metaphysical fables, and so "projected" them outward onto the universe around them. For him, Gnostic myth was really just a poignantly confused way of talking about the universal human tragedy of the ego's alienation from the unconscious, which each of us enacts in growing out of childhood. The infant dwells in the superpersonal unity of the unconscious, so the story goes, wholly unaware of any duality of self and other; but with age comes progressive individuation, which involves the ego's traumatic emergence from that original state of blissful plenitude into the winnowing drama of personality. And the same story, says Jung, unfolds itself in the development of human society; cultural phylogeny, so to speak, recapitulates psychological ontogeny. Primitive cultures remain just at the boundary of the infantine state, half dreaming in the tender dawn-light of the nascent ego, effortlessly projecting the contents of the unconscious onto the world in the forms of gods, spirits, ghosts, and demons. The somewhat more mature civilized peoples of the ancient world then transformed those projections into rigid religious systems, thus abandoning the flowing immediacy of dreams for the static day-lit objectivity of doctrines. Modern persons abandon myth and creed alike, in favor of the subtler projections of ideological and social prejudice. In each case, though, a tragic internal division persists, and is even hardened over time. All of us have lost touch with that inner world in which our souls were born, and remember it only in the alienated forms of imaginary external forces and principles.

According to Jung, it was the special distinction of the ancient Gnostics in some sense to have understood this: to have recognized that the stories we usually tell about the world are in fact just projections — just fabrications — behind which lies the true tale we have forgotten, the perennial story of that primordial catastrophe that has shattered each of us within. Unfortunately, not having the benefit of Jung's "scientific" psychology to explain their spiritual distress to them, the Gnostics inevitably fell back upon projections of their own. They imagined the unconscious as a divine *pleroma* from which the spirit had literally suffered a prehistoric fall. They interpreted the latent but restless presence of the unconscious behind the ego's elaborate plaster facade as the imprisonment of a divine scintilla in the vast dungeon of the cosmos. They dramatically transcribed their inchoate awareness of inner inhibitions and confusions into a figural language of hostile cosmic archons. They transformed the ego's denial of its dependency upon the unconscious into the story of the "god" of this world, who proudly denies that there is any God above himself, whose creature he is. And they mistook the dreamlike deliverances rising from their own inner depths for the voice of a savior descending from beyond the sphere of the fixed stars. All understandable errors, Jung thought, but with some singularly unfortunate consequences. In Gnostic thought, the primal human longing to overcome the ego's alienation from the unconscious was distorted into a yearning for a final escape from spiritual exile and a return to a divine unity transcending world and ego alike. But that, thought Jung, stripped of its mythic garb, is nothing more than a pathetic longing for the ego's disappearance into its impersonal ground. That would be to trade one tragedy for another. The only true rescue from the human predicament lies not in a retreat from the ego back into the abyss of the unconscious, but in one's reconciliation with one's own primordial depths, achieved by raising the unconscious up into consciousness without sacrificing one's individuality or autonomy. In the end, he concluded, psychic alienation can be conquered only through Jungian psychotherapy. The only true *pneumatikos*, it turns out, is a psychiatric patient (one whose psychiatrist likes to talk a great deal about archetypes).

I am omitting many details, admittedly, but I doubt it matters. What is truly astonishing about this sort of psychologistic reductionism is its absolute inversion of the spiritual aspirations it is meant to explain. It certainly explains how it is that *The Red Book* seems to preserve the most ungainly aspects of ancient Gnosticism — its boringly rambling symbolic narratives, the pretensions of its spiritual patriciate, its self-absorption and ethical sterility — but none of its genuinely sympathetic religious qualities: its ennobling sorrow, its tragic sense of estrangement from the world, its delightful paranoia. Behind all of that lay not simply some need for personal accommodation, psychological integrity, or mental health, but a true hunger for a transcendent Other with the power to set the soul free from the bleak circumscriptions of the self: a longing not just for the ego's reconciliation with its own hidden depths, but for a final revolt against everything — height and depth, principalities and powers, the frame of this "present evil order" — that separates the soul from the truth that can waken it from illusion and death.

TO TELL THE TRUTH, I find *The Red Book* a rather disconcerting document, not simply because I regard it as essentially an expression of arrested pubescence, lurching clumsily between the morbid and the hilarious in its attempts at profundity, but because I cannot shake the feeling that it is somehow a real reflection of the spiritual situation of our times. It seems to me that ours is one of those epochs that is hospitable to a gnostic sensibility. Certainly, the newer religious movements that have flourished most abundantly in the developed world over the last century and a half (including a great deal of American evangelicalism) have often assumed strikingly gnostic forms; and the smaller sects that keep springing up at the margins (Scientology, for instance) are even more acute manifestations of the same spiritual impulses. Gnostic themes, moreover, have been a persistent and recurrent element in Western literature since the Romantic age — from Blake to Baudelaire, from Hugo to Patrick White, and so on — and all the arts of the modern age, high and low, often express spiritual longing in gnostic terms (the science fiction film that is really a gnostic allegory, for instance, is in danger of becoming a cliché). And most of us now are susceptible to the psychologistic assumption that spiritual disaffection is something to be cured by discovering and decoding some forgotten, half-effaced text inscribed somewhere within the self. I suppose it may all have something to do with the constant erosion of the spiritual ecology of Christendom over the past few centuries, and with the final collapse of the old social order of the West in the twentieth century's political and ideological storm winds, and with all those seas of human blood that overwhelmed its ruins. With the loss of all the seemingly stable institutions and tacit accords that once provided the grammar of belief, it is only to be expected that religious yearning should express itself in ever more individualist, transcendentalist, and psychological forms. It may also have a great deal to do with that seemingly irreversible alienation from the natural world that defines modernity: dark satanic mills, air conditioners, split atoms, industrial waste, biological weapons, the dissolution of any natural sense of space and time in the fluent instantaneity of modern communications, medicines that actually heal, opiates that genuinely obliterate pain, entertainments that relentlessly cretinize, constant technological change, the mutability of the "transparent society," the shrill fragmentariness of the "society of the spectacle," ubiquitous advertising, market fetishism, and so on. The realm of the senses has become ever more remote *from* us, and ever less meaningful *for* us.

Moreover, the metaphysical picture of reality that the West has embraced ever more unreflectively since the rise of the mechanical philosophy is one that forcibly expels the transcendent from the immanent. At one time, it seemed enough simply to open one's eyes to see the light of the divine reflected in the mirror of creation: the cosmos was everywhere the work of formal and final causes, and of a pervasive divine wisdom, an endlessly diverse but harmonious *scala naturae* rising up from the earth to heaven. The whole universe was a kind of theophany, and all of reality participated in those transcendental perfections that had their infinite consummation in God. Now, however, we have learned, generation after generation, to see nature as only a machine, composed from material forces that are inherently mindless, intrinsically devoid of purpose, and therefore only adventitiously and accidentally directed toward any end, either by chance or by the hand of some demiurgic "Intelligent Designer." And, with the rise of Darwinism, the latter hypothesis has come to seem largely otiose. In the context of the mechanistic narrative, at least, the story of evolution appears to be only a mindless process of violent attrition and fortuitous survival, random force and creative ruin, in which order is the accidental residue of chaos and life the accidental residue of death. In such a cosmos, nothing of the "here below" seems to show us the way to the "there above," and it is hardly surprising that many of us should come to imagine transcendence solely as an absolute absence of God from the world, a beyond ever further beyond, of which we become aware not through the beauty or order *of* the world, but precisely through our estrangement *from* the world — through our distrust of its seductive illusoriness, and through an insistently dissonant voice within each of us announcing that this is not our true home.

Yet, even so, there remains an essential disparity between that voice as we hear it now and as it was heard by the ancient Gnostics. For them, the inner "call of the stranger God" remained an expression — however tragically muted and distorted — of a perennial and universal spiritual longing: the wonder at the mystery of existence that is the beginning of all philosophy and all worship, the restlessness of the heart that seeks its rest in God, that luminous elation clouded by sorrow that is the source of all admirable cultural achievements and all spiritual and moral heroism. Even at its most despairing, the Gnostic religious sensibility still retained some vital trace of a faith that, in more propitious circumstances, could be turned back toward love of the world, and toward a vision of creation as a vessel of transcendent glory. Our spiritual situation may be very different indeed.

ABOVE, I MADE passing reference to the figure of Izdubar in *The Red Book*, the god made lame by the dire "magic" of modern science; but I did not mention that, as the story advances, Jung heals Izdubar of his infirmity. He does this by convincing the god to recognize himself as a fantasy, a creature of the imaginary world. This does not mean, Jung assures him, that he is nothing at all, because the realm of the imagination is no less real than the physical world the sciences describe, and may in its own way be far more real. Once Izdubar accepts this, Jung is able to shrink him down to the size of an egg, and then to give him a new birth as a god whom no modern magic can harm. "Thus my God found salvation," writes Jung. "He was saved precisely by what one would actually consider fatal, namely by declaring him a figment of the imagination." This is, I think, a rather monstrous story. A kinder and less narcissistic man would have allowed Izdubar the dignity of a god's death rather than reduce him to a toy to be kept in a cupboard in the unconscious. The deep human longing for transcendence is ultimately inextinguishable, and can always be stirred and provoked and compelled anew by moments of beauty, love, creative exultation, spiritual ecstasy, and so forth. For the Platonist, it is a longing that can be satisfied only when one sees that the world of ordinary experience is a cave filled with flickering shadows and so learns to seek the true sun of the Good. For the Christian, this is a fallen and wounded world, but also one groaning in expectation of the glory that one day will be revealed in it.

For the Gnostic, the world is a prison from which the spirit must flee altogether in order to find the true light of truth. In each case, though, what remains constant is the real hope for an encounter with a divine reality greater than either the self or the world. Our spiritual disenchantment today may in many ways be far more radical than even that of the Gnostics: we have been taught not only to see the physical order as no more than mindless machinery, but also to believe (or to suspect) that this machinery is all there is. Our metaphysical imagination now makes it seem quite reasonable to conclude that the deep disquiet of the restless heart that longs for God is not in fact a rational appetite that can be sated by any real object, but only a mechanical malfunction in need of correction. Rather than subject ourselves to the torment and disappointment of spiritual aspirations, perhaps we need only seek an adjustment of our gears. Perhaps what we require to be free from illusion is not escape to some higher realm, but only reparation of the psyche, reintegration of the unconscious and the ego, reconciliation with ourselves — in a word, therapy.

That may be, if nothing else, the best palliative for psychological distress that we can produce these days. But, if so, there is a cultural cost to be borne. The gnostic expression of spiritual longing is the most extreme and hazardous religious venture of all; it is the final wager that the soul makes, placing the entire universe in the balance in its search for redemption. If it should be subdued by the archons of the age, the only spiritual possibilities left are tragic resignation or banal contentment. Beyond that point, for a culture or an individual, lies only one drearily predictable terminus: the delectable nihilism of Nietzsche's Last Men, the delirious diversions of consumption and expenditure, the narcotic consolation of not having to think about death until it comes. This, at least, is the troubling prospect that *The Red Book* poses to my imagination. It may truly be possible for an essentially gnostic contempt for the world to be inverted into a vacuous contentment with the world's ultimate triviality. Jung quaintly imagined he was working toward some sort of spiritual renewal for "modern man"; in fact, he was engaged in the manufacture of spiritual soporifics: therapeutic sedatives for a therapeutic age. For us, as could never have been the case in late antiquity, even distinctly gnostic spiritual tendencies are likely to prove to be not so much stirrings of rebellion against materialist orthodoxies as dying convulsions of resistance. The distinctly modern metaphysical picture of reality is one that makes it possible to regard this world as a cave filled only with flickering shadows and yet also to cherish those shadows for their very insubstantiality, and even to be grateful for the shelter that the cave provides against the great emptiness outside (where no Sun of the Good ever shines). With enough therapy and sufficient material comforts, even gnostic despair can become a form of disenchantment without regret, sweetened by a new enchantment with the self in its particularity. Gnosticism reduced to bare narcissism — which, come to think of it, might be an apt definition of late modernity as a whole.

At least, that is how I often tend to see the spirits of the age. This is no cause for despair, however. Every historical period has its own presiding powers and principalities on high. Ours, for what it is worth, seem to want to make us happy, even if only in an inert sort of way. Every age passes away in time, moreover, and late modernity is only an epoch. This being so, one should never doubt the uncanny force of what Freud called *die Wiederkehr des Verdrängten* — "the return of the repressed." Dominant ideologies wither away, metaphysical myths exhaust their power to hold sway over cultural imaginations, material and spiritual conditions change inexorably and irreversibly. The human longing for God, however, persists from age to age. A particular cultural dispensation may succeed for a time in lulling the soul into a forgetful sleep, but the soul will still continue to hear that timeless call that comes at once from within and from beyond all things, even if it now seems like only a voice heard in a dream. And, sooner or later, the sleeper must awaken.

# THIRTY-FOUR

# *Seeing the God*

For the first ten of its eleven chapters, the *Metamorphosis* or *Golden Ass* of Apuleius (c. 125–c. 180) seems to be nothing more than a diverting, frequently ribald burlesque; but then, in the closing pages, the tone entirely changes, and all at once the farce gives way to one of the loveliest and most devout expressions of faith in a compassionate divine savior in all of ancient literature. Lucius — the tale's protagonist and narrator, who has endured nearly a year in the form of an ass — wakes one night near the sea at Corinth and, seeing the full moon above him, purifies himself in the tide and prays to this "shining goddess" and "Queen of Heaven" that she deliver him from the magic that binds him. When he then falls asleep upon the strand, the goddess visits him in a dream, rising out of the sea in all her beauty. Her hair is unbound, her head wreathed with flowers and crowned with a gleaming lunar disc set in a silver circlet, her body clad in radiant white, crocus yellow, and rose red; draped from one shoulder, she wears a black, flower-hemmed cloak whose dark folds, aglow with an unearthly splendor, are adorned with coruscating images of the stars and the moon at midmonth. "Moved by your supplications," she tells Lucius, "I am come to you: I the begetter of everything in nature, mistress of all elements, firstborn of the ages, the supreme deity, queen of the souls of the dead, first among all those in heaven, the single form of all gods and goddesses — I who by my will superintend the shining summits of heaven, the wholesome breezes of the sea, and the pitiable silences of the underworld — I whose single divinity is venerated throughout the world under numberless aspects." She recites some of the names by which she is known among the nations, but reveals that it is the Ethiopians and Egyptians who call her by her true name, Queen Isis. She promises Lucius that she will restore him to human form on the morrow, but charges him to remember that now and until the day he dies he has been dedicated to her service. She assures him, however, that she will grant him a long and glorious life, and that when at last he descends to the dead he will see her shining among the shadows of Acheron, reigning in the Stygian firmament, and she will bring him into the Elysian Fields.

The next day, during public festivities in her honor, the goddess fulfills her promise and Lucius, now dressed in the white garment of a votary, joins in a triumphal procession of her worshipers. He even resolves to enter her priesthood, despite his initial doubts about the vow of sacerdotal chastity, and finally presents himself at her temple to be inducted into her mysteries. He never directly divulges what the sacraments of initiation are, but after submitting to them he does report — apparently quite earnestly — that the experience was a profound one: he drew near, he says, to the very border of death and placed a foot upon Proserpina's threshold, and then was ravished through all the elements, and saw the sun shining in its full glory at midnight, and was even allowed to approach both the chthonian and celestial gods to adore them in person. Once the rites have been concluded and several days have passed, just before his reluctant departure from the temple to return home, he falls down before the image of Isis and utters a fervent prayer to the goddess who has saved him. "O You," he says, "truly holy and eternal redemptrix of humankind, be ever generous to the mortals whom you cherish, bestowing a mother's sweet love upon the miserable in times of trial. Neither day nor night nor the smallest single moment is devoid of your blessings, for you protect men at sea and on land, and you chase away life's storms by stretching forth your saving right hand, with which also you unwind the inextricably tangled weave of fate and calm Fortune's tempests and restrain the baneful courses of the stars. The gods above worship you, the gods below venerate you, you turn the earth, you give the sun its light, you rule the world, you trample down hell. It is you the stars obey, you for whom the seasons return, you in whom the gods rejoice, and you the elements serve. . . ."

It is a remarkable (and hauntingly familiar) inventory of divine powers and blessings. Isis creates and nourishes and sustains; Isis loves and protects; Isis defeats death and hell; Isis saves. Moreover, Lucius learns all of this in a moment of revelation and personal conversion, an experience of the profoundest inner transformation, of which his outer transformation from beast to man is only a symbol. And his new life among the saved becomes actual for him only through a sacramental initiation that carries

him beyond the power of death, borne up by the grace of divine and omnipotent love.

THERE WAS a brief period in the early, heady days of the anthropology
of religion, when James Frazer was still in fashion, during which it was
regarded by many as something of a scandal that so many seemingly
common elements could be found in both the developed Christianity of
the early centuries and many of the pagan devotions of late antiquity. To
this day, in fact, there are Christians who become terribly anxious at the
suggestion that the early church, in many places, had something of the
form of an Asiatic or Hellenistic mystery cult, or that other sects that offered salvation through sacramental association with a savior deity cherished something of the same religious aspirations of Christianity. Really,
though, there is nothing alarming or even surprising in the discovery
that the gospel spoke to religious hopes that existed outside its corporate
boundaries, or that early Christian devotion should have been expressed
in forms not wholly alien to the culture and language of its time. What
is genuinely worth reflecting upon, however, is the particular way — at
once so recognizable in its time and yet also so very subversive — in which
Christianity answered the religious expectations of much of the ancient
world. For example, as the great classicist Walter Otto argued with such
penetrating insight, the very essence of a great deal of ancient piety (as
Apuleius's book so strikingly shows) was the longing for theophany: a
genuine vision of the god one worshiped, vouchsafed through a gracious
divine condescension. The whole of temple worship revolved around this
desire: the figure of the god or goddess in his or her shrine, gazing through
the temple doors out toward the courtyard and altar, was understood not
simply as a decorative offering *to* the divine, but as a revelatory disclosure
*of* the divine, in the house in which the god or goddess was pleased to dwell
on earth. To see the divine face — the face of God — was the great passion
that animated pagan religion, in a vast variety of its native expressions.

Early Christianity certainly spoke to this deep and deeply pious yearning, but in a way that was not only quite unprecedented but also probably
impossible, within the context of pagan culture, to have been imagined.
Something of extraordinary cultural significance occurred when Christianity succeeded (over a few centuries) in both preserving and overturn-
ing the religious logic of theophany, by offering humanity a vision of the
face of God, but one visible only in the face of a crucified peasant, and
thereby in the face of every neighbor who demands our love. I suppose
one might call it a kind of *Aufhebung* (in the Hegelian sense): a dialecti-

cal moment of synthesis that both preserves and destroys what has gone before — or that preserves *by* destroying. Whatever one calls it, however, it constitutes one of those rare historical transitions that separate one epoch from another irrevocably, a shift in moral imagination that somehow remakes the world. Whatever the case, what pagan and Christian culture both shared in common in this regard was the conviction that the vision of God is possible because it is somehow continuous with the entire reality of life within the spiritual economy of the natural world. For pagans and Christians alike, the entire cosmos is already a revelation of divine glory, a mirror of transcendent beauty and power, shaped and illuminated by a truth that shines through it in every instant. This is the common world of both pagan and Christian culture, however radically the understanding of that world may have been altered as one creed yielded to the other. It may be, moreover, that modernity constitutes yet another irrevocable epochal transition, but one more radically alien to both the pagan and Christian visions than either ever was to the other. At least, this was the thought that flitted through my mind as I was rereading Apuleius this week. For better than three centuries, we moderns have been training ourselves to think of the physical world in purely mechanistic terms; we have — perhaps for the first time in human history — dedicated ourselves to seeing the universe about us as a reality from which every possibility of theophany has been scrupulously excluded. That is a revolution in spiritual sensibility whose ultimate possible cultural consequences, I am fairly sure, do not bear contemplating.

# THIRTY-FIVE

# Is, Ought, and Nature's Laws

There is a long, rich, varied, and subtle tradition of natural law theory, almost none of which I find convincing, but much of which I have to admit to be — within the intellectual world in which it was gestated, and according to the premises it presumes — internally consistent. And, whatever reservations I may have regarding the methods and manners of natural law philosophy, I certainly endorse its guiding vision of a harmony between cosmic and moral order, sustained by the divine goodness in which both participate, even if I do not believe that that harmony can be discerned or described with anything like the precision that many in this tradition imagine it can. In recent years, however, especially in America, a version of natural law theory has taken shape — under the pressure of public debates conducted solely in terms dictated by the modern political order — that tries to import the logic of the tradition into the arena of the secular forum. In that setting, it seems to me, the very idea of natural law becomes irretrievably incoherent. What I have in mind is a style of thought currently popular among certain kinds of "Thomists" (I shall name no names), which assumes that compelling moral truths can be deduced from any truly scrupulous contemplation of the principles of cosmic and human nature, quite apart from special revelation, and within the context of the modern conceptual world. In many of its most significant details, it is simply traditional natural law theory. It begins, entirely correctly, from the recognition that the movement of the human will is never purely spontaneous, and that all volition is evoked by and directed toward an object beyond itself. It presupposes, moreover, and perfectly reasonably, that beyond the immediate objects of desire lies the ultimate end of all willing, the Good as such, which in its absolute priority makes it possible for any finite object to appear to the will as desirable. It asserts, as would I, that nature is governed by final causes. And, finally, it takes as given that the proper ends of the human will and the final causes of creation are inalienably analogous to one another, because at some ultimate level they coincide (for believers, because God is the one source of both). Thus, it would seem, in knowing the causal ends of nature we can know the proper moral ends of the will, and vice versa, and can even discover the relative validity and authority of those moral ends.

So far so good, I suppose. But problems immediately arise when — in part out of a commendable desire to speak to secular society in ways it can understand, in part out of some tacit quasi-Kantian notion that moral philosophy must yield clear and universally binding imperatives, but mostly out of philosophical naïveté — the natural law theorist insists that all of this should be perfectly evident to any freely reasoning mind, regardless of religious belief or cultural formation. Thus, allegedly, the testimony of nature should inform us, when reason is rightly attentive to it, that abortion is murder, or that contraception is wrong, or that marriage should be monogamous, or that we should value social justice above personal profit, or that it is wicked — and extremely discourteous — to eat members of that tribe that lives in the valley on the other side of the mountains. Nature, however, tells us nothing of the sort, at least not in the form of clear commands or hierarchies of moral obligation. In neither an absolute nor a dependent sense — neither as categorical nor as hypothetical imperatives, to use the Kantian terms — can our common knowledge of our nature or of the nature of the universe at large, of itself, instruct us clearly in the content of true morality.

Let me, for the sake of argument, approach this matter from the vantage of a very late modern person, well tutored in the casual voluntarisms and nihilisms of modernity in its senescence. For one thing, as far as any *absolute* morality is concerned, and despite the obstinate refusal of many, say, traditional Thomists to grant the point, it is quite impossible to get around David Hume's bluntly stated — if frequently misunderstood — assertion that it is not clear logically how to derive an "ought" from an "is." Even if one could exhaustively describe the elements of our nature, the claim that we are morally obliged to act in accord with them, or to prefer "natural" uses to "unnatural," could be made only as something additional and adventitious to the whole ensemble of facts that this description would comprise. Otherwise we could not see it as a *moral* good at all, but only as a negotiable feature of private taste. The assumption that the natural and moral orders are connected to one another in any but a purely pragmatic way must be of its nature antecedent to our experience of the world. I know of many stout defenders of natural law who are quick to dismiss Hume's argument, but who — when pressed to explain themselves — can do no better than to resort to a purely conditional argument: *if* one is (for instance) to live a fully human life, one must then . . . (etc.). But, in supplementing a dubious "is" with a negotiable "if," one certainly cannot arrive at a morally *categorical* "ought."

And, frankly, it is difficult to say what natural law theory, abstracted from religious or metaphysical tradition, can really tell us about the relative worthiness of the employments of the will. There are, of course, generally observable facts about the things characteristic of our humanity (the desire for life and happiness, the capacity for allegiance and affinity, the spontaneity of affection for one's family or native heath) and observable facts about those things that generally conduce to the fulfillment of innate human needs (health, a well-ordered family and polity, sufficient food, aesthetic bliss, a sense of spiritual mystery, leisure, and so forth); and if we all lived in a Platonic or Aristotelian or Christian intellectual world, it would be fairly easy to draw a connection between these two sets of facts that nearly everyone would find morally persuasive. As we do not live in that world, however, at least outside certain little philosophical island communities of mutual support, we do not enjoy the luxury of presuming any necessary moral analogy between the teleology of nature and the proper objects of the will.

It is, after all, simply a fact that many of what we take to be the plain and evident elements of universal morality are in reality artifacts of cultural traditions. Today we generally eschew cannibalism, slavery, and wars of conquest and spoliation because of a millennial process of social evolution, the gradual universalization of certain moral beliefs that entered human experience in the form not of natural intuitions — at least, not in any simple sense — but of historical events. We have come to find a great many practices abhorrent and a great many other practices commendable not because the former transparently offend against our nature while the latter clearly correspond to it, but because at various moments in human history we found ourselves addressed by uncanny voices that seemed to emanate from outside the totality of the perceptible natural order and its material economies. One may choose to believe that those voices in fact awakened us to natural truths, and that it was for that very reason that they proved morally persuasive to us; but how could one possibly prove that, when our concept of human nature has so obviously been contingent upon the history of these moral ideas?

The truth is that we cannot talk intelligibly about natural law if we have not first agreed upon what nature is, and if we do not all accept in advance that there really is a connection between what is and what should be. Even then, even if it were clearly demonstrable that, for the majority of persons, the happiest life is the most wholesome, and that most of us can procure spiritual and corporeal contentment for ourselves and for others by observing a certain "natural" mean — still, the daringly disenchanted moralist might ask, what do we owe to nature? What is one to say if I assert that, to my mind, the good is not contentment or justice, but the extension of the pathos of the will — as Nietzsche would put it — the poetic labor of the will to power, the overcoming of the limits of the merely human, the justification of the purely fortuitous phenomenon of the world through its transformation into a supreme aesthetic event? What if I believe the most exalted object of the will to be the *Übermensch*, that natural prodigy, that fortunate accident, which now must become the end to which human culture consciously aspires? Denounce me if you will for the perversity of my convictions. But, after all the *hypothetical* imperatives one can imagine have been adduced, and after every possible appeal has been made to the general good, still no argument could be offered — barring the total *spiritual* conversion of my vision of reality — that would logically oblige me to alter my thinking. In the end, that is to say, belief in natural law is inseparable from the idea of nature as a realm shaped by final causes, oriented in their totality toward a single transcendent moral Good: one whose dictates cannot simply be deduced from our experience of the natural order, but must be received as an apocalyptic interruption of our ordinary explanations that nevertheless, miraculously, makes the natural order intelligible to us as a reality that opens up to what is more than natural. That, however, is not a vision of moral truth that can be meaningfully translated into the language of modern secular society's public policy debates.

# THIRTY-SIX

# Si Fueris Romae

In 1919, Davidson Black — today chiefly remembered as a colleague of Teilhard de Chardin — was made a professor in the Peking Union Medical College, an institution principally endowed by the Rockefeller Foundation. His American benefactors had given him his post with the strict stipulation that he dedicate his energies to creating a respectable department of human anatomy, which he did as scrupulously and as tirelessly as he could. But his real interests lay elsewhere. He had wanted to come to China in order to pursue his interests in human evolutionary history, and in particular to search for fossil remains of earlier hominids in the limestone caves near the village of Zhoukoudian in the hill country outside the capital. It was there that the German naturalist K. A. Haberer had discovered, among the bones of various extinct animals, a tooth that almost certainly had come from a precursor of *Homo sapiens*, and there also that the Swedish paleontologist John Gunnar Andersson wanted to institute a systematic search for traces of humanity's phylogenic forebears. The administrators of the Rockefeller Foundation, however, had no intention of subsidizing quixotic expeditions into China's asperous hinterlands, or investigations in the new and recondite field of paleoanthropology, and so did everything they could to discourage Black's whims. To keep his employers happy, Black was obliged to devote most of his official working hours to anatomical study and to save his evolutionary researches for his private lucubrations. And his daily labors necessarily entailed spending a great deal of time dissecting human cadavers. Of these, fortunately, there was a ready supply available from the municipal constabulary, which was responsible not only for arresting and detaining suspects but also for executing convicts; and the police were all too happy to be relieved of the task of disposing of the corpses themselves, and gladly heaped them into the beds of trucks to send along to the college.

It was a convenient arrangement on the whole, but not ideal. In those days, Chinese criminals were executed by decapitation, and so the cadavers that arrived in Black's operating theater were for the most part headless. One can see the problem. Even if the police remembered to send the severed heads along with the corpses — and the record is unclear here — Black was still working with damaged specimens: the cervical connective tissues, muscles, nerves, and vertebrae were all too mangled for accurate study. And then, one assumes, there would have been the difficulty of determining which head belonged to which body, and so the near impossibility of reconstructing the natural liaison between them or of establishing whether there were any discernible rules governing correlations between cephalomorphism and somatomorphism (and so on). Finally, pleased though he was with the abundance and freshness of his inventory, but frustrated by this single persistent defect, Black sent an inquiry along to the city's police prefecture, asking whether it might be possible to procure cadavers that were still intact. Once again, the police were entirely willing to oblige. The very next day a consignment of condemned prisoners, in chains and under guard, arrived at the college, accompanied by a letter graciously inviting Black to put them to death in any manner he thought might best suit his purposes. It was a generous offer, I think we would all agree; but Black was scandalized all the same. He refused the gift and sent the prisoners back to the police (and to their deaths, of course). Thereafter, he took no further deliveries of convicts, dead or alive, and chose instead to avail himself only of the more irregular supply of corpses he could obtain from the city morgue.

WELL, I IMAGINE something similar has happened to all of us now and then while traveling abroad. Awkward moments of this sort are more or less inevitable when one ventures any appreciable distance from native harbors. Sooner or later one is all but certain to dismay a French hostess by delicately sipping from the finger bowl, or to perplex a Greek interlocutor with one's Anglo-Saxon reserve by continually backing away from his amiably insistent propinquity, or to alarm an Italian by making the impertinent suggestion that one might actually come to dine at his home one evening, or to disgust a *mir-shikar* by failing to deliver a competent *coup de grâce* during a wild boar hunt in the Punjab, or to wound a central Asian tribesman's pride by accepting the hospitality of his yak-hide yurt but refusing the offer of his youngest wife for the night. Tact can go only so far in such circumstances. So I think we can all comprehend Black's plight, even as we enjoy the special piquancy of his story: there the hapless fellow was, after all, squandering his nights striving to fathom the deep inscrutabilities of evolutionary anthropology, trying to pierce the heavily accumulated veils of geological time and to reach down into the long hidden past in the hope of laying hold of the mystery of humanity's origins, suddenly awakened from his reveries by a startling encounter with the even more impenetrable mysteries of profound cultural difference. How could he hope, in that appalling instant, to respond in a way at once in keeping with his own principles and also sufficiently decorous to show that he was sensible of the courtesy he had been extended?

By the same token, however, we can certainly also spare a moment's sympathetic chagrin for the poor police official who sent those chained convicts to Black. The gesture had such a quality of demonstrative generosity to it, of guileless gallantry — something of the Gascon's exuberant display of spontaneous largesse or of the Cavalier's sonorous "Your servant, sir!" and deep bow from the waist and sweeping flourish of the doffed panache. To have his gift so unceremoniously returned must have been at least a little humiliating. And, really, he was doing nothing obviously unreasonable. From his vantage, it was probably the case that these wretches, having been duly condemned, were for all intents and purposes already only so much rubbish to be disposed of. It may well have been that, as far as he was concerned, the difference between sending Black a freight of carcasses before they had actually been executed rather than after was little more than a technical detail. It really is all a matter of cultural perspective.

After all, what made Black recoil from the killing of those prisoners may have been in part some vague superstition regarding the unique legitimacy of properly exercised jurisprudential violence, but it was almost certainly in greater part an intuition inscribed on his soul by a long process of cultural formation, both personal and historical. He was in the moral habit, so to speak, of believing that an individual human life is never wholly devoid of moral significance, no matter what its legal status, and that therefore any violence he might commit against any person would have some sort of determinate consequence for his own moral identity. That intuition — that particular way of understanding the meaning of each human being — is not a universal property of human society; it is a result of the particular cultural and (inevitably) religious tradition. It is worth recalling, however, that Black hardly occupied a position of moral superiority in this matter. By all accounts he was a decent man, but he seems also to have been strangely inattentive to the reality of his situation, in the supremely abstracted manner that men of clinical temperament often are. Surely he ought to have been aware, simply from the quantities of corpses he had been receiving from the police, that a great many of the convicts whose bodies he was examining had been sentenced and executed for crimes that in his own country would have carried no graver penalty than imprisonment or perhaps a fine, and that the Peking magistracy probably operated with a far looser sense of evidentiary procedure than a Western court would have done. He may not have had much occasion to consider the matter before being confronted by a consignment of convicts still in a not quite postmortem state, but it is hard not to think he should have reflected before then upon the moral ambiguities of the college's pact with local law enforcement.

Really, though, it is hard to judge him very harshly, given the far more conscious compromise our government and (more broadly and deeply) our culture of insatiable consumption have reached with the current government of the People's Republic. Decade upon decade, we hear of the arrest, imprisonment, torture, and murder of China's religious minorities (house church Christians, Tibetan Buddhist monks, and so on), of the cruel measures taken to enforce the nation's one-child policy, and of countless other chronic atrocities, but our response consists in little more than a sporadic susurrus of disapproval, just loud enough to flatter ourselves that we have principles but not so loud as to allow those principles to interfere with fiscal or trade policy. We try to shame the ruling party with pious panegyrics to "human rights," as though the concept had any appreciable weight outside the cultural context that makes it intelligible, but we buy and borrow from the party, and profit from its policies, without hesitation or embarrassment. I think the government of the People's Republic of China might be pardoned for concluding that our actions, and not our words, indicate where our true values lie.

# THIRTY-SEVEN

# Nature Loves to Hide

Not long ago, I spoke ill of a modern form of natural law theory that unsuccessfully attempts to translate an ancient tradition of moral reasoning into the incompatible language of secular reason. Because of an obscurity I allowed to slip into the fourth paragraph, several readers imagined that I was speaking *in propria persona* from that point on, rather than on behalf of a disenchanted modern rambling among the weed-thronged ruins; and some were dismayed. Edward Feser, for instance, issued a confused and slightly hysterical condemnation wherein, with bludgeoning brio, he accused me of numerous logical errors I did not really commit and then pronounced me a Humean modernizer who doubts reason's natural orientation toward the Good. The piece missed the mark by a league or two; but, in its favor, it did contain a number of genuinely interesting conceptual mistakes, chief among them a simplistic use of such words as "revelation" and "supernatural." There is an old argument here, admittedly. Somewhere behind Feser's argument slouches the specter of what is often called "two-tier Thomism": a philosophical sect notable in part for the particularly impermeable partitions it erects between nature and grace, or nature and supernature, or natural reason and revelation, or philosophy and theology (and so on). To its adherents, it is the solution to the contradictions of modernity. To those of more "integralist" bent (like me), it is a neoscholastic deformation of Christian metaphysics that, far from offering an alternative to secular reason, is one of its chief theological accomplices. Whatever the case, however, its approach to natural law is ultimately incoherent.

Before completing that thought, however, it might help to rehearse just a few of the conceptual obstacles our age erects in the path of natural law theory. So:

1. *Finality's fortuity.* Most traditional accounts of natural law require a picture of nature as governed by final causality: for every substance, there are logically prior ends — proximate, remote, or transcendent — that guide its existence and unite it to the greater totality of a single cosmic, physical, moral, social continuum embraced within the providential finality of the divine. They assume, then, that from the "is" of a thing legitimate conclusions regarding its "ought" can be discerned, because nature herself — through her evident forms — instructs us in the elements of moral fulfillment. In our age, however, final causality is a concept confined within an ever more beleaguered and porous intellectual redoubt. One can easily enough demonstrate the reality of finality within nature, but modern scientific culture refuses to view it as in any sense a cause rather than the accidental consequence of an immanent material process. Within any organic system, for instance, ontogeny is fruitfully determined by strict formal constraints, but these are seen as the results of an incalculably vast series of fortuitous mutations and attritions, and therefore only the residue of an entirely stochastic phylogeny. Hence nature's finality indicates no morally consequential ends (much less the supereminent finality of the Love that moves the stars), but is rather merely the emergent result of intrinsically *meaningless* brute events.

2. *Dame Nature, serial murderess.* Even if final causality in nature is demonstrable, does it yield moral knowledge if there is no clear moral analogy between natural ends and the proper objects of human motive? For Thomas Aquinas, only a moral disorder can make one claim ignorance of the reality of the God who, as the source of one's being, is supremely worthy of love. True in principle, of course. Even so, the "failure" to find a moral dimension in one's intrinsic ontological contingency may not be *entirely* culpable. Our modern narrative of nature is of an order shaped by immense ages of monstrous violence: mass extinctions, the cruel profligacy of an algorithmic logic that squanders ten thousand lives to fashion a single durable type, an evolutionary process that advances not despite, but because of, disease, warfare, predation, famine, and so on. And the majestic order thus forged? One of elemental caprice, natural calamity, the mercilessness of chance — injustice thrives, disaster befalls the innocent, and children suffer. Why, our deracinated modern might ask, should we believe that nature's organizing finality, given the kinds of efficient causes it prompts into action, has *moral* implications that command imitation, obedience, or (most unlikely of all) love?

3. *Elective priorities.* Assume, however, that we can establish the existence of a moral imperative implicit in the orderliness of the world, as

perceived by a rational will that, for itself, must seek the good: Does that assure that we can prove what hierarchy of values follows from this, or how we should calculate the relative preponderance of diverse moral ends? Yes, we may all agree that murder is worse than rudeness; but, beyond the most rudimentary level of ethical deliberation, pure logic proves insufficient as a guide to which ends truly command our primary obedience, and our arguments become ever more dependent upon prior evaluations and preferences that, as far as *philosophy* can discern, are culturally or psychologically contingent. Consistent natural law cases can be made for or against slavery, for example, or for or against capital punishment, depending on which values one has privileged at a level too elementary for philosophy to adjudicate. At some crucial point, natural law argument, pressed to disclose its principles, dissolves into sheer assertion.

4. *Theory's limits.* The most gallant of Feser's non sequiturs is his claim that, because reason necessarily seeks the good, there exists no gap into which any Humean distinction between facts and values can insinuate itself. But obviously the gap lies in the dynamic interval between (in the terms of Maximus the Confessor) the "natural" and "gnomic" wills. The venerable principle that the natural will is a pure ecstasy toward the good means that, at the level of gnomic deliberation, whatever we will we desire *as* the good, but not that philosophical theory can by itself *prove* which facts imply which values, or that the good must *naturally* be understood as an incumbent "ought" rather than a compelling "I want." Feser asserts that "purely philosophical arguments" can establish "objective true moral conclusions." And yet, curiously enough, they never, ever have. That is a bedtime story told to conjure away the night's goblins, like the Leibnizian fable of the best possible world or the *philosophe*'s fairy tale about the plain dictates of reason.

THE QUESTION relentlessly begged in all of this is what "reason" is. It is perfectly possible to both believe that the whole natural dynamism of our reason and will is toward the good and still deny that natural law theory provides a sound model of how the intellect can know moral truths. There is nothing scandalous in this unless one creates a false dilemma by imagining a real division between the discrete realms of supernatural and natural knowledge. Feser speaks of revelation as an extrinsic datum consisting in texts and dogmas, and of the supernatural as merely outside of nature, and thinks there really is such a thing as purely natural reason. From that perspective, one cannot deny philosophy's power to demonstrate objective moral truth without denying reason's innate capacity for the good. Like a Kantian (the two-tier Thomist's alter ego), one must believe that philosophical theory's limits are also reason's.

These divisions are illusory. What we call "nature" is merely one mode of the disclosure of the "supernatural," and natural reason merely one mode of revelation, and philosophy merely one (feeble) mode of reason's ascent into the light of God. Nowhere, not even in the sciences, does there exist a "purely natural" realm of knowledge. To encounter the world is to encounter its being, which is gratuitously imparted to it from beyond the sphere of natural causes, known within the medium of an intentional consciousness, irreducible to immanent processes, that grasps finite reality only by being oriented toward a horizon of transcendental ends (or, better, "divine names"). There is a seamless continuity between the sight of a rose and the mystic's vision of God; the latter is in fact implicit in the former, and saturates it, and but for this supernatural surfeit nothing natural could come into thought. It does not then represent some grave failure of natural reason that philosophy cannot achieve definitive moral demonstrations, or that true knowledge of the good is impossible without calling upon other modes of knowledge: the (ubiquitous) supernatural illumination of a conscience — a heart — upon which the law is written, Platonic *anamnesis* (of the eternal forms or of what your mother taught you), cultural traditions with all their gracious moments of religious awakening (Jewish, pagan, Christian, Hindu, Taoist, Buddhist, Muslim, Sikh, and so on), prayer, inspiration, the cultivation of personal holiness, love of the arts, and so on. There is no single master discourse here, for the good can be known only in being *seen*. Certain fundamental moral truths, for instance, may *necessarily* remain unintelligible to someone incapable of appreciating Bach's fifth Unaccompanied Cello Sonata (or perhaps Carmen McRae singing Dave Brubeck, or the exquisite choreography of a well-turned double play). For some it may seem an outrageous notion that, rather than a fanciful collection of purportedly incontrovertible proofs, the correct rhetoric of moral truth consists in a richer but more unmasterable appeal to the full range of human capacities and senses, physical and spiritual. I, however, see it as rather glorious: a further confirmation that our whole being, in all its dimensions, is a single gracious vocation out of nonexistence to the station of created gods.

# THIRTY-EIGHT

# Purpose and Function

I cannot say that I have warmed to the theme of natural law theory, but I am definitely beginning to derive a certain morbid pleasure from the passions it can excite. This is an unwholesome entertainment, however, so I shall make a last observation and then leave the topic alone.

The story to this point: Some months ago, I admitted here that I find very little natural law theory persuasive, but granted that classical forms of the tradition are cogent given the religious and metaphysical assumptions with which they work; of attempts to forge an effective natural law theory without the support of those assumptions, agreeable to the temper of modernity, I was dismissive. In a subsequent issue, I laid out some of the reasons why the late modern view of reality is one to which I think no current natural law theory can successfully accommodate itself and made some provocative assertions on the limits of "purely natural" ethical reasoning. Both columns provoked some attacks: some judicious, others marked by an emotional incontinence eerily reminiscent of some of Daniel Dennett's more infamous "letters to the editor," none (as far as I have seen) particularly germane to my arguments or in any way solvent of them.

Perhaps some of that is my fault. Given the necessarily condensed nature of columns with word limits, I may have been guilty of a few cryptic formulations. At least, one of my critics seems especially pertinaciously committed to the *idée fixe* that my concern was to argue for the impotence of philosophical moral reasoning in order to promote the intellectual hegemony of theology. I suppose, therefore, that my denial of the existence of any "master discourse" on ethical matters as well as my rejection of any strict division of philosophy from theology were less incandescently perspicuous than I had imagined they were. I seem also to have failed to make adequately clear that my skepticism regarding the power of a "purely natural" philosophy to establish the reality of a moral dimension in natural ends arises not from doubts regarding the powers of natural reason, but rather from doubts regarding the powers of philosophical dialectic when it artificially confines itself to "purely natural" principles.

Mind you, much of the disagreement vanishes if the central question is only whether, to borrow a line, "there is common ground between all human beings, and particularly between religious believers and non-believers, on which moral disagreements can be rationally adjudicated." I am not sure I could sneak so minimalist a definition of natural law theory past, say, the piercing eyes of Russ Hittinger; but, by all means, if we are talking only about principles upon which we all agree in advance, then only details remain. I, however, do not believe everyone agrees on those principles anymore, even when it seems they might. I think traditional moralists today will inevitably find that any "natural" terms they employ have very different meanings for their interlocutors, and invite very different conclusions. And they will find also that no philosophical arguments *simply* from the evident natures of things will suffice to prove the validity of their presuppositions. That is not really all that provocative a claim, so long as one remembers to distinguish principles from proofs. In my second column, I stated that purely natural philosophical arguments have "never, ever" succeeded in establishing "objectively true" moral conclusions. Again, though, apparently I should have been clearer. I was not denying the rational obviousness of a great many "innocuous" moral truisms — one ought not to torture babies, for instance, or one ought not to punish the innocent, and so on — but I certainly was denying that what is rationally obvious is always therefore some kind of objective *fact* that philosophical dialectic can prove to be true from a synthetic judgment about nature. The moral content — the imperative — in such principles resides nowhere within the ensemble of natural facts that philosophy can enumerate. These are truths that attest to themselves before an illuminated conscience, and one must have an immediate grasp of them to be capable of any ethical reasoning at all.

Anyway, argument is not necessary here. One need only supply an invincibly complete, *purely* natural argument for some clear moral conclusion to prove me wrong; and this would not dismay me. I do not think that will happen, however, and right now my real interest lies elsewhere. I simply cannot shed the suspicion that many of us today fail fully to grasp the sole true intellectual achievement of modernity: the creation of a fully developed, imaginatively compelling, and philosophically sophisticated tradition of metaphysical nihilism.

MY GREATEST FAILURE in my second column, however, seems to have been in neglecting to explain that, in providing a brief description of the late modern, neo-Darwinian picture of nature, I never meant to accuse natural law theorists of suffering from a naïve obliviousness to the sheer redness of nature in tooth and claw. The issue for me was never one concerning the violence of nature, of which everyone is perfectly well aware, but one concerning modernity's overarching narrative — physical and metaphysical — of what nature is. The late modern picture of reality is, culturally speaking, something altogether unprecedented. In the days of, say, Thomas Aquinas, there was no particularly cogent alternative to seeing nature as a rationally ordered continuum in which all things witnessed to a final good, at once cosmic and moral. Even if one did not concur with Thomas's (often very questionable) moral judgments, one could scarcely reject many of his metaphysical presuppositions; and so one might not notice the covertly theological nature of those judgments. Not so now. The modern person's failure to find a moral meaning in nature's forms is not simply attributable to a perverse refusal to recognize objective truths. There is now a story that makes nihilism — in the technical sense of disbelief in any ultimate meaning or purpose beyond the physical — plausible and powerful.

With the rise of the mechanical philosophy, modern persons began to conceive of natural ends not as inherent purposes, but merely as useful functions. Even those who believed that the exquisite clockwork of the universe had been assembled by an intelligent designer still regarded physical nature as an amalgam of intrinsically aimless energies upon which order had been extrinsically imposed, and so not as a natural revelation of the divine *logos* pervading all things. Then, with the rise of Darwinism, and finally of an essentially mechanistic genetocentric neo-Darwinism, an entirely new and seemingly exhaustive account of physical order and causality came into being, one in which there were no such things as intrinsic natures, but only local coalescences of diverse and meaningless material forces. Within this view of things, organisms are cohesive but farraginous assemblages of the various "desiring machines" (to use Deleuze's phrase) that compose bodies and psyches. Not only is there no single universal rational form dictating the proper end of *this* or *that* individual organism; there is no single proper purpose inherent in any aspect of an organism. There is only a warring multiplicity of genetic and organic propensities and uses — temperamental, chemical, erotic, creative, destructive, and so on. Prescriptions regarding what tends toward the flourishing of distinct natural kinds refer, then, only to a proximate and pragmatic calculus of what works in general, but have nothing to say about what is morally incumbent upon any individual instance of life's energies.

Now, of course, the late modern "naturalist" or "physicalist" view of reality suffers from innumerable logical lacunae, most particularly at the level of ontology; and there are phenomena it can never adequately explain, such as intentional consciousness. But a sufficiently complacent metaphysical nihilist can "logically" dismiss logic as a flawed instrument, crafted fortuitously by mindless forces, without any bad conscience. Happily for them, natural law theorists will only rarely find themselves arguing with anyone consciously committed to so extreme a naturalist perspective. In most persons there is enough moral sentiment and habit — enough nostalgia for the absolute — for them to be open to persuasion. But sentiment and habit are fragile and perishable things; and the nihilist narrative is far more tacitly pervasive than we are always aware. This is because it is appealing. It is all part of the great ideological project of modernity. The metaphysical demotion of nature's order from purposiveness to functionality is a license to believe that there is no meaning to life that we do not impute to it or — more excitingly — impose upon it. Metaphysical nihilism is a formula for a limitless voluntarism, the exhilarating adventure of the will to power. To many this seems like liberation from the tyranny of the absolute, and so the very form of freedom. To others, more traditionally inclined, it seems like cruel exile from participation in creation as a natural and supernatural order, and so slavery to nothingness. All that can mediate between these two views of reality is the rhetoric of conversion — in all its philosophical, cultural, empirical, religious, and affective registers — but I know of no school of "purely natural" moral reasoning that can convince anyone but the already converted. Again, though, I am more than willing to be proved wrong.

# THIRTY-NINE

# No Enduring City

O ne of the temperamental advantages to be gained from a belief in divine providence is serenity in the face of history's ambiguities. This may be one of the more subdued and unheroic expressions of faith, but for Christians trying to make moral sense of the story of Christendom — from its once quite unpredictable rise to its now quite indubitable collapse — it is an absolutely indispensable one. For, if indeed God became incarnate within history in order to reconcile time to eternity, then it only stands to reason that the event of Christ should be one that never ceases to unfold in time, with discernible consequences and in substantial forms. An unutterable, inconceivable, entirely transitory interruption of history might suffice to liberate the occasional captive soul from the prison house of an alien cosmos, by the "grace" of a paradox, but it could not alter the relation between creation and God. And yet the actual historical record of Christian society hardly encourages confidence: marvelous cultural and ethical achievements, of course, but almost all of them inseparably associated with innumerable institutional betrayals of the gospel. Hence the need for a generously indeterminate trust in the mysterious workings of God's will *sub contrario.* Otherwise the believer is apt to become trapped at one pole in a tedious dialectic of indignant rejection and credulous celebration, indulging either in sanctimonious denunciations of "Constantinianism" or in triumphalist apostrophes to the spiritual greatness of "Christian" culture, in either case reducing the very concept of grace to an empty cipher. A little prudent providentialism, however, relieves one of the anxious urge to pronounce some absolute verdict on Christian history as a whole, or to pretend to understand how the Holy Spirit might or might not reweave the tangles of human sin into unexpected occasions of charity or truth. It allows one simply to accept the inscrutable complexities of a world that, if it has been redeemed, nevertheless still groans in anticipation of a glory yet to be revealed, and so of a world in which all good is inextricably bound up with moral failure.

On the other hand, however, the hiddenness of God's counsels ought not to become a license to complacency. Living as they now do in the long aftermath of Christendom's political, social, and cultural collapse, able to gaze out across its twilit ruins from a certain critical and disenchanted distance, modern Christians are peculiarly well situated to consider anew what the true relation between Christianity and the native forms of human society is. At least, they possess an unprecedented perspective from which to pose the question. As witnesses to the ultimate failure of Christendom's attempted accommodation between a living cultural consciousness of Christ and the concrete structures of human political and social power, they can at least ask whether the end of the old Christian order should be understood as something on the order of an immense historical accident or as instead something much more like an ineluctable destiny. After all, there is no genuinely faithful proclamation of the gospel that does not involve a very real and irreducible element of sheer contrariness toward the most respectable of human institutions. When the peasant Christ tells the aristocrat Pilate of his kingdom not of this world, or when Paul warns Christians against any commerce with the works of the god of this cosmos, or when Christ commands his followers to forgive those who wrong them in excess of all natural justice, or likens the wealthy citizen at heaven's gate to a camel attempting to slip through a needle's eye — as well as at countless other junctures in the New Testament — the gospel is announced as something essentially subversive of the accustomed orders of human power, preeminence, law, social prudence, religion, and government. A radically new story is being told, one meant to reorient and, to a very great degree, invert the stories that human beings have told about themselves from time immemorial. And this creates a certain irresoluble tension in any attempt to make sense of the Christian past, because it has been only within the stable institutional and cultural configurations of an all-too-human history that the gospel's more subversive story has been audibly proclaimed over two millennia, and has continued to produce material and intellectual consequences. Perhaps, though, I should offer some illustration of what I mean.

CONSIDER TWO EPISODES — nearly contemporaneous with one another — from the Italy of the High Middle Ages.

The first occurred on 25 August 1256, when the *podestà* and *capitano del popolo* of Bologna summoned the citizens of the *commune* to the city's Piazza Maggiore to announce the abolition of all bonded servitude within the city's civil and diocesan jurisdictions. Some 5,855 serfs were redeemed from their *signori* — who were remunerated out of the communal treasury at a total price of 54,014 lire — then placed under ecclesiastical authority, and then granted their liberty. An irrevocable abolition of slavery in Bologna was then issued in a short text known as the *Liber Paradisus*, in which was indited the name of every emancipated serf. Historians have occasionally speculated on the economic benefits that Bologna may have reaped from this decision — for one thing, freedmen were eligible to pay taxes — but the actual cost of the manumission, immediate and deferred, was so exorbitant that it is rather difficult to see how the municipal administration could have calculated any plausible profit from its actions. Perhaps, then, one should take seriously the motives that the *Liber Paradisus* itself actually adduces: "Paradisum voluptatis plantavit dominus Deus omnipotens a principio," it begins, "in quo posuit hominem, quem formaverat, et ipsius corpus ornavit veste candenti, sibi donans perfectissimam et perpetuam libertatem" ("In the beginning, the Lord God Almighty planted a paradise of delight, in which he placed man, whom he had formed, and whose body he had adorned with the garb of radiance [a shining raiment], endowing him with perfect and perpetual freedom"). It was only by sinning, the argument proceeds, that humanity bound itself in servitude to corruption; God in his mercy, however, sent his Son into the world to break the bonds that hold humanity in thrall, that by Christ's own dignity all of us should have our natural liberty restored. Thus all persons currently bound in servitude by human law should have their proper freedom granted them, for they along with all the rest of us belong to a single *massa libertatis* wherein now not so much as a single *modicum fermentum* of servitude can be tolerated, lest it corrupt the whole. This was, needless to say, an extraordinary declaration. Its logic extended far beyond the immediate practicalities of a local writ of emancipation, and into the realm of universally binding theological truths. It was an altogether radical proclamation of an intrinsic incompatibility between the concrete realities of the prevailing social order and the language of the gospel that Christian society professed to obey.

The second episode, however, which to our sensibilities might seem the more outlandish of the two, was for its time far and away the more ordinary. Some twelve to fifteen years after the promulgation of the *Liber Paradisus* (the date cannot be more precisely determined than that),

Thomas Aquinas put the finishing touches on that famous (or infamous) passage in the *Summa Theologiae* (II-II, q. 11, art. 3–4) where he defends the practice of executing heretics. The argument he laid out there was quite a simple one, consisting in only two points, both of which he considered more or less incontestable: First, as regards the heretics themselves, their sin by itself warrants both excommunication and death. Second, as regards the church, the graver evil of heresy is that it corrupts the faith, which gives life to the soul; and so, if we execute forgers for merely corrupting our currency, which can sustain only temporal life, how much more justly may we deal with convicted heretics not only by excommunicating them but also by putting them to death. Of course, Thomas adds, out of her mercy toward each man who has strayed, the church hesitates to pronounce a final condemnation until "the first and second admonition" have both failed; but then, if the heretic remains obstinate, "the church, no longer hoping for his conversion, turns itself to the salvation of others, by excommunicating him and separating him from the church, and furthermore delivers him over to the secular tribunal so that the latter might remove him from the world by death." Nor can ecclesial compassion extend any further than this. Recidivism, for instance, even of the most transient kind, is unpardonable. Says Thomas, "at God's tribunal, all who return are always received, because God is a searcher of hearts, and knows those who return in sincerity. But the church cannot imitate God in this, for she presumes that those who relapse after being once received are insincere when they return; so she does not obstruct their path to salvation, but neither does she shield them from the sentence of death."

Now, making whatever allowances we wish for historical context when considering these two episodes — for, say, the possibly somewhat mixed motives of the government of the Bolognese *commune* in freeing its bonded population, or for the good intentions of Thomas in hoping to preserve as many souls as possible out of the general ruin of this fallen world, and so on — their juxtaposition provides a perfect epitome of the spiritual contradictions inherent in Christendom. In the one case, the laymen of the municipal government of Bologna — drawing upon their catechetical and devotional formation as educated Christians, and upon the scriptural language of the culture in which they had been reared, but upon no theological formation beyond that — were able to grasp, articulate, and act decisively upon a rich and rather beautiful theological principle, quite in defiance of the received social and economic practices of their age, and with fairly radical results. In the other case, one of the greatest speculative minds of Western Christian tradition recommended that, when confronted by the preacher of aberrant doctrine, the church should (albeit reluctantly) assume the role of Caiaphas, and encourage the secular arm to discharge the part of Pilate. I know that may seem an offensive analogy: Jesus before his accusers was in the right, after all, and the heretic in the wrong; and Thomas was concerned for the salvation of souls; and so on and so on. But there can be no mitigation here of the offense against Christian charity. Christ may indeed have stood upon the side of truth, over against the verdicts passed upon him by both Caiaphas and Pilate, but the truth to which he bore witness was among other things a very particular rule of life, a clear and concrete way of inhabiting the world, a very specific practice of the presence of God among human beings; and it was one absolutely antithetical to the violence of religious and political power. So, granting that Thomas and his order were products of their times, still the use of coercion and murder to defend the church cannot be anything other than a betrayal of the gospel far graver than any mere doctrinal deviation could ever be. Thomas's argument is entirely consonant with the principles (social and moral) of Christendom, and yet entirely alien to the principles of Christianity. And that even so powerful an intellect as Thomas's could have failed to grasp this is, to the say the very least, troubling.

So, then, in the case of the Bolognese emancipation, we encounter an extraordinary event produced by the total saturation of a culture — generation after generation — in the language of the gospel, in the narrative of Scripture, and in the logic of Christian theological tradition: an event that could not possibly have occurred apart from the historical reality of Christendom, in all its cultural intricacy and depth and layerings and efflorescences. In the case of Thomas's argument, however, we encounter a monstrous deformation of Christian teaching also produced by the historical reality of Christendom: by the inherited mythology of the Constantinian accommodation and by a long-indurated cultural habit of viewing the church and Christian society as a single, immense, integrated machine for the manufacture of baptized souls. Rather than the new pattern of corporate human life inaugurated in Christ's ministry — the practice of a life redeemed by God, the vital shape of a social order that executes neither heretics nor forgers — the gospel had now become merely the deposit of sacred doctrine, which must be defended, if necessary, by the power of the sword; for it is occasionally expedient that, for the sake of a Christian nation, one man should die. We may now be naturally disposed, correctly, to celebrate the one episode and lament the other. But how, practically speaking, in the realm of concrete social history, can one disentangle the cultural possibilities that allowed for the one from those that allowed for the other? Conversely, was the obvious contradiction between them merely one of those ambiguities that the vagaries of history inevitably generate, or was it instead the inevitable consequence of any attempt to forge a functioning alliance between the gospel and the social structures of human power?

CHRISTIANITY FIRST ENTERED the world of late antiquity not as an institution, nor as a fully developed creed, but first and foremost as an event that had no proper precedent or any immediately conceivable sequel. In its earliest dawn, the gospel arrived in history as the proclamation of a convulsive disruption *of* history, a truly subversive rejection of many of the most venerable cultic, social, and philosophical wisdoms of the ancient world. And the central event that the gospel proclaimed — the event within the event, so to speak — was the resurrection of Christ, which, according to Paul, had effectively erased all sacred, social, racial, and national boundaries, gathered into itself all divine sovereignty over history, and subdued all the political and spiritual agencies of the cosmos: the powers and principalities, the thrones and dominions, the "god of this world." The language of the book of Galatians is especially uncompromising with regard to the implications of this "interruption." There Paul states that the event of salvation in Christ was a complete liberation from the constraints of elemental existence (the *stoicheia*), but also from the power of law; for even the law of Moses, holy though it is, was defective, having been delivered only by an angel through a mere human mediator, and had operated only as a kind of provisional "disciplinarian" (*paidagogos*) till Christ had set us free.

In a very real sense, then, Christianity entered human consciousness not primarily as an alternative set of religious obligations and credenda, but first and foremost as the apocalyptic annunciation of the kingdom and its sudden invasion of historical and natural time alike. Within the spiritual world of Judaism, it was intelligible, but principally as a prophetic announcement made out of season — "This day is the scripture fulfilled in your hearing" — which impetuously demanded immediate assent to what seemed a preposterous claim. More to the point, in the larger world of the empire it was, as René Girard correctly notes, positively irreligious in its implications: a reversal of established sacred truths, the instant in which the victim of social and religious order was all at once revealed as the righteous one, the innocent one, even God himself. The pattern established in Christ — especially in the inexhaustibly suggestive story of his confrontation with Pilate — was one of martyrdom as victory, of power as the willingness to become powerless before the violence of the state and thereby to reveal its arbitrariness, injustice, and spiritual falsehood. In its original form, therefore, the gospel involved a pressing command to all persons to come forth, out of the economies of society and cult, and into the immediacy of that event: for the days are short. And, having been born in this terrible and joyous expectation of time's imminent end — its first "waking moment" being the knowledge that the kingdom was near — the church was not at first quite prepared to inhabit time except in something like a condition of sustained crisis. There was at first no obvious medium by which a people in some sense already living in history's aftermath, in a state of constant urgency, could enter history again, as either an institution or a body of law or even a religion. It would take a little time, and some adjustment of expectations, and perhaps a degree of disenchantment as well, for so singular an irruption of the eschatological into the temporal to be recuperated into stable order again. Still, of course, the church quickly assumed religious configurations appropriate both to its age and to its own spiritual content. Jewish scripture provided a grammar for worship, while the common cultic forms of ancient society were easily adaptable to Christian use. There was a certain degree of natural "pseudomorphism" in the process, a crystallization of Christian corporate life (with all its novelty) within the religious space vacated by the pagan cults it displaced. This was inevitable and necessary; a perfectly apocalyptic consciousness — a consciousness subsisting in a moment of pure interruption — could not really have been sustained beyond a certain, very brief period. Even then, the alloy was never entirely stable. At least, it has often seemed as if the Christian event is of its nature something too refractory — the impulse to rebellion too constitutive of its own spiritual logic — to be contained even within its own institutions. This might be one of the reasons why Christianity over the centuries not only has proved so irrepressibly fissile (as all large religious traditions, to some degree, are), but has also given rise to a culture capable of the most militant atheism, and even of self-conscious nihilism. Even in its most enduring and necessary historical forms, there is an ungovernable energy within it, something that desires not to crystallize but rather to disperse itself into the future, to start always anew, more spirit than flesh or letter.

I am not speaking, I hasten to add, of some supposed "inner essence" of the faith, some pure *Wesen des Christentums* that somehow became trapped in the amber of subsequent tradition. I am speaking, rather, of a distinct element of Christianity's power that cannot be ignored without fundamentally ignoring the very character of the gospel, an element that may occasionally generate certain *intrinsic* stresses within the church, but that could not help but produce a far greater and more chronic tension once an *extrinsic* accommodation had been reached with political authority. It was, of course, a fruitful tension, producing as it did all the immense social goods of the Christian order: the cultural creativity, the slow amelioration of laws, the birth of the hospital, the establishment of an immeasurably richer moral grammar than the West had ever known, a whole vast and various range of artistic, technical, and scientific achievements — all of which were inseparable in one way or another from the radical revision of the understanding of the human being and of nature that Christianity introduced into the world. Yet its moral failures were no less astonishing or numerous. And now we live in the time after Christendom, amid the rapidly vanishing fragments of its material culture, bound to it by only a few lingering habits of thought. Modernity is the post-Christian age, the reality of a culture that was shaped by the final failure of that accommodation. So, again, more simply: Why exactly did it fail?

MODERNITY, TAKEN AS a definable cultural project or epochal ideology, understands itself as the history of freedom. Or rather, I suppose I should say, the one grand cultural and historical narrative that we as modern persons tend to share, and that most sharply distinguishes a modern from a premodern vision of society, is the story of liberation, the ascent of the individual out of the shadows of hierarchy and subsidiary identity into the light of full recognition, dignity, and autonomy. It is a story that does not, obviously, amount to a single ideological program; rather, it gives rise to a bewildering variety of analogous but often incompatible ideologies; but it does determine what our highest or most central value is, to which all other values are subordinate. And it is quite easy to call attention to those movements of late medieval and early modern theological and philosophical reflection that helped to produce our specifically modern understanding of freedom: voluntarism, nominalism, an ever greater tendency to imagine God's freedom in terms of the absolutely undetermined sovereignty of his will, the gradual migration of this image of freedom from God to human beings, and so on. Having made something of a cottage industry of such observations myself, I shall refrain here from repeating myself at length. Suffice it to say that what the word "freedom" has generally come to mean for most of us now, when our usage is at its most habitual and unreflective, is libertarian autonomy and spontaneous volition, the negative freedom of the unrestrained (or at least minimally

restrained) individual will. It is a concept of freedom not only impoverished, but ultimately incoherent (but that is an issue for another time).

Here, however, I want to point out that there is another side to the
story as well. Simply said, all of modernity's tales of liberation, in all their
diversity and frequent contradictoriness, are also variations unfolded
within or springing up in the shadow of the very particular history of the
gospel's proclamation. Resistance to or flight from the authority of the
law — or, rather, a sense of the law's ultimate nullity — has from the first
been a vital part of the moral sensibility of the gospel. And in every modern demand for social and personal recognition as inherent rights there
is at least a distant echo of Paul's proclamation of the unanticipated "free
gift" found in Christ. The peculiar restlessness, the ferment, of modern
Western history — great revolutions and local rebellions, the ceaseless
generation of magnificent principles and insidious abstractions, politics
as the interminable ideological conflict between Edenic nostalgias and
eschatological optimisms, the ungovernable proliferation of ever newer
"innate" rights and ever more comprehensive forms of "social justice" —
belongs to the long secular sequel of the declaration that the kingdom has
arrived in Christ, that the prince of this world has been judged and cast
out, that the one who lies under the condemnation of the powers of this
age has been vindicated by God and raised up as Lord. It is a sort of "oblivious memory" of Paul's message that all the powers of the present age have
been subdued, and death and wrath defeated, not by the law — which, for
all its sanctity, is impotent to set us free — but by a gift that has canceled
the law's power over against us.

This is not a claim that can be adequately defended in a few pages, of
course. At the very least, however, it seems obvious to me that Christian
culture could never generate any political and social order that, insofar as
it employed the mechanisms of state power, would not inevitably bring
about its own dissolution. Again, the translation of Christianity's original apocalyptic ferment into a cultural logic and social order produced a
powerful but necessarily unstable alloy. For all the good that it produced
in the shaping of Western civilization, it also encumbered the faith with
a weight of historical and cultural expectation wholly incompatible with
the gospel it proclaimed. When Christianity became not only a pillar of
culture, but also a support of the state, and thereby attached itself to that
human reality that necessarily sustains itself through the prudential use
of violence, it attempted to close the spiritual abyss separating Christ and
Pilate on the day of their confrontation in Jerusalem. At the same time,
however, it created a cultural reality animated or at least haunted by the

language of the gospel: the often tacit but always substantial knowledge that all of human power's pretenses and delusions and deceits have been exposed for what they are, and overthrown by God's incarnation as a man who was the victim of all the enfranchised religious, political, and social forces of his time and place. There was no way for such an alliance to avoid subverting itself.

I am not saying only — though I am saying — that the concrescence of Christianity into Christendom necessarily led in the West, over the course of centuries, to its gradual mortification, its slow attrition through internal stress, and finally its dissipation into the inconclusiveness of human history and the ephemerality of political orders. I am saying also that Christendom could not indefinitely survive the corrosive power of the revelation that Christianity itself had introduced into Western culture. Christian culture's often misunderstood but ultimately irrepressible consciousness of the judgment that was passed upon civil violence at Easter, by God, was always the secret antagonist of Christendom as a political order. Certainly, reflective intellectual historians have often enough noted the ironic continuity between the early modern rise of principled unbelief and the special "apocalyptic vocation" of Western culture; and the observations of Ernst Bloch and many others on the "inevitable" atheistic terminus of the Christian message are, while not exactly correct, at least comprehensible: for modern Western atheism is chiefly a Christian heresy, and could not have arisen in a non-Christian setting. Which yields the troubling thought that perhaps the historical force ultimately most destructive of the unity of the Christian culture of the West has been not principally atheism, materialism, capitalism, collectivism, or what have you — these may all be secondary manifestations of some deeper problem — but Christianity. Or, rather, I suppose I should say, an essential Christian impulse that, as a result of the contradictions inherent in Christendom, had become alienated from its true rationality and ultimate meaning.

ANYWAY, TO RETURN to my point of departure, a belief in providence is an ineffably precious thing at times. It seems to me rather absurd when Christians feel obliged either to celebrate or to lament the conversion of Constantine — to proclaim it either as the victory of the true faith over its persecutors or as the victory of the devil over the purity of the gospel — rather than simply to accept it and all its historical sequels as part of the mysterious story of grace working upon fallen natures: to love everything good and splendid that it produced, to deplore everything sordid and evil, and then to recognize as well (and this is the most challenging task of all) that the tale of Christendom's failure and defeat is also enfolded within those same workings of grace. Christendom was that cultural reality that was constitutionally, materially, morally, intellectually, and religiously disposed to hear the gospel as a cosmic truth, to which it was therefore always open, if not necessarily very obedient. For that, Christians would be churlish to be ungrateful. All of that, however, is now an exhausted history, one at least as tragic as it was joyous. The sheer banality of modern secular culture, and of its curiously rationalistic brutalities, may be a catastrophe for Western civilization; but it is also the inevitable result of a confusion between two orders that can never be one, and between which any real alliance can be at most a dialectic of reciprocal enrichment and impoverishment, in which each draws strength from the other only by surrendering something of its own essence. So perhaps the best moral sense Christians can make of the story of Christendom now, from the special vantage of its aftermath, is to recall that the gospel was never bound to the historical fate of any political or social order, but always claimed to enjoy a transcendence of all times and places. Perhaps its presence in human history should always be shatteringly angelic: it announces, even over against one's most cherished expectations of the present or the future, a truth that breaks in upon history, ever and again, always changing or even destroying the former things in order to make all things new. That being so, surely modern Christians should find some joy in being forced to remember that they are citizens of a kingdom not of this world, that here they have no enduring city, and that they are called to live as strangers and pilgrims on the earth.

# FORTY

# The True Helen

Having been stricken blind, he believed, for his poetic defamations of Helen — whom the Laconians of his day adored as a goddess — Stesichorus (c. 640–555 BC) regained his sight by composing an expiatory palinode, in which he proclaimed that the Spartan queen had never really eloped with Paris, that the Achaeans and the Trojans had fought their great war over a phantom, and that the true Helen (ever virtuous) had gone instead to Egypt to live under the protection of the pharaoh Proteus. Euripides (c. 480–406 BC) later elaborated upon the tale in his play *Helen*, claiming that Paris had abducted a mere *eidolon* fashioned from ether by Hera, while Hermes had carried the true Helen away to Memphis. And Herodotus (c. 484–425 BC) recorded a somewhat less fanciful variant of the story. But the legend is of far more ancient provenance.

It was known in Sparta even when Menelaus and Helen still reigned, and had begun to spread along the Eurotas Valley before Troy fell, and was the common lore of Lacedaemonian artisans and peasants before the ship bearing their king and queen sailed into the dark waters of the port of Gytheion. Helen herself heard of it the day after reaching harbor, from one of the Helot girls given to her as handmaidens for the triumphal procession to Therapne; and it provided her a few moments of amusement to think how foolish it made Menelaus look to suggest that he had returned from the war not with his recreant wife, but only with a dream of a woman. But for the next few days she gave the tale no thought.

In the following weeks, however, as the hideously gradual royal progress crept across the alluvial plains stretching between the looming gray ridges of Taygetus and Parnon, and wound along the edges of dry ravines, skirting farms and villages and olive groves, often accompanied by the discordant songs of the local rustics, Helen reflected upon the story more and more frequently, with an ever deeper fascination. Sometimes at night, after Menelaus had fallen asleep, she would leave her tent and look toward the far rises where distant shepherds' fires gleamed in the darkness like stars floating above the ocean, as if this land she despised had melted altogether away, and she allowed herself the fantasy that, rather than the dreary hovels of Sparta or the pale argillaceous foothills to the north or the prospect of the grim Dorian citadel awaiting her, the morning would reveal a fabulous land of sparkling sands, vast temples, emerald river basins . . .

How thoroughly she had forgotten Sparta's squalor, she often thought to herself during that journey. And already how remote seemed her memories of Troy's great golden walls, the opulence of Priam's palace, the high bright houses of the city. Now she must return to this rude, hard people she had never cared for, with their sullen satisfaction in their own terseness and their impatience with subtlety. She had loved the Trojans' oriental delight in periphrasis and elegant bombast, and their insatiable appetite for everything splendid, intricate, and oblique, and even the languid postures and inhuman aspects of their gods — like that hauntingly terrific image of Poseidon on Tenedos.

But perhaps, she thought, it really was all an illusion. Or perhaps she was the illusion, and her memories only the dreams of a phantom. True, she recalled it all. Above all she recalled, with an aching tenderness, how that lissome youth, with his long perfumed locks and his almost epicene beauty, had borne her away at night and lain with her for the first time among the fragrant grasses of the island of Kranai, while soft salt breezes poured over them from a sea made violet and sapphire in the morning twilight. Yet now even that seemed as if it had hardly ever happened. This was not an entirely new feeling. Even as a young girl, she had occasionally suspected that the world she knew was somehow false, that it was not her true home, that she was not who she seemed to be (even to herself). And now she found it almost plausible that every man who had embraced her, from that night on Kranai onward, had been like Ixion coupling with Nephele, and that she had all along been only her own phantom, and that her true self had been — and still was — somewhere else, very far away.

In the long years after her return to Sparta, Helen often dreamed that she was standing on the high walls of Troy, looking down to where the Scamander glittered among dark grasses and bone-white rocks as it flowed down to the blue and silver sea. But occasionally, and far more vividly, she dreamed that she was wandering at evening in the porches of a great temple built in a strange style, among immense statues of bulls and of gods with the faces of beasts — cats and crocodiles — and that far off she could see a verdant river plain, and still further off a sea of golden sand stretching to the horizon, shimmering beneath a sky of deep translucent blue and a moon that shone like burning glass.

WHEN THE SAMARITAN sorcerer Simon had found her in a brothel in Tyre, Helen had been barely more than a girl, though she had practiced her trade for seven years. Her uncommon beauty had made her a favorite of the house's clientele of merchants and sailors, as well as a source of considerable profits, and so she was astonished when she learned that this odd and troubling stranger, who it seemed made his living as some kind of itinerant holy man, had possessed the wherewithal to buy her away from her owners. At first she was afraid of him, though there was also something about him she found compelling: something in the entrancing limpidity of his dark eyes, and in the strangely melodious intonations of his voice (despite the harsh Levantine accent of his Greek), and in the guileless earnestness with which he disclosed to her his secret teachings about himself — and about her.

The same night in which he led her away from the brothel he sat with her on a low harbor wall and, as they gazed out at a brilliant moon shining upon the sea, he told her that he was God incarnate, who had descended from a divine Fullness, a realm of eternal light, to find her and deliver her from captivity, and through her to bring salvation to all. She was, he told her, the divine *Epinoia*, the first emanation of the divine mind, who had languished in bondage to malign angels age upon age, passing through countless lives of degradation, again and again, fettered in flesh and forgetfulness. Most of what he said she found incomprehensible. But he went on for hours, telling her of the divine All, of *Nous* and *Epinoia*, of the Hebrew Demiurge, of the Archons and Angels who had created the world and then enviously imprisoned her, their mother, in matter; he recounted how in each age she had been an object of contention among the angels, and so also among men, and how as Helen of Troy she had been fought over by gods and nations . . .

Here, at least, was a name she recognized. A few years before, a young tutor of wealthy merchants' sons had made surreptitious use of her services on several occasions, and on account of her name had related to her the story of the Trojan War more than once; and she, starved for any diversion, had taken it in and held it in memory. She could not help, therefore, but take some pleasure in the thought that she had once been the most beautiful and famous of women, the object of every desire. But she found the Samaritan's words preposterous.

In the year that followed, she traveled as his consort, spoke the words he gave her to speak, watched him perform wonders, and hid her boredom well during the long discourses with which he enchanted his followers. And sometimes she allowed herself to wonder whether indeed he had not, amid the nonsense of his elaborate mythologies, touched upon the truth about her, or upon some portion of the truth. Ever since childhood, and certainly ever since she had been made a prostitute by those who owned her, she had known moments when she had felt as if it were all a terrible dream, an illusion visited upon her by some invisible but redoubtable power of spite, and as if she were not truly there at all, and as if this world were not her true home. And even now she could not avoid sometimes feeling that perhaps her true self had always been — and still was — somewhere else, in a place of light, far away.

At night, she often dreamed of the brothel and of her misery there, and would sometimes wake in tears. Occasionally, though, and more vividly, she dreamed she was gazing from high city walls upon a shining river flowing across a plain of white rocks and dark grasses, down toward a pale strand where dark ships were drawn up upon the sands, and out into a vast glittering silver bay. And on very rare occasions, far more vividly still, she dreamed that she lay with a beautiful youth in the morning twilight, among fragrant island grasses stirred by soft breezes, fresh with salt, blowing in from a violet and sapphire sea.

# FORTY-ONE

# Dante Decluttered

*The Divine Comedy.* Dante Alighieri. Translated by Clive James.
Liverwright Publishing. 560 pages. $29.95.

For me, the appearance of Dan Brown's newest Robert Langdon novel,
its dust jacket adorned with Dante's flinty profile and a misappropri-
ated title, poses a purely historical question: Has there ever been another
case anywhere in the annals of the printed word of a literary figure as
majestically imposing as Dante — or of a work as monumental as the *In-
ferno* — featuring as the central "motif" (or theme, or plot device, or Mac-
Guffin, or whatever) in a book by a writer as ineffably horrid as Brown? (It
seems unlikely, by several orders of statistical magnitude.) Another question it prompts, and one probably of more immediate cultural concern,
is whether Dante today can command the attention of even a vanishingly
minuscule fraction of the readers that Brown can summon from the four
quarters of the wind with a single inept metaphor. (Here too, I suppose, the
answer is obvious.) One should not worry, of course. The flame of Dante's
greatness will continue to shine out, quietly but persistently, through our
current Dark Ages and long into the future, while the nerve-wracking
fluorescent glare of Brown's celebrity will turn pink and finally fade away
whenever its mercury is exhausted. At least we have to believe that, as long
as some vestige of civilization remains, readers will continue to return to
*The Divine Comedy* for its astonishing imaginative scope, its moral and
spiritual passion, its lyrical genius, and so on. The few valid complaints
against it, such as they are, will consistently recur: that the ghastly solidity
of Dante's imagined hells often seems so much more absorbing than those
shimmering saints floating in his pale impalpable heavens; that by the end,

dull theological discourses have largely crowded out the gripping personal narratives that had carried the poem all the way up from the dark wood of Dante's midlife wanderings to the terrestrial paradise where Beatrice was waiting for him; that Dante's final description of the Trinity encircled by the celestial rose conjures up an image about as engrossing as what one might see in a kaleidoscope bought on a boardwalk. But the poem will never lose its hold on the discerning.

All of which being said, it is nevertheless the case that the full power of the *Comedy* lies beyond the grasp of the great majority of readers, for two simple reasons: most must rely on inadequate translations, and very few indeed possess the specialized knowledge necessary to make sense of Dante's innumerable personal, political, historical, and theological allusions. Regarding the former problem, only so much can be done. No translator can ever satisfactorily render a poem of genius into another tongue. In English, there are now far more versions of the *Comedy* than can easily be recalled, ranging in tone from the torpid fustian of Cary and Longfellow to the ostentatious virtuosity of Laurence Binyon to the fluent plainness of C. H. Sisson. None of them can do more than adumbrate, often only very wanly, the glittering concision and constantly varying music of Dante's Tuscan. Regarding the latter problem, the solution established over the past several decades is that of the critical apparatus. The standard form of recent editions of the *Comedy* includes the original text in facing counterpoint to its translation, as well as an enormous number of footnotes or endnotes explaining every obscure reference to ancient metaphysics, medieval Italian politics, Dante's biography, and whatever else the modern reader is unlikely already to know much about. It is a somewhat awkward arrangement, but largely necessary. Even the very best recent renderings of the poem, such as that of the Hollanders or that of Anthony Esolen, require the reader to clamber over these critical barricades to get to the verse itself, and then still invite the eyes of the deficient linguist to flit back and forth between the original and translated texts. The result, inevitably, is one of (for want of a better word) deceleration. This is something of a pity. Much of the immediate poetic power of the *Comedy* lies in its unrelenting rapidity: the continuous stream of imagery, the compulsive movement of the narrative, and above all the unarrested coursing of the poetry itself, which perfectly unites consummate economy of language and overflowing fullness of aesthetic effect. For the most part, the books we read when we set out to read Dante are all immensely longer than the glorious book that Dante actually wrote. It is difficult properly to appreciate the grace, force, and agility of a great dancer when one can watch his dance only in slow motion, interspersed with numerous stills.

CLIVE JAMES'S new translation of the *Comedy* is an attempt to reverse the effect of the now standard critical editions. James has returned to the older model of English translations and has produced not another text consisting largely in Talmudic layerings and annotations, but a poem in English written upon the pattern of the original, meant to be taken in as a single continuous experience of an unfolding narrative: no halts, shifts in modality, or epicyclic reversions; no dizzying descents into the Dis of the critical apparatus or rapturous ascents to the unadulterated vision of the pure Italian text. It is a noble aspiration, if nothing else; and in many places it is a success. No one familiar with James's writings over the years can really doubt that he is an immensely talented, witty, intellectually voracious, readable, and (for the most part) judicious critic. He is also a novelist of some skill, and his memoirs (at least, in the first volume thereof) are splendid. And he is a genuinely accomplished poet. He has also, unfortunately, been guilty of a great deal of dreadful dabbling in popular culture, and his career as a television "personality" in Britain has involved him in numerous projects over which posterity, if it has so much as a shred of mercy, will draw the thickest veils of oblivion; his 1993 series *Fame in the Twentieth Century* was often so molar-grindingly fatuous that to call it froth would be vastly to exaggerate its substantiality.

Still, when he is good he can be very good. The best of his poetry exhibits an admirable combination of deceptively unpretentious diction and tense lyric control. At times, it has something of the plain yet almost oracular plangency of his beloved Philip Larkin, and perhaps something of the dry but oddly evocative eloquence of Keith Thomas as well. And it may be only because he is an Australian expatriate living in England, but I think some of his poetry reminds me of Peter Porter's. Whatever the case, he has an estimable gift. And, as he has demonstrated in such pieces as "Poem of the Year (1982)," he is quite adept at long verse forms. His version of the *Comedy* is not mannered in the way the older Victorian renderings were, even if it betrays certain mannerisms that smack a little too much of James and too little of Dante, but it is written in a formally strict English verse. It is also, for the most part, quite fluid, uncluttered, and even lovely. James has elected — God bless him and his issue forever — *not* to attempt to reproduce Dante's *terza rima*, a form that English simply does not possess a sufficient quantity of natural rhymes to sustain over extended periods. Instead he writes in quatrains, in iambic pentameter, at which he is an old practiced hand.

He also, however, takes liberties with the text, both larger and more numerous than he seems willing to own up to in his introduction. Principally, in order to avoid the delays created by long footnotes to the text, he has chosen to integrate much of the information that those notes would contain directly into the poem itself. He attempts to reduce these explanatory interpolations to their barest essentials — a few clipped phrases, sometimes only a few words — but they still have an inflationary effect on the narrative. In his desire to produce a poem, rather than an ocean of critical commentary with a bit of poetry bobbing about like flotsam at its center, James has still managed to give us a book that is substantially longer than Dante's original. The aim remains noble, but the execution is of rather mixed effect. Moreover, there is a certain capriciousness about James's choices regarding which information to convey and which to omit. I suppose that there was simply too much that he might have said regarding who Beatrice was, so he decided not to say anything at all.

IN THE END, HOWEVER, cavils aside, I think James's Dante is a success, in precisely the terms he has dictated for himself. It is a long poem, and naturally it is not of uniform quality throughout; and since it is a translation it necessarily shows occasional signs of forced phrasing; and some of the easy unpretentiousness gets a little too easy and unpretentious for me. But for the most part the verse is delightful, its flowing diction often apparently effortless, its cleverness obvious but not flamboyant. Needless to say, the scintillating beauty of Dante's poetry cannot be magically reproduced in another language; but it is possible to create an occasionally analogous loveliness that serves, if nothing else, as a genuinely reverent tribute to the original. And this James achieves in many places. Take, for instance, this passage from his rendering of the *Purgatorio*:

> A sweet unchanging air
> Fondled my brow, the soft force of a breeze
> Bending the trembling boughs to that point where
> The mountain's shadow first falls. At their ease
> The boughs were swayed, and still remained upright
> Enough for all the little birds to sing
> Out of the tree-tops where they spent the night
> And now turned their fine arts to welcoming
> The morning hours, ecstatic in the leaves
> Which gave an undertone to their sweet rhymes
> As, near Ravenna, the Sirocco cleaves

The air — one of the winds, in ancient times,
Locked up by Aeolus — and the pine wood
Murmurs from branch to branch.

I suppose I could do without that last, somewhat needless amplification upon Dante's *quand' Ëolo scilocco fuor discioglie*, but I would still say that there is some real element of Dante's music here: the union of terseness and delicacy, of simplicity and elegance. And, taken solely as English verse, it is very enjoyable. That is more than enough justification for including James's Dante among one's favored translations of the *Comedy*, and even for reading it through once or twice, just for the pleasure it affords. There will always be time for footnotes on other occasions.

# FORTY-TWO

# Emergence and Formation

A few months ago, I began reading a book by the sociologist Christian Smith called *What Is a Person?* — concerning which, though it is very interesting, I have nothing of consequence to report just at the moment. I mention it here only because its early chapters reminded me of a topic upon which I have intended to write for some time. Among the most crucial supports for Smith's central argument, you see, is an extremely strong concept of natural "emergence": that is, the seemingly simple idea that in nature there are composite realities whose peculiar properties and capacities emerge from the interaction of their elements, even though those properties and capacities do not reside as such in those elements themselves. An emergent whole, in other words, is more than — or at any rate different from — the sum of its parts; it is not simply the consequence of an accumulation of discrete powers added together extrinsically, but the effect of a specific ordering of relations among those powers that produces something entirely new within nature. This proposition is, of course, quite true in a general sense; but it is also quite false in several specific senses, and most especially in the sense that Smith gives it. According to him, an emergent reality is one that, though remaining ever dependent upon the native properties of the elements composing it, nevertheless possesses new characteristics that are wholly "irreducible" to those properties. But this is certainly false. At least, as a claim made solely about physical processes, organisms, and structures — in purely material terms — it cannot possibly be true. If nothing else, it is a claim strictly precluded by most modern scientific prejudice. From a genuinely "physicalist" perspective, there are no such things as emergent properties in this sense, discontinuous from the properties of the prior causes from which they arise; anything, in principle, must be *reducible*, by a series of "geometrical" steps, to the physical attributes of its ingredients.

Those who think otherwise are, in most cases, merely confusing irreducibility with identity. Smith, for instance, uses the example of water, which, though composed of the two very combustible elements hydrogen and oxygen, possesses the novel property of extinguishing fire; therefore, says Smith, water "is irreducible to that of which it is composed." But it is nothing of the sort. Yes, water's resistance to combustion is not *identical* with any property resident in either hydrogen or oxygen molecules, but it is most definitely *reducible* to those special molecular properties that, in a particular combination, cause hydrogen and oxygen to negate one another's combustible propensities. A seemingly more promising example adduced by Smith is that of a computer, which (he notes) is composed of silicon, metal, plastic, electrical impulses, and so on, but which possesses functions that are not present in any of its parts and that are qualitatively different from a mere aggregation of the properties of its parts in some sort of total sum. Here, however, Smith compounds his earlier error by failing to notice that what distinguishes a computer's powers from those individually possessed by its various elements is not any *emergent* property at all, but rather the causal influence of a creative intellect acting upon those elements from without. Taken as a purely physical phenomenon, nothing that a computer does — as distinct, that is, from what an intending mind does with a computer — is anything more than the mathematically predictable result of all its physical antecedents. At the purely material level, whatever is emergent is also reducible to that from which it emerges; otherwise, "emergence" is merely the name of some kind of magical transition between intrinsically disparate realities.

In any event, I have no great quarrel with Smith. In the end, he is quite correct that a computer is not reducible without remainder to its physical components. He is even more correct in arguing — as is the purpose of his book — that human personality is not reducible to purely physical forces and events. The problem with his argument is merely a matter of the conceptual model of causation that he has adopted. For, in the end, what reductionism fails to account for, and in fact fails even to see, is not the principle of emergence, but the reality of formal causality. In the case of the computer, for instance, its functions are more than the sum of the properties inherent in its physical constituents because a further, adventitiously informing causality, itself directed by a final causality, has assumed those physical constituents into a purposive structure that in no meaningful sense can be said to have emerged from them. (The captious physicalist, of course, would want at this point to assert that the mind and actions of the computer's designer are themselves only physical events, and so the computer is still emergent from and reducible to a larger ensemble of material causes; but that is both beside the point and, as it happens, entirely wrong.)

WHY IS THIS DISTINCTION particularly important? Principally because it seems quite clear to me that there are realities in nature that are indeed irreducible to their physical basis, and that this fact renders materialism — or physicalism, or naturalism — wholly incredible. Existence itself, for what it is worth, is the prime example of an indubitable truth about the world that is irreducible to physical causes (since any physical causes there might be must already exist). But consciousness is perhaps an example more easily grasped. And, just to refresh our memories, we should recall how many logical difficulties a materialist reduction of mind entails.

The most commonly invoked is the problem of *qualia*, of that qualitative sense of "what it is like" that constitutes the immediate intuitive form of subjectivity, and that poses philosophical difficulties that even the tireless and tortuous bluster of a Daniel Dennett cannot entirely obscure. There is also the difficulty of abstract concepts, which become more dazzlingly difficult to explain the more deeply one considers how entirely they determine our conscious engagement with the world. And of course, there is the problem of reason: for to reason about something is to proceed from one premise or proposition or concept to another, in order ideally to arrive at some conclusion, and in a coherent sequence whose connections are determined by the semantic content of each of the steps taken; but, if nature is mere physical mechanism, all sequences of cause and effect must be determined entirely by the impersonal laws governing the material world. One neuronal event can cause another as a result of physical necessity, but certainly not as a result of logical necessity; and the connections among the brain's neurons cannot generate the symbolic and conceptual connections that compose an act of consecutive logic, because the brain's neurons are connected organically and interact physically, not conceptually. And then there is the transcendental unity of consciousness, which makes such intentional uses of reason possible and which poses far greater difficulties for the materialist than any mere neurological "binding problem." Then, of course, there is perhaps the greatest difficulty of all, intentionality, what the great Franz Brentano regarded as the supreme "mark of the mental," inseparable from every act of consciousness: the mind's directedness, its "aboutness," its capacity for meaning, by which it thinks, desires, believes, represents, wills, imagines, or otherwise orients itself toward a specific object, purpose, or end. On the one hand, the mind knows nothing in a merely passive way, but always has an end or meaning toward which it is purposively directed, as toward a final cause; yet, on the other, there is absolutely no intentional reciprocity between the mind and the objects of its intentions (that is, thoughts can be directed toward things, but things, at least taken as purely material events, cannot be directed toward thoughts). Intentionality is finite and concerned with its objects under specific aspects, whereas material reality is merely an infinite catenation of accidental events; and so the *specific* content of the mind's intentions must be determined by consciousness alone. One could never derive the specific *meaning* of a given physical event from the event itself, not even a brain event, because in itself it *means* nothing at all; even the most minute investigation of its physical constituents and instances could never yield the particular significance that the mind represents it as having. And so on.

Not that there is room here to argue these points. Nonetheless, there are very good reasons why the most consistent materialist philosophers of mind — when, that is, they are not attempting to get around these difficulties with nonsolutions like "epiphenomenalism" or incoherently fantastic solutions like "panpsychism" — have no choice in the end but to deny that such things as *qualia* or intentionality or even consciousness as such truly exist at all. The heroic absurdism that, in differing registers, constitutes the blazingly incandescent core of the thought of Daniel Dennett, Alex Rosenberg, Paul and Patricia Churchland, and other impeccable materialists of the same general kind follows from the recognition — not very philosophically sophisticated as a rule, but astute nonetheless — that consciousness can exist within the world of nature only if matter is susceptible of formation by a higher causality, one traditionally called "soul." And the soul, as such a formal cause, is precisely that which cannot simply "emerge."

# FORTY-THREE

# *From a Lost World*

This year, 2014, marks the centenary of the beginning of the end. It was in July of 1914 that European civilization entered its final death throes, the last convulsions of which would not subside for more than thirty years. After that, not even the illusions remained. The great Western project of secular modernity that had begun with the wars of the emergent nation-state back in the sixteenth and seventeenth centuries (conflicts that history, with her superb talent for hidden ironies, calls the "Wars of Religion") had reached its logically ineluctable conclusion, carrying away the feeble remnants of Christendom on tides of human blood. Since then, the great moral mission of western European society has been to arrange the debris in as attractive a style as possible, and to try to translate irreversible decline and disenchantment into some kind of humane ethos. Even though, however, we cannot help but *commemorate* the start of the Great War this year, it is not an event we can really *remember* — and not only because practically no one is now alive who has any personal recollection of it. We owe some sort of reverent reflection to those who perished over the following four years (at least, I like to think we do), but the sheer scale of the cataclysm simply defies the scope of any rational imagination. There are those still among us, true, who have vivid memories of the utter brutality of the Second World War. My father, who passed away just this last year, lived through some of the most savage fighting in the European theater, during the push across France into Germany — in the Vosges Mountains, at Bitche, street to street in Heilbronn, and so on — and he experienced horrors that he never related to me or my brothers when we were growing up, but that left an indelible impress upon his mind. Yet even he, he told me more than once, found it impossible imaginatively to encompass the sheer barbarity and madness of the Great War.

For myself, in my private meditations, if I want to do some sort of justice to the memory of those whose lives were stolen away by the monstrous imbecility of the war that began in 1914, I have to think in epitomes. One can lament millions of deaths, but not really properly mourn them; it is possible, though, to fix one's thoughts and, to some degree, one's emotions on certain individuals. And lately, as I have been considering this approaching centennial, I have been thinking repeatedly about two figures, out of the very many who might have occurred to me: Henri Alban-Fournier (1886–1914), the French novelist who wrote under the name of Alain-Fournier, and George Butterworth (1885–1916), the English composer.

AS THEIR DATES INDICATE, neither man lived long; and, consequently, neither left behind him a particularly weighty collection of completed works. Both produced art of extraordinarily wistful tenderness, in some ways unfinished or even immature, but perhaps for that very reason almost excruciatingly evocative; and everything they created bore unambiguous signs of genius. But there is not much of it. Alain-Fournier is remembered principally as the author of a single novel, *Le Grand Meaulnes* (1913), a small glittering masterpiece whose popularity has never waned in France, and a book that is among the most widely and frequently translated of the twentieth century. Butterworth's entire published oeuvre consists of three short exquisitely lyrical orchestral pieces — *Two English Idylls* (1911), *A Shropshire Lad* (1911), and *The Banks of Green Willow* (1913) — a song cycle of poems by W. E. Henley called *Love Blows as the Wind Blows*, which exists in three variants (1911–1914), and twenty-six other song settings (many of poems by A. E. Housman); there also exists a suite for string quartet (1910), but it is never performed or recorded. One can read Alain-Fournier's novel in an afternoon, and can listen to all of Butterworth's music (including all three versions of the song cycle) in just under two hours. And yet it would be difficult to find two artists whose work more forcefully summons up a sense of what the Great War and its historical sequels destroyed forever. Exactly why this is so is not easy to say. *Le Grand Meaulnes*, for example, is a book whose hold on the reader's imagination seems so much greater than the sum of its parts. Every young person — or, at any rate, every young man — should read it around the age of nineteen, when the emotions it touches upon are still new. The plot hovers beautifully, if perhaps a little preposterously, between sentimental romance and fairy tale; and at no point does it descend from its dreamy altitudes down to the hard earth of a France on the verge of a devastating war. At its center is the tale of a young man one night happening upon a mysterious chateau — where celebrations for a wedding that will not take place are being held, and where he falls hopelessly in love with a beautiful girl — but which he cannot find again the next day or for a long time thereafter. And, when at last he is reunited with his lost love, the complications of the plot that ensue are both tragic and almost hallucinatory in their remoteness from reality. As for Butterworth's music, its lyricism is so lush and earnest that only a young man could have written it. This is not to say that it is saccharine or gushing, like those interminable chromatic meanderings of Delius; it is rigorous in form, and no piece lasts a second longer than it should. But it is also an innocent music, perfectly timeless in its flowing beauty, betraying no hint of the darkness gathering on the horizon; and it is absolutely saturated by a feeling of gentle melancholy, of a longing for something fading away, or already lost.

For me, this is where the peculiar genius of both men lay: in their ability to evoke a sense of something always just at one's back, which one cannot turn around quite quickly enough to glimpse — the sense of a lost country at whose border one can only drift, or of a lost memory whose tremulous edge one cannot quite grasp. Theirs is an art pervaded by the ache of exile, the feeling of something now gone that was always both perilously fragile and deeply loved: a vanished childhood or early youth; departed innocence; the loveliness of rural France and England, with their woodlands and copses soon to be cleared away for development, and their fields and country lanes soon to be covered over by metaled motorways; an older social consensus, sustained by a rosier set of illusions; a fairyland fading in the light of dawn; a squandered and immemorial paradise; or whatever else. Above all, in long retrospect, it summons up images of a generation of children who grew up in the long, serene Edwardian spring, but who would not grow old enough to have children of their own.

PERHAPS SOME OF THAT is attributable to the accidents of personal history. Had either Alain-Fournier or Butterworth lived a full life, the symbolic power of his youthful works might not now seem so overwhelming. But the former was only twenty-seven when he died in battle near Vaux-lès-Palameix (his body remained unidentified until 1991), and the latter only thirty-one when he was killed in a trench near the Somme (his body was never recovered); and it is difficult to encounter their art without the transience of their lives at least *modulating* how one reacts to it. But, really, that is not the only reason for the effect their works have. Both men, despite their youth, possessed a positive genius for nostalgia. That is a significant gift. All memory is tragic in the end: the failures, humiliations, betrayals, sufferings, or calamities that we recall for the most part cannot now be undone; the joys, triumphs, discoveries, and raptures that we recall are for the most part long gone. All memory is haunted by the traces of a fall from grace or of an Eden to which we cannot return. So any artist who masters the medium of nostalgia has the power to render us all but defenseless. It is impossible to outgrow Alain-Fournier or Butterworth, no matter how sophisticated one's sensibility might become, because the further one is removed from the naïveté of youth, the more deeply one is moved by recollections of the enchantments of innocence. That is why both men serve as such painfully vibrant symbols of the world that was lost in the first half of the last century. For those of a mind to do so, I recommend marking the centenary of the Great War at some point in the coming year by reading *Le Grand Meaulnes* and listening to all of Butterworth's surviving compositions. It would be very hard to think of two figures whose art and whose lives, taken together, so perfectly remind us of an innocence that perhaps our entire culture has now lost — and remind us also that some things, once lost, can never be recovered or restored.

# FORTY-FOUR

# A Phantom's Visit (C.B.)

I could tell at once that he was a ghost. There was a certain translucency about him: the sallow light of the lamp on my library desk shone out not only behind him but through him, acquiring an emerald tint from the specter of his velvet smoking jacket as it did so. I also, nearly as quickly, recognized whose ghost he was. I knew that fierce gaunt face from the few nineteenth-century photographs that we have of him. It was the latter realization, rather than the former, that caused a gasp of wonder to escape my lips. To meet a ghost has never seemed to me a particularly astonishing eventuality; but to meet one of such eminence, and in my own home . . .

"You must excuse me," he said after a moment, in a voice that some-how was both perfectly audible and yet, at the same time, seemed to em-anate from a very great distance. "It was not my intention to cause you alarm." He had only the slightest trace of a Parisian accent, I noticed.

I assured him that, to the contrary, he had done me a great honor by dropping by.

He smiled a bleak smile. "Neither was that my intention," he said, turning his eyes to the shelves nearest him. "Sometimes, when I feel the need to walk about the world again, I find myself drawn to places where copies of my books can be found. I see you own many" — he swept a silent finger across the spines of several volumes — "and I felt a very palpable pull upon me."

He looked at me again and drifted a few feet nearer. "I am touched. Still, I should not have intruded had I known you would come in here so late at night. After all, the greatest virtue of the dead is their silence. Hav-ing passed beyond the boundaries of the utterable, and having thereby lost the privilege of utterance, they can no longer bore the living with tedious inventories of regrets or, worse, burden them with the fruits of hard-won wisdom. We are supposed to keep our quiet vigils in that inner sanctuary into which the living must not peer and from which not so much as a whisper should escape. So forgive me for stepping through the veil that hides the last and most terrible mystery from view. And, to tell the truth, it always causes some awkwardness in the politer circles of deceased society when one of us cavalierly disregards the cardinal rule of postmortem etiquette."

I assured him again that I was in fact delighted to have found him in my house. "To meet greatness in the flesh . . . ," I began to say, but then caught myself. He seemed not to notice my embarrassment, but I felt the need to divert the conversation into another channel as quickly as possible. "When you make your visits from . . . from the other side, are you ever surprised by the current state of things?"

With something like a contemptuous laugh, he drifted away again, to look at the books on another shelf. "Things are more or less what I always assumed they would be," he said after a moment. "Modern man is as he ever was. His chief distinction is his disbelief in original sin and, consequently, his inability to strive against it. And by disbelief I do not mean some sort of brave rejection of the doctrine, some defiant demand flung at heaven for possession of one's own soul; I mean merely the impotence of an imagination that finds the very notion of sin incomprehensible, the conscience of a man who is sure that, whatever sin might be, it surely lies lightly upon a soul as decent as his own, and can be brushed off with a single casual stroke of a primly gloved hand; I mean a habitual insensibility to the illuminations and chastisements of beauty, a condition of being wholly at home in a world from which mystery and sin and glory have all been banished, and in which spiritual wretchedness has become material contentment. To that man, the bliss that calls to him in the beautiful would seem only an intolerable accusation, its gracious invitations only a perverse condemnation of his well-earned and lavishly vegetal happiness."

He paused. His voice had begun to grow harsh, and I had the impression that he had surprised himself. He looked at me with a mild expression. "Forgive a phantom his prejudices." I said that there was nothing to forgive.

"But really," he said, his voice almost immediately becoming angry again, "how else should I think of the world into which I was born? How else can I make sense of that complacent love of moral squalor, that luxuriant triteness, that was the single spiritual achievement of that age? Where every bourgeois had been poisoned by the banality of Voltaire — that philosopher of the concierges — and where every good citizen heard the voice of progress and enlightenment in the inane prattle of journalists, with all their childish laicism?"

I could see that he was becoming lost in his own reflections. He was no longer talking to me so much as to himself; and, in fact, he turned his back to me as he continued:

"How did they ever come to that place, those desolate multitudes, gathered under Satan's ashen skies? It was never any use asking them. They remembered only, as in a dream, departing from frozen harbors bathed in twilight, sailing over dark waters lit by a sickly moon, in groaning barks borne on torpid currents past shores where sheer granite cliffs or walls of iron-gray thorns forbade any landing, and at last drawing up into those oleaginous waters, alongside dreary quays wanly gleaming with rime. If they could only have cast their minds further back, perhaps they might have recalled a lost paradise: green and yellow meadows stirred by tender winds, umbrageous forests and emerald groves, glass-blue mountain peaks melting into azure skies, glittering bays whose diamond waters break in jade and turquoise surges on sands like powdered alabaster — where the rain falls gently, and is transformed by the setting sun into shimmering curtains of gold — where, beyond verdant valleys and limestone caves, lies a palace filled with every delight the senses can endure, enclosing garden courtyards where crystal fountains splash in porphyry basins, intoxicating perfumes hang upon the breezes, undying flowers of every hue shine out amid the greenery's blue shadows. . . .

"If only they could have recalled. . . . But, of course, they did not wish to do so. Occasionally they might hear a distant dolorous echo, a faint fading rumor of forgotten bliss, carried to them over the purple sea, but they only turned away and thrust their hands into their pockets, anxiously feeling for their purses. Their triumph was their diabolical drabness, their pitiless sobriety. And what is perfect sobriety other than the rejection of love, of communion — of the God who is the love that gives itself with the recklessness of a drunkard? They wanted no paradise more opulent than the contentment they had already achieved."

Now he did turn to me again.

"The moral quantum within my own dissipations . . . which were never so extravagant as I made out in my poems. To play the flaneur, the dandy delicately glistening upon the boulevards, can be an act of rebellion against an age in which dreariness has become the face of sensualism, in which men cosset their appetites precisely by coarsening and deadening them. For what the modern age has taught us is that the kingdom of hell is essentially a respectable place, where the devil is best served by remaining incognito, where sin and remorse and penitence trouble no one with their curbside importunities — 'Please, sir, only a sou!' — where no one frets about angels or devils, where all good men apply themselves to becoming machines among machines, without sin because without souls.

"What world, after all, could be more respectable than one without sin? Where the only transgression anyone truly deplores is to deny that the highest happiness is prosperous mediocrity? Where the only indecency is to suggest that, among the ashes of the modern heart, there might linger a spark of divinity that, blown upon with but a little breath, could be kindled into flame?"

I said nothing, but merely nodded.

"In such a world," he continued, "those who uphold public morals and serve the public weal do so only for Satan's ends. They can rise to no higher god than he. They are guardians of the world of commerce, where everything is valued only as it might be bought or sold, where all giving and receiving are governed by the satanic law that each must try to take more than he gives, where everything is plunged into the abysmal shadow of that insatiable Typhon called America — that gaslit desert of barbarism, with its infantile, gigantic, exuberant vulgarity, its monstrously guileless delight in affluence, its omnivorous vacuity." He ceased speaking suddenly, looking all at once abashed. "Have I offended you?" he asked.

"Not in the least."

He smiled, almost forlornly, then turned back to my books again. "May I borrow a copy of *The Wind in the Willows*?" he asked after several moments, quite unexpectedly.

"Yes," I replied, "of course."

# FORTY-FIVE

# Nabokov's Supernatural Secret

In 2009 the remains of Vladimir Nabokov's unfinished last novel, *The Original of Laura*, were published, more than three decades after the dying author had asked his son Dmitri to destroy them. In 2012 Nabokov's first large literary work, a play entitled *The Tragedy of Mister Morn*, appeared in English translation, nearly nine decades after the author had set the Russian text aside. Both releases were occasions of some excitement even though, to be honest, neither work was an especially astonishing performance. The novel, even in its fragmentary form, amply confirms that the late decline in Nabokov's literary powers — flickeringly evident in *Ada* (1968), blazingly obvious in *Transparent Things* (1972) and *Look at the Harlequins!* (1974) — was both inexorable and steep. The play, on the other hand, is full of glints and glimmers of the literary triumphs to come, and it contains certain motifs — an exiled king incognito, for instance — that would flower magnificently in more mature works; but in itself it is inconsequential. Nabokov is something of an addictive substance to the susceptible, however, and his admirers tend to be grateful for even the meagerest scraps of "new" material (even his lepidopterological papers have enthusiasts who, I think it fair to guess, have little real interest in entomology). What is really significant about these two most recent releases, it seems to me, is that, taken together, they afford us privileged glimpses of, respectively, the somber dusk and rosy dawn of a literary career that during its long golden day was among the most mysteriously captivating of the twentieth century. First as a Russian émigré in Western Europe writing in his native tongue and then as an American writing in English, Nabokov produced a number of books that, simply as feats of narrative enchantment, came perilously close to perfection. His greatest works — a category that unquestionably comprises *The Defense* (1930), *The Gift* (1938), *Lolita* (1955), *Pale Fire* (1962), and *Speak, Memory* (1967), and that arguably also includes *Despair* (1934), *Invitation to a Beheading* (1936), *The Real Life of Sebastian Knight* (1941), and *Pnin* (1957) — bear witness to their author's almost uncanny ability to make his own delight in the act of creation immediately felt by his reader. But precisely how he achieved his effects is not always entirely clear.

IN PART, this is because, as an artist, Nabokov was about as *sui generis* as they come. He may not have been quite the parthenogenetic marvel he seemed to imagine he was (to hear him, he had never been influenced by anyone at all as a writer, but had sprung fully formed from Zeus's brow with a pen in one hand and a butterfly net in the other), but it is certainly true that his sensibility and his craft were so distinctively his own that he cannot be classed in any school or tradition. He can be *compared* to other writers, of course, but the analogies always seem oblique at best. Perhaps, in one way or another, he is "like" Kafka, Joyce, Proust, Musil, Svevo, Walser, Gombrowicz, Krúdy, Beckett, Cortázar, Borges, or Robbe-Grillet — or Flaubert, Pushkin, Sterne, Lewis Carroll, or Gogol — or Bruno Schulz, Boris Vian, Mikhail Bulgakov, Norman Douglas, Sadegh Hedayat, or Machado de Assis — or Platonov and the Odessa school of Olesha, Babel, Krzhizhanovsky, and Ilf and Petrov — or . . . (and so on). But, really, he is much more *unlike* them, and unlike anyone else too, and all attempts at plausible homology quickly dissolve, having provided no real insight into the strange power of his art.

This is not to say that it is wholly unaccountable. The formal mastery of Nabokov's best work is obvious. A great part of the pleasure his books afford comes from his prose, which in English often seems all the more beguiling for its ever so slightly foreign accent. There is also his gift for exquisitely rendered details, astonishing concrete images, and unexpected metaphors. He was also a brilliant humorist. And one can scarcely exaggerate the elegant complexity of which he was capable, or the unerring sense of order (for instance, in the way he beautifully linked together the glittering miniatures that constitute *Pnin*, a novel so charming that one hardly notices how brilliant it is). Yet, all that being granted, there remains something more. It is not solely the formal ingenuity of his writing that enchants us, but also an element present in the text that seems to exceed the form of the text altogether. Or perhaps it is not so much present as enticingly hinted at: something always out of sight, just beyond the boundaries of the book. At its most absorbing, his is an art of the palpably withheld, of a story truer than the one he is telling, constantly adumbrated but never quite disclosed, hiding below the surface of the words on the page, or far below many layers of narrative involution. This impression of some mysterious surfeit — of an answer or a secret at once delightfully and infuriatingly elusive, or of an invisible context within which the book must mean something more than it seems to mean on the surface — reaches its consummation in that labyrinth of mirrors that is *Pale Fire*, a work of such exuberant intricacy that no satisfactory solution to all its enigmas will ever be produced (though Nabokov clearly had one in mind). But it is a sense imparted in some measure by almost all of his books. And in recent years many critics, who on the whole had been reluctant to address Nabokov's more "spiritual" preoccupations, have come around at last to the realization that a rather crucial ingredient of his art's peculiar power over our imaginations is what is often called his "metaphysics." That is not really the right word, though. Nabokov had no metaphysics in the strictly technical sense, since he had neither the patience nor the aptitude for abstractions. It is better to say, still somewhat vaguely, that the "secret" concealed in Nabokov's texts, of which the reader catches only occasional, fleeting, and obscure glimpses, is a supernatural one.

NABOKOV SAW patterns everywhere, and in everything: art, nature, history, individual and collective fates . . . chess (at which he was a master, but in which he took his principal pleasure by devising exquisitely delicate problems to be solved on paper). His whole experience of reality was shaped by pervasive teleological intuitions, and his response to those intuitions was one of delight and curiosity, as well as a happy conviction that beyond all the patterns he could see lay more extensive and deeper and more wonderful patterns, which he could only sense. And, the greater the complexity, subtlety, and grace of the patterns he perceived, the more certain he was of the presence of creative intelligence in the fabric of things, a dimension of intentional meaning at once communicating itself and yet concealing itself from direct scrutiny. One might almost say that, for him, there really was no ultimate formal distinction to be made between nature and art: practically everything is, if approached with a sufficiently responsive sensibility, a poetic achievement. I suspect that this explains his distaste, as a lepidopterist, for any purely genetic, molecular taxonomy of the creatures he studied so lovingly. He remained to the last defiantly faithful to an essentially morphological approach to his butterflies not because, as is often said, he was the last old-fashioned autodidactic gentleman naturalist, but because he believed that one could not penetrate the mysteries of nature without cultivating in oneself a feel for nature's endlessly ingenious artistry. And, if that seems a little quaint, I would point out that it was his fastidious, fatiguingly microscopic attentiveness to morphology that allowed him to postulate back in 1945 not only that the group of lepidoptera known as *Polyommatus* blues was not quite the cohesive biological family it was thought to be, but that the blues had, over millions of years, arrived in the Americas in five successive waves from Asia, over the Bering Strait. It seemed an extravagant hypothesis at the time, but the newest techniques in gene sequencing have, in just the past few years, confirmed it in every detail, right down to the order of the separate migrations. (Perhaps his own vindication by geneticists would have improved Nabokov's opinion of molecular biology.)

More to the point, this fascination with form accounts for Nabokov's sense that the natural world everywhere exhibited signs of conscious artistry, of the most elegant — and sometimes whimsical — kind. He was captivated by instances of mimicry, for example, especially when the result seemed to be far more accomplished than evolutionary imperatives could possibly warrant: the appearance of oozing poisons imitated "by bubble-like macules on a wing (complete with pseudo-refraction)," or a moth resembling a certain kind of wasp so exactly as to walk and move its antennae in ways alien to moths, or a butterfly in whose shape and color "not only were all the details of a leaf beautifully rendered but markings mimicking grub-bored holes were generously thrown in," and so on. For him, concepts like "natural selection" and "the struggle for survival" were simply explanatorily inadequate "when a protective device was carried to a point of mimetic subtlety, exuberance, and luxury far in excess of a predator's power of appreciation." And it was chiefly here, in what seemed to him a constant victory of the beautiful over the needful in nature, and in the specular harmonies and morphological allusions that passed between species, that he believed he had found signs of something like a conjuror's pleasure in complex illusions. "I discovered in nature," he wrote, "the non-utilitarian delights that I sought in art. Both were a form of magic, both were a game of intricate enchantment and deception." And where there is artistry, surely, there must be consciousness.

But what does that mean? What sort of consciousness was it, precisely, whose workings Nabokov thought he could discern in all the glorious and devious patterns by which he found himself surrounded? One answer — not particularly satisfying perhaps, and certainly not final, but correct nonetheless — is "spirits." There was perhaps more than a hint of Russian silver age spiritualism in Nabokov's thinking, a propensity inherited from his mother (who, he said, always possessed a powerful sense of the reality of the other world); but, more to the point, there was also a tendency toward a kind of idealism, a conceptually vague but imaginatively rich picture of all of reality as a communion of minds. He believed not only in the immortality of the soul, but in the soul's participation in the design of things; and he suspected that those souls who have passed beyond this life have been set free to take a more deliberate part, from the other side of the loom (so to speak), in weaving the larger pattern of reality. Nabokov's belief in fate, which ran very deep indeed, was of a piece with this peculiar view of things. No less than in nature and in art, he thought he could see the weavers' hands in the destinies of individual lives. He seemed to believe, for instance, that his father and a certain foreordained bullet had been circling one another in a kind of grim dance for many years — with occasional premonitory near approaches — until at last they converged in Berlin in 1922, where Nabokov's father was killed by an assassin. And, frankly, Nabokov's own private history was so extravagantly improbable and yet so eerily symmetrical that it would have been very odd indeed had he not felt that the whole course of his experiences had been elaborately orchestrated for him. His life unfolded as a kind of chiasm, with four distinct phases of roughly two decades each: an Edenic youth of vast wealth, idyllic estates, and pure imaginative and aesthetic delight; an anxious young adulthood of penury, exile, and finally grave danger; a stable but only moderately comfortable middle age in a new homeland, where his reputation slowly began to take root and blossom; and then, unexpectedly, a last period of vast wealth, idyllic mountain meadows, and pure imaginative and aesthetic delight once more. It was no mere figure of speech when, in *Speak, Memory,* Nabokov spoke of those moments when he could contemplate the "magic carpet" of his memories, as though outside of time, and feel a "thrill of gratitude . . . to the contrapuntal genius of human fate or to tender ghosts humoring a lucky mortal."

THIS, AT ANY RATE, is one very large part of that secret — that seeming surfeit of meaning in Nabokov's works — of which I spoke above. His are in a significant sense haunted books. Far more often than one might suspect, especially on a first reading, there are ghosts hovering just beyond the margins of the page. They are not the phantoms of horror fiction, and they rarely if ever intrude too forcibly upon the action of the tale. Rather, they are subtle beings, possessed of enchanting powers, quiet presences mysteriously and winsomely insinuating themselves into the narrative, and even on occasion into the very form of the text. In the short story "The

Vane Sisters" (1951), for instance, only the most alert of readers is likely to notice that the tale's two eponymous ladies (both deceased) have playfully invaded its final paragraph, quite unbeknownst to its putative author, with an acrostic message. And, unless one is paying close attention, one will fail to see that the narrator of *Transparent Things* is in fact a dead man, and that in the book's final sentence he is gently ushering the soul of his protagonist into the next life. Even when the ghosts are somewhat more recessive presences in the text, though, they are often vital to the action, and the reader who is wholly unaware of them will inevitably miss something of the largely invisible design that expresses itself, however circuitously or ambiguously, in the visible design of the narrative. Again and again, Nabokov's books prove to be, if not transparencies, at least translucencies, luminous veils through whose secondary patterns the primary patterns of the other world can be descried. I agree with Brian Boyd, for instance, in principle if not in every detail, that *Pale Fire* is as much a story about the threshold between this life and the next, and about those who cross that threshold in either direction, as it is a brilliantly hilarious fantasy about a poet writing his final masterpiece and a lunatic who fantasizes that he is an exiled king. Specifically, I agree that a pervasive but unseen presence throughout the book is John Shade's dead daughter Hazel, and that the *Vanessa atalanta* butterfly that briefly plucks at her father's sleeve just a few moments before his death is quite likely her revenant.

Whatever the case, all these hauntings — all the silent disembodied presences, all the faint spectral whispers and gleams and vibrations at the edges and in the interstices of the texts — are expressions of Nabokov's convictions that consciousness is something like the ground or essence of all reality and that the soul, being pure consciousness, is indestructible. If, though, these convictions possessed any more precise theoretical content than that, there is no record of precisely what it was. The nearest thing we have is a tantalizingly promising sentence in his most "metaphysically" suggestive piece, the lecture "The Art of Literature and Commonsense": "That human life is but a first installment of the serial soul and that one's individual secret is not lost in the process of earthly dissolution, becomes something more than an optimistic conjecture, and even more than a matter of religious faith, when we remember that only commonsense rules immortality out." But just here, poised on what appears to be the brink of Nabokov's most explicit pronouncement upon the soul, two pages have disappeared from the sole surviving typescript of the text; when the argument resumes on the far side of the caesura, it has already moved on to another topic (which irresistibly suggests, at least to me, some sort of mischievous posthumous editing on Nabokov's part). Perhaps the missing pages would only have reinforced the enigma. As I have noted, precise philosophical formulations were not in Nabokov's line. What we can say with near certainty is that he spoke for himself in the epigraph he set at the beginning of *Invitation to a Beheading* (attributed there to the wholly fictional Pierre Delaland): "Comme un fou se croit Dieu, nous nous croyons mortels." We can also reasonably assert that he thought of the passage from this life to the next as — at least, for most souls — a wonderful transformation, in which consciousness achieves a richer existence, a far greater fullness than it enjoys within the enclosures of embodied life: to die is to awaken into an incomparably more expansive reality, a vaster dimension of thought and sensibility. He may even have regarded this metamorphosis as something like a necessary phase within the soul's "natural cycle." Nabokov was quite adamant in rejecting the suggestion that his lepidoptery was anything but a purely scientific passion; it was, as far as he was concerned, wholly uncorrupted by the pathetic need to see butterflies as symbols of the spiritual within nature, or as trite metaphors for the immortal soul. But I only half believe him. For instance, an Atlas moth breaking from its cocoon at the end of his early short story "Christmas" serves as a fairly straightforward image of life beyond death. As stridently as Nabokov the artist proclaimed his repugnance for facile symbolisms, the butterflies that throng his fictions often appear to be more than incidentally associated with moments where the partition between worlds seems particularly thin. And certainly he could not have been insensible to what is so deeply evocative about a holometabolous species whose transfiguration from a humbly earthbound larva into a winged and gloriously lovely *imago* is achieved by way of a kind of death, entombment, and resurrection.

The most Orphic or gnostic expression among Nabokov's works of his belief in the soul's immortality is found in *Invitation to a Beheading*, which is also the nearest thing to a purely surreal novel that he ever wrote. There, as nowhere else in his writings, the metaphysical atmosphere is one of stark dualism. The book's protagonist, Cincinnatus C., is clearly imprisoned in a reality to which he does not properly belong, and which in fact is far less real than he. The world around him is repeatedly revealed to be little more than hastily assembled collections of canvas, pasteboard, painted wood, and plaster, ringed about by crudely daubed theater scenery, cluttered with poorly constructed props, and populated by secondary characters whose identities are so fluid that they themselves are scarcely more than masks or stage puppets. At one point, Cincinnatus briefly removes his own body, disassembling it like an articulated armor and setting it aside; at another, he imagines his soul as a pearl ring swallowed by a shark and now deeply embedded in its fat; at yet another, he recalls once inadvertently taking a stroll high up in midair, to the angry consternation of the onlookers below. At the end of the novel, just as he is being put to death by the miserable imps among whom he has lived his entire life, but who find his "gnostical turpitude" and impenetrable spiritual "opacity" intolerable, he realizes that he believes neither in them nor in death, and so he rises from the executioner's block like a giant, breaks the false world into fragments, scatters its now tiny and transparent inhabitants in terrified flight, and strides off in a direction from which he thinks he hears the voices of other beings like himself.

The note of spiritually aristocratic gnosticism, however, is far more muted in Nabokov's other books. For one thing, despite his well-deserved reputation for personal hauteur and his ill-deserved reputation for "coldness" as an author, his writings betray a fiercer sense of justice and a deeper reserve of compassion than he is usually given credit for. For another, his love of nature was too intense for him ever to imagine it to be in any sense illusory; as much as persons of a cruel or unimaginative cast of mind might have the power to create an artificial hell for others here on earth, the true world of the senses and of the sensitive mind is intrinsically benign, and at times paradisal. That said, the sensible realm also remained for him, however ineffably, a fabrication: not in the sense of something false, but in the sense of something born from rational imagination and artistic elation. In the end, one could say, everything is a manifestation of soul. One of the tenderest and perhaps most revealing moments in all of Nabokov's fiction is the scene in *Bend Sinister* (1947) in which Adam Krug reflects on the marvelous depth of his love for his own son: "a little creature, formed in some mysterious fashion . . . by the fusion of two mysteries, or rather two sets of a trillion mysteries each . . . and then permitted to accumulate trillions of its own mysteries; the whole suffused with consciousness, which is the only real thing in the world and the greatest mystery of all."

WHEN TRYING to make sense of Nabokov's conception of reality, and of his belief in a creative collaboration of souls shaping the world of experience — a kind of collective Dreamtime, I am almost tempted to say — one sooner or later must ask what Nabokov believed the essential origin or ground of consciousness to be. It seems clear to me (if only because of the cumulative impression left on me by various veiled intimations scattered throughout his works) that he imagined all souls as belonging to a hierarchy of intelligence, the consummation of which is a single source of creative consciousness: the supreme enchanter, the ultimate artist. He was utterly indifferent to religion, true. The one Divine Liturgy he attended as a boy so bored him that his father told him he need never attend again. He was pleased that his mother's conversion late in life to Christian Science afforded her such happiness, but he was not even mildly tempted to investigate her beliefs. Creeds, rituals, devotions, and dogmas were to him all little more than specimens of local folk custom, which was something he found unbearably tedious.

Still, in the end, his is a vision of reality that is all but unintelligible apart from some concept of God. Yet he seems to have found the very word distastefully indiscreet, and perhaps too commonplace to describe his own intuitions. On the one occasion when he made any sort of public declaration on whether he believed in God, in a 1964 interview with Alvin Toffler, he pulled off the impressive trick of affirming that he did precisely by affirming nothing whatsoever: "I know more than I can express in words, and the little I can express would not have been expressed, had I not known more." This may be Nabokov's sole known contribution to apophatic theology. Everything else he had to say on the matter he expressed with exquisite evasiveness, and principally by making himself, in his role as author, a kind of allegory of the divine. Often, he accomplished this simply by allowing the designer's hand to be glimpsed at unguarded breaches in the walls of the text. In *Pnin* he did it simply by occupying the roles both of an omniscient observer and of a character within the story. He did it most unambiguously at the end of *Bend Sinister*, where he unexpectedly enters his own novel from above, as a kind of omnipotent *deus ex machina*. Adam Krug, lying in a prison cell not long after learning of the brutal murder of his young son, awakes from "the bottom of a confused dream," dimly perceives something ominously meaningful in the patterns of light and shadow around him, and is just on the verge of recalling the horrible truth; but "then," writes Nabokov, "I felt a pang of pity for Adam and slid towards him along an inclined beam of pale light — causing instantaneous madness, but at least saving him from the senseless agony of his logical fate." A few pages later, at the moment of Krug's death, the narrative shifts midsentence from Krug's world to the world of his creator, who at that point rises from his writing desk, attracted by the sound of a moth striking the screen of his window. As Nabokov stares out into the night, he reflects upon the fate he has devised for his creature, and momentarily takes note of "an oblong puddle invariably acquiring the same form after every shower because of the constant spatulate shape of a depression in the ground" — a puddle, he tells us, that somehow "Krug had perceived through the layer of his own life." And this, of course, makes one wonder whether Nabokov too might at that moment be glimpsing a trace of a yet fuller reality, through the layer of his own life.

Beyond that, Nabokov disclosed nothing about his ultimate beliefs. We simply cannot give a proper name to his "spiritual" or "theological" convictions. But, then again, neither could he. He was, I think one can say, a sort of visionary of the aesthetic realm. His perspective upon reality as a whole was not that of the mystics, the philosophers, or the religiously devout; and yet it was one that allowed him to see — through the mystery of consciousness and of the beautiful intricacy of the world of experience — the primordial and final reality of spirit in all things. What he recognized above all, and what he was able occasionally to describe with incomparable artistry, was the mind's essential and original ecstasy toward form and complexity and beauty, and the way in which the world answers that ecstasy with its ever-deepening patterns and enigmas and signs of creative intelligence. It was, for him, a recognition most fully expressed in the dauntless curiosity of science and in the irrepressible inventiveness of art, but not one that could be reduced to an argument or a logical demonstration. One either sees or one does not; and, for those who do not, there may be no remedy for their defect of sensibility. And that, as it happens, may be a lesson well worth taking from Nabokov's works, whatever else one might or might not be able to take as well: that the materialist is not simply someone who lacks the mystic's immediate insight into the transcendent, or the philosopher's grasp of the ontology of the absolute and the dependent, or the religious devotee's experience of the rationality of faith, but is also — and perhaps much more essentially — a philistine.

# FORTY-SIX

## *Roland on Consciousness*

A few months ago, the morning before my eldest brother was to return home to Norway after a long visit, I dreamed that I had just awakened in the early light of dawn to find my dog Roland sitting at the end of my bed, a bar of softly glaucous shadow — cast by the central casement frame of my double window — draped over his shoulders like a prophet's mantle. Roland is of middling size, with a shorthaired coat of mottled white, brown, and black, and with a handsome face with a coal-black nose and deep brown eyes; and I recognized at once the profound melancholy in both his posture and his expression. "What's wrong?" I said, after a moment of uneasy silence.

He slowly shook his head, and then — in a voice plangent with sadness — replied, "I have to leave you. I have to go to Norway with your brother."

I was astonished. For one thing, I could not recall ever hearing Roland speak before, at least not this clearly; I certainly did not know he had a voice so much like Laurence Harvey's (though with a warmer, furrier tone). For another, he had given no indication before this of any intention of leaving us; and, given the depth of his attachment to my wife, the very notion would have been inconceivable to me. "Why?" I asked. "What do you mean?"

He sighed, bowed his head for a moment, then raised it again to look into my eyes with the frankest of gazes. "Your brother and I knew each other long ago," he said. Then, seeing my bewilderment, he immediately added, "Oh, not in this life, of course. I'm only three years old, after all. In another life, very long ago, countless *kalpas* in the past, in a better age than this our present *Kali-yuga*. In those days, you see, I was a god in the *Tushita* heaven, and your brother was my little pet monkey T'ing-T'ing.

We were quite inseparable." An amused smile appeared on Roland's face and he gave his head a gentle, obviously affectionate wag. "What a scamp he was. How often he would don a small chaplet of silver bells, clamber up onto the back of my throne of jade and gold, cavort in merry little capers above my head, and then suddenly tumble down into my lap. Even Maitreya and the goddess bodhisattva Guanyin couldn't help laughing, and the tender warmth of their mirth flowed down even into the deepest *narakas* and momentarily eased the torments of the damned."

"I had no idea," I said after a moment.

Roland was still lost in his memories, however. "Some of his antics were terribly mischievous, and I was often urged to exercise more discipline over him. But I couldn't — he delighted me so. On a few occasions, he raided the banqueting table of the gods before they'd seated themselves. Sometimes he stole flagons of wine and made himself drunk. Twice he slipped into the divine orchards and gorged himself on the peaches of celestial longevity. Once, when the demons of *Pratapana* mounted one of their pathetically futile escalades against the ramparts of the heavens, he sat high up on the walls pelting them with peach-stones and screeching with unseemly laughter. But I loved him so."

Here Roland paused to bite at an itch on his haunch and then to smooth his fur with his tongue.

"Anyway," he resumed, "our long idyll reached its end when each of us exhausted his stores of good karma, and we both plunged back down into the spawning-ditches of *punabbhava*, and into the tangled meshes of *pratitya-samutpada* . . . a humiliating, but inevitable, dégringolade. *Anitya*, you know. Thereafter our karmic paths diverged for aeons. But now we've found one another. How could we bear to be parted again?" And a lugubrious sigh escaped his lips. "Oh," he said, his manner suddenly brisker, "that black bear came back last night and got into the trash again."

"I thought I heard you barking at something . . . ," I began.

"Yes, I saw him from the living room window. I caught a glimpse of gleaming ursine teeth in the moonlight and I'm afraid that, when I recognized what I was looking at, an atavistic thrill of pure terror set me off. Irrepressible canine instinct, I'm afraid. I'd help you clean up the debris, but I have no thumbs." He turned his head as if about to jump down from the bed, but then paused and turned back to me. "You know, that's a very potent word, really — recognized, I mean . . . recognition . . ."

"How so?"

"Well, I've been pondering the problem of consciousness a great deal lately, and how impossible it is to fit it into a truly mechanistic account of life or of evolution — I mean at the most elementary level. Take simple recognition of something, for example: there you have an instance of seemingly irreducible intentional consciousness, right? But we know what a thorn in the side of materialism intentionality is: it's a conspicuous example of final causality right there in the midst of supposedly aimless mechanical events . . . its content is eidetic . . . you know, dependent on mental images, and so on conscious thought . . . it supplies a specific, finite *meaning* to experience that the physical order can't provide . . . Well, simply said, it doesn't fit into the mechanistic story, does it? And so, as I understand it, the really consistent materialist position is that consciousness and intentionality are all secondary, even illusory, the epiphenomenal residue of purely mechanical processes. Supposedly, if you delve down deeply enough — into the body's neural machinery or into the dark backward and abysm of evolutionary time — you'll find that all intentional activity dissolves into a series of unconscious, aimless physical functions, which natural selection has refined into such a complex order that it generates the illusion of unified conscious intention."

He paused to scratch the back of his ear with a hind paw, then resumed: "Take my silly fright at that bear's teeth. Allegedly that would be just a neural agitation that only seems to have a rational content and purpose — survival — but that's really just the fortuitous result of an accidental juxtaposition of physical effects, mechanically coordinated by evolution. If you could trace my instinctive fear back in time, you'd arrive at some primitive organism without eidetic consciousness or intentional awareness, in which just by chance the shape of a bared tooth would — for no *reason* — provoke the neural response of flight. And then, since this would accidentally have the salutary effect of helping preserve that organism's life, that neural tendency would be preserved and transformed over generations into an indurated genetic predisposition. Only later would the elaborate stage-trickery of consciousness arise out of all that biochemistry, like vapors from a swamp. Well, do you believe that? Could any mechanical coincidence that bizarrely pointless and rare ever be sufficiently specified by natural selection? Do you really think that that neural reaction could even have occurred without some kind of eidetic recognition — some formal idea — present?"

"Well . . ."

"Of course not," he continued. "These materialists say it's mechanism all the way up — or at least up to some inexact point where some kind of phylogenic or neural alchemy, which we hazily call 'emergence,' magically produces consciousness as a kind of tinsel party-crown atop the machine.

Nonsense, I say. Nonsense! It's just the opposite: consciousness and intentionality go all the way *down*, in varying degrees but continuously. Really, consciousness is at the ground of everything — it *is* the ground. Oh, did you remember to pick up some of those rawhide treats I like? I want to put some in my luggage for the flight."

"Look," I said. "Do you really have to go to Norway? They'll probably put you in quarantine for a month when you arrive. And you know how prissy Europeans get about long-term visits by foreign animals without visas."

Now an almost pitying expression appeared on his face. "I'm sorry, but I must. T'ing-T'ing needs me . . . for spiritual guidance."

Knowing my brother as I do, I could think of no further plausible demurral, so I said nothing, merely nodding my head in resignation.

"You know," Roland added, "this whole business of consciousness reminds me of something that occurred to me the other day regarding superposition."

"Sorry — regarding . . . ?"

"Superposition. You know, the measurement problem, double-slit experiments, whether there's a collapse of the wave function — I certainly think there is — all that sort of business. You see, it occurred to me . . ."

Just then, however, a shrill, intolerably raucous claxon sounded. In a moment, the entire scene had melted away and I found myself emerging from sleep, savagely groping for my abominable alarm clock.

To awaken from an interesting dream before it reaches its end is always irksome; but I have to admit that my chief emotion, once the mists in my mind had begun to evaporate, was relief. It was very good to know that Roland would not be leaving on the evening flight with my brother. It was comforting, moreover, to have my sense of normality restored: I have no cause to believe, for instance, that Roland is a Mahayana Buddhist, much less a quondam Taoist deity once enthroned in a syncretic Buddhist heaven. So I was at peace. My only real regret on rising from bed, and for several days thereafter, was that, in all likelihood, I should never now find out what it was my dog had wished to tell me about quantum mechanics.

# FORTY-SEVEN

# The Love of Wisdom

I went in at the sign of the Temulent Termagant (a frowsy slattern asplay in a shallow ditch along the wayside, with toes pointing upward, cheeks feverishly flushed, hair and bonnet and skirts wildly disordered, and a fist angrily raised at a rachitic child hobbling by on crutches). A public house I had known well in youth, it was a building beneath whose peeling lintel I had not passed for two decades. It took me only moments to find the Philosopher; I spied him through clouds of tobacco smoke and melancholy, seated alone at a table in a corner, both his glass and the bottle of whiskey beside it about half empty. I had not seen him recently, and, as he lifted his head at my approach, I was astonished at his appearance: hair uncropped and disheveled, complexion waxen, the rheum about his pale blue eyes making it seem they peered at me through minute pellicles of hoarfrost. He said nothing when I reached the table, but invited me to sit by extending a hand whose nicotine stains looked like indelible varnish.

"Hello, Phil," I said after a moment. "I'd thought you might be here."

He stared at me vaguely for a few seconds, coughed phlegmily, and said, "Well, you've found me. Have a drink." His voice was weary, quiet, harsh.

"Maybe later," I said. "What's all this about you and Sophie?"

He emitted a single morose laugh, emptied his glass in one swallow, and filled it again. "Lady Sophia, if you please," he snarled sardonically. "Don't let's forget her pedigrees. We mustn't be guilty of insolent familiarity, sir — of *lèse-majesté*." Then he sighed and lowered his head, and his voice became at once gentler and sadder: "It's all over between us this time. There's no going back."

"Did she say that?"

"No need. I just know. It's been coming for some time, honestly. The distance between us has been growing . . . getting colder . . . oh, I can't say how long. It was ridiculous of me to think . . . to hope . . . I mean, we're from different worlds. This was inevitable."

I hesitated only a moment before asking, "What did you do, then? What did you say?"

He raised his head and stared directly, if hazily, into my eyes. "Well, how predictable. Of course, everyone assumes I'm the one to blame . . ."

"Well, I've known Sophie . . . known the lady for some time myself," I said, "and you have to grant that . . ."

"Right, that she's the pure, irreproachable one. That I'm the one who couldn't bear the difference in our social derivations, because class consciousness rises up from below — doesn't it? — like a vapor from the mire. But her, she's as sweet and temperate as sunlight at dawn. Just shines down on everyone with unadulterated, unprejudiced, disinterested benevolence. Doesn't care tuppence about class. I heard it before I met her. *Sapientia verecunda et pudens*, they said, *casta et irreprehensa*. Well, maybe she's not quite as verecund or pudent as you all think. Maybe sometimes the truth is more, you know, *Sapientia — ista meretrix!*"

It was as if an electric shock had shot through me. "Look," I said, struggling to restrain my anger. "I'm not judging. Your bitterness is making you ungallant. There's nothing meretricious about her . . ."

"Says the man who's sat at her table but never caressed her." He drank, nearly emptying his glass again. "Sorry, that's unfair. But you don't understand. Remember, she drew me to her first. I wouldn't have been that brave. She's a girl who knows the power of her own beauty, believe me. And such beauty too — those ruby lips, those glistening sable locks, those shining eyes, that flawless skin, that curvaceous figure . . ." A quiver passed through him, and he finished his drink and poured out another. "It was so easy. She deftly cocked a coquettish oeillade in my direction — one appraising glance from those glorious eyes, one approving smile from those delectable lips — and I was vanquished. She knew what she was doing. She inveigled me. She's a seductress, all the more irresistible because she seems so chaste . . ."

I was about to reply still more sternly, but he seemed to know what I would say and raised a hand to prevent me.

"No, no," he said, his tone altering yet again, now becoming audibly contrite. "You're right. It's true. I'm to blame. She's put up with my moods and vacillations and frustrations for years now, without complaint. I know I'm the one who always makes things go wrong." Tears were now coming into his eyes. "I'm the one who's ruined it all . . ."

Pity overcame me. "How long have things been going bad?" I asked gently.

He sat back in his chair, breathed deeply, and stared into space. "I can't say. At first, it was sheer bliss. All soft spring days and softer summer nights. Laughter and love . . . like innocent children at play. And I was wholly hers. Every day I brought her tokens of my devotion, like the guileless boy I was: all the choicest flowers of Platonic contemplation, blossoms of Pythagorean mysticism, bouquets of visionary idealism, little punnets of berries — not ordinary, ephemeral, seasonal berries either, but the finest, rarest, eternal hyperouranian berries, gleaming, unique, and imperishable. And she delighted in my gifts, and lavished her love on me. I thought it couldn't end. But then . . . I don't know exactly when . . . I began trying to please her more and more, to impress her, I suppose, for fear she would tire of me. And the harder I tried, the more uncertain her responses became, the more forced her praise . . . the more tepid her thanks. Then we began to argue. It seemed the more I did, the less she appreciated my efforts."

"What were you doing exactly?"

"Trying to show her I loved her, I thought. My gifts became more exotic, so she wouldn't lose interest. Specimens of exquisite, scholastically logic-chopped bric-a-brac, none of which appeared on her mantelpiece. 'Too fussy,' she said when I pressed her. I sent her flurries of Cartesian sonnets — I thought we could renew our romance with a new start — but she was disdainful. 'They seem to be more about you than about me,' she said. I couldn't please her, and I kept making things worse. When I sang Kantian ballads in the garden below her window, she merely gazed down enigmatically, blew me a perfunctory kiss, and lowered the sash. The next day I received this by post . . ." — he drew out from an inner jacket pocket and unfolded a leaf of heliotrope stationery that looked as if it had been held often between clenched hands — "'My Dear Boy,' she begins. See how she condescends even when she's trying to be tender? Dear Boy. Then she tells me that I'm being silly, that the repudiation of traditional metaphysics is just drastic emotionalism, and not sincere at all. She says that causality is already a logical category that's prior to the empirical, and only my unreflective servility to mechanistic thought makes me think it can't be extended analogically beyond the sensible. She says she's beginning to doubt the earnestness of my professions of love. And . . . all sorts of things." He folded the letter and thrust it away again. "So I changed. I sent her witty, ironic postmodern triolets. She accused me of vulgarity, of playing the Bohemian. She said these shifts of mood were disconcerting, frightening. Then . . ." He paused.

"What, for God's sake? What did you do?"

"I gave up. In pique — no, in despair — I wrote her a long series of analytic propositions. I even . . . used a great deal of formal logical notation."

I was appalled. I fought for words. "You didn't," I said at last. "That's barbaric . . . depraved."

He looked at me with utter resignation in his eyes. "I knew it was the end — she couldn't forgive me — she'd believe I'd completely forsaken her. Oh, Lord, what now?" He shook his head and struck the table with his open hand. "Never to taste the nectar of her kisses again . . . never to hear the sweet music of her voice melt in silvery peels of doting laughter . . . Never."

A terrible silence reigned between us for nearly a minute. Then I spoke. "You damned fool," I said coolly, "you've never understood women. She doesn't want to tell you what she wants from you — no woman does. She wants you to know. She wants to know you've been listening to her, that you've *seen* her. She doesn't need all these spasms and convulsions of sentiment from you, all these apocalyptic renunciations and absurd dramatic gestures. That's all about you, not her. You're performing, acting out not what she means to you, but how you'd like to imagine yourself in her eyes. There's still time, if you'll just sober up. Go back to the beginning, recapture the magic of that first thrill of love she woke in you. Stop trying to captivate her when she's already yours. Be sublimely negligent of method. Speak to her again in the lilting, halting, innocent language of myth, of genteel dialogue, of piercing poetic metaphor — of Platonism. Every other philosophical style is folly, vainglory, or nihilistic spite. Show her that you still cherish her as she truly is. Show her herself in your heart's glass of visions . . . Show her that you *see* her."

He stared at me with wide eyes for several seconds. Then, quietly, he said, "Is that still really possible?"

"Yes," I replied, "if you love her. She will never cease loving you."

# FORTY-EIGHT

# Gods and Gopniks

Journalism is the art of translating abysmal ignorance into execrable prose. At least, that is its purest and most minimal essence. There are, of course, practitioners of the trade who possess talents of a higher order — the rare ability, say, to produce complex sentences and coherent paragraphs — and they tend to occupy the more elevated caste of "intellectual journalists." These, however, are rather like "whores with hearts of gold": more misty figments of tender fantasy than concrete objects of empirical experience. Most journalism of ideas is little more than a form of empty garrulousness, incessant gossip about half-heard rumors and half-formed opinions, an intense specialization in diffuse generalizations. It is something we all do at social gatherings — creating ephemeral connections with strangers by chattering vacuously about things of which we know nothing — miraculously transformed into a vocation.

All right, I suppose that all sounds a little spiteful. I take it back. I am perfectly aware that there are quite a few men and women of considerable gifts laboring in the fields of journalism, and that some figures of genuine literary eminence have risen from the ranks of the profession. My affection for H. L. Mencken verges on the idolatrous. I can think of a half-dozen writers I admire who began (and in some cases ended) their careers writing for the popular press. And, after all, I am not entirely certain how I should classify what I am doing in writing a regular column. Still, it seems fair to me to note that what a journalist does for a living does not, in itself, require him or her to be a scholar, an artist, a philosopher, or even particularly good at sorting through abstract ideas. And, really, it is hard both to meet a regular deadline and also to pause long enough to learn anything new, or waste much time even following one's own arguments.

Which brings me to Adam Gopnik, and specifically his *New Yorker* article of 17 February 2014, "Bigger Than Phil" — the immediate occasion of all the rude remarks that went coursing through my mind and spilling out onto the page overhead. Ostensibly a survey of recently published books on (vaguely speaking) theism and atheism, it is actually an almost perfect distillation of everything most depressingly vapid about the cogitatively indolent secularism of late modern society. This is no particular reflection on Gopnik's intelligence — he is bright enough, surely — but only on that atmosphere of complacent ignorance that seems to be the native element of so many of today's cultured unbelievers. The article is intellectually trivial, but perhaps culturally portentous. Simply said, we have reached a moment in Western history when, despite all appearances, no meaningful public debate over belief and unbelief is possible. Not only do convinced secularists no longer understand what the issue is; they are incapable of even suspecting that they do not understand, or of caring whether they do. The logical and imaginative grammars of belief, which still informed the thinking of earlier generations of atheists and skeptics, are no longer there. In their place, there is now — where questions of the divine, the supernatural, or the religious are concerned — only a kind of habitual intellectual listlessness.

FOR FULL DISCLOSURE'S SAKE, I should note that my most recent book is among those Gopnik discusses (sort of). It seems clear he did not read it — at least not as far as, say, the introduction — given the bizarre description he provides of its argument. "As the explanations get more desperately minute, the apologies get ever vaster," he writes:

> David Bentley Hart's recent "The Experience of God: Being, Consciousness, Bliss" doesn't even attempt to make God the unmoved mover, the Big Banger who got the party started; instead, it roots the proof of his existence in the existence of the universe itself. Since you can explain the universe only by means of some other bit of the universe, why is there a universe (or many of them)? The answer to this unanswerable question is God. He stands outside everything, "the infinite to which nothing can add and from which nothing can subtract," the ultimate ground of being. This notion, maximalist in conception, is minimalist in effect. . . . A God who communicates with no one and causes nothing seems a surprisingly trivial acquisition for cosmology.

Excuse the sigh of vexation; I cannot help it. If only he had read at least the first chapter. Well, setting aside the nonsense about desperately minute explanations, which cannot possibly be relevant to any argument of mine, the God described in my book is the creator of everything, who communicates with all persons in a constant and general way, and with many individuals in an episodic and special way. Whatever originality I might claim for certain aspects of my argument, its metaphysical content is entirely and ecstatically derivative: pure "classical theism," as found in the Cappadocians, Augustine, Denys, Thomas Aquinas, Ibn Sina, Mulla Sadra, Ibn Arabi, Shankara, Ramanuja, Philo, Moses Maimonides . . . well, basically, just about every significant theistic philosopher in human history. (Not to get too recherché here, but one can find most of it in the Roman Catholic catechism.)

Then again, reading the book would not necessarily have helped Gopnik much. Anyone who imagines that the propositions "God is the source of all existence" and "God creates everything" are antitheses, or that divine transcendence involves God simply standing "outside everything," or that defining God as the Absolute precludes defining him as the Unmoved Mover, enjoys an understanding of philosophical tradition that is something less than luxuriant. Fair enough. He is in another line of work, and probably should have avoided these issues altogether. The real problem with his article is not its dialectical deficiencies so much as its casual inanities. The dazzling moment of truth comes when Gopnik claims that what unbelievers "really have now" is

> a monopoly on legitimate forms of knowledge about the natural world. They have this monopoly for the same reason that computer manufacturers have an edge over crystal-ball makers. . . . We know that men were not invented . . . that the earth is not the center of the universe . . . and that, in the billions of years of the universe's existence, there is no evidence of a single miraculous intercession with the laws of nature. We need not imagine that there's no Heaven; we know that there is none, and we will search for angels forever in vain.

Did Gopnik bother to read what he was writing there? I ask only because it is so colossally silly. If my dog were to utter such words, I should be deeply disappointed in my dog's powers of reasoning. If my salad at lunch were suddenly to deliver itself of such an opinion, my only thought would be "What a very stupid salad." Before all else, there is the preposterous temerity of the proprietary claim; it is like some fugitive from a local asylum appearing at the door to tell you that "all this realm" is his inalienable feudal appanage and that you must evacuate the premises forthwith. Precisely how does materialism (which is just a metaphysical postulate, of extremely dubious logical coherence) entail exclusive ownership of scientific knowledge? Does Gopnik think he can assert rights here denied to Galileo, Kepler, and Newton? Or to Arthur Eddington, Werner Heisenberg, Max Planck, Erwin Schrödinger, Paul Dirac, Anthony Zee, John Barrow, Freeman Dyson, Owen Gingerich, John Polkinghorne, Paul Davies, Stephen Barr, Francis Collins, Simon Conway Morris, and (yes) Albert Einstein? The tiny, thwarted blastema of a thought that seems to be lurking in Gopnik's words is the notion that we have only lately discovered that God cannot be found as a discrete physical object or force within the manifold of nature, and that this is somehow a staggering blow to "that hypothesis" — though, curiously enough, Augustine or Philo or Ramanuja (and so on) could have told him as much: God is not a natural phenomenon. Is it really so difficult to grasp that the classical concept of God has always occupied a logical space that cannot be approached from the necessarily limited perspective of natural science?

IT DOES NOT MATTER. Nothing is happening here. The conversation has never begun. The current vogue in atheism is probably reducible to three rather sordidly ordinary realities: the mechanistic metaphysics inherited from the seventeenth century, the banal voluntarism that is the inevitable concomitant of late capitalist consumerism, and the quiet fascism of Western cultural supremacism (that is, the assumption that all cultures that do not consent to the late modern Western vision of reality are merely retrograde, unenlightened, and in need of intellectual correction and many more Blu-ray players). Everything else is idle chatter — and we live in an age of idle chatter. Lay the blame where you will: on the Internet, 940 television channels, social media, the ubiquity of high-fructose corn syrup, whatever you like. Almost all public discourse is now instantaneous, fluently aimless, deeply uninformed, and immune to logical rigor. What I find so dismal about Gopnik's article is the thought that it represents not the worst of popular secularist thinking, but the best. Principled unbelief was once a philosophical passion and moral adventure, with which it was worthwhile to contend. Now, perhaps, it is only so much bad intellectual journalism, which is to say, gossip, fashion, theatrics, trifling prejudice. Perhaps this really is the way the argument ends — not with a bang but a whimper.

# FORTY-NINE

## Roland in Moonlight

In my dream, I had just entered the sitting room of my house. It was still several hours before dawn, but music was quietly playing: I heard the last lines and fading chords of Schubert's "Der Leiermann," in the recent recording by Jonas Kaufmann, before silence fell. I was confused at first, but I soon spied my dog, Roland, sitting on the carpet in front of the large bay window seat, staring out into the night. A soft, pure lunar light, shredded by the pine branches outside the glass into long glistening ribbons of pale silvery blue, poured gently into the room and over his mottled fur of white, brindled brown, and cobalt gray, and for a few moments it almost seemed as if he were himself little more than a pattern of shadows and moonlight. The illusion vanished, however, when he turned his head and held me for an instant in the cool gleam of his eyes, before returning his gaze to the window. "I'm sorry," he said in that warmly resonant voice of his (so hauntingly similar to Laurence Harvey's), "did the singing rouse you? I thought I had the volume down low enough to disturb no one."

"I don't think it woke me," I said. "I really can't recall."

"I suppose it's inconsiderate of me," he said. "It's just that I have many things on my mind, and it's only during these hours that I can get time to myself, just to think about things. During the day, my time is so taken up with domestic responsibilities — playing those games of fetch you all love so, letting you scratch my stomach, and so on. In these watches after midnight, though, I can reflect on things."

A memory began to rise to the surface of my thoughts. "Yes," I said, "weren't you going . . . yes, weren't you going to Norway with my brother?"

"Oh, I changed my plans. I really can't leave Mama" — he meant my wife — "all alone with you lot. I'll visit your brother in the summer, with your mother. That's not what I was thinking about now." He sighed. "Do you like that recording?"

"It's gorgeous."

"It is, isn't it? I'm so used to the *Winterreise* being sung by a baritone, by Fischer-Dieskau especially, and that dark ghostly timbre his voice had; but here's this marvelous tenor singing it with every bit as much pathos and power and mystery . . . It's a piece that never seems to loosen its grip on me. Now that I'm four and my ears are more mature, and my heart wiser, it's more entrancing than ever. I mean, how did Schubert do it, the poor perishing ape? Such ineffable tenderness, such dulcet resignation, so much . . . leave-taking. That last *Lied* in particular. No other composer ever produced that exquisite combination of shattering melancholy and whimsical buoyancy. What to call it? Merry sorrow? No. Tragic jaunti-ness? No, that's awful." He shook his head. "It's unbearable but beautiful, whatever it is — sweet nostalgia, under the shadow of death's wings. You just know that when he wrote those songs he could hear the angel drawing near. But that's how it often is. We frequently know . . . more than we know . . . anticipate more . . . Like those wonderful elephants."

"I'm sorry," I said. "You've lost me."

Roland turned and then rose and trotted over to me, wagging his tail. "I'd be happy to explain. But, first, do you happen to have any of those lovely bacon treats about you? I could do with a little something just now."

I brought three treats from the pantry, sat in the window seat, and tossed them to him one after another. He devoured them quickly (and a little noisily, to be honest), then sniffed and tentatively licked my finger-tips, then rolled onto his back so that I could rub his stomach, and finally stretched, turned over, and sat up again.

"Thanks," he said. "One gets peckish. As for the elephants . . . well, there are many delightful stories about those magnificent creatures, about their intelligence and sensitivity, their capacity for devotion and grief, and so on. But I was thinking of the day that Lawrence Anthony — you know, the 'elephant whisperer' — died in 2012 at his house on that huge South African game preserve that's more than a day's journey in size, and the herds of rogue elephants he had rescued and tended all arrived within a couple of hours to pay their respects . . . to mourn, I suppose. I think I read about that in one of your old *New Atlantis* issues. Amazing. They'd been away for well more than a year, and then there they were. How did they know? What summoned them across all that wilderness, so they could intone their subsonic threnodies?" He shook his head wonderingly. "How do souls reach out across the limits of time and space? There's just no end to the mysteries of spiritual beings." He paused, almost with a start, and looked into my eyes with an expression of faint suspicion. "You don't have any sympathies for the degenerate views of those fellows that deny that elephants are spiritual beings, with immortal souls, do you? Like traditionalist Thomists and whatnot?"

The question alarmed me. "Oh, absolutely not," I said emphatically.

"And . . . and . . ." His brow furrowed, his eyes narrowed. "And dogs?"

"Look," I said, trying not to take offense. "You've known me all your life. You must know that I believe all conscious beings possess spiritual natures and have spiritual destinies, and that beasts partake of rational spirit. I'll admit" — I shrugged — "I sometimes have my doubts about certain kinds of Thomists. I mean, I've known a few who, if they have souls, keep them well hidden. But that's the exception that proves the rule."

His features relaxed. "I'm sorry. A silly question, really. Mind you, these days you have philosophers out there who deny that anyone at all — canine, anthropine, or lower on the scale of nature — has rational consciousness. We're all just organic machines to them. And as for extraordinary acts of consciousness, like those elephants . . . well, they just deny they ever occur. And this means they have to pretend that vast regions of universally attested experience are just delusions and fabrications."

"Such as?"

"You know — fatidic dreams, knowledge of remote events, that sort of thing."

"Oh," I said uncertainly. "You mean the paranormal?"

Roland winced slightly. "I don't care for that word. But, well . . . I mean, ordinary consciousness isn't really reducible to purely physical causes, of course, but you know how these materialist savages, with all their abominable superstitions, can convince themselves it is. But what if there really are phenomena of mind that defy mechanistic paradigms completely? That violate locality, separability, causal contiguity . . . ? I mean, well, look: Have you ever dreamed something in precise detail before it happened, something you could not have predicted?"

"Yes," I said.

"And known others who had the same experience?"

"Yes. My father had some very vivid dreams like that."

Roland sighed and momentarily turned his eyes back to the moonlight beyond the window. "I miss your father. He was so kind."

Words would not come, so I simply nodded my head.

Roland looked at me again. "Have you ever suddenly known of

something happening far away, something that you also could not have predicted?"

"On three occasions, definitely," I said. "All three were dreadful."

"Well, there you have it," said Roland. "I could go on too. But the point is, haven't most of us had those experiences? Or at least known others who have — other people we trust? Aren't there enough examples of these moments when the walls of material nature become like transparent glass — when a peregrine breeze momentarily lifts the veil aside and grants us a glimpse of what we shouldn't be able to see if we were just biochemical machines — to qualify as established data? To merit investigation? Or just curiosity?"

"Oh, you know," I said, "there's so-called 'paranormal' research, but I doubt it's very fruitful. If nothing else, these things are so episodic, and the causal logic is impossible to make sense of . . ."

Roland yawned loudly and scratched his right ear with his hind paw. "Balderdash. Anyway, I'm not talking about laboratory research, really. I just mean that scientists and philosophers who want to make sense of consciousness aren't going to do the subject much justice if they simply rule out any evidence that doesn't fit into a machine picture of the mind. The problem isn't method, but metaphysics. Dogmatic materialism makes them look for only mechanical causes, and to pretend that these other events never occur. It's all just fanaticism . . . fundamentalism. But, again, even ordinary mental events should make them surrender their prejudices — intentionality is every bit as fabulous and uncanny as telepathy — but they can't. I don't understand it. Dogs aren't like that. We're not . . ." He paused and laughed quietly. "We're not dogmatic. Sorry about that. Your father, with his taste for horrid puns, would have liked that."

"Yes, I'm afraid so."

Roland closed his eyes and lifted his nose, as if drawing in the moonlight as a fragrance. Then he looked at me and smiled. "I really do miss your father."

"So do I," I said, as the dream faded or changed (I cannot recall which).

# FIFTY

# Ad Litteram

W hen lecturing undergraduates on Kafka's *Metamorphosis* — during his otherwise idyllic American years, when he had to make his principal living in the classroom — Vladimir Nabokov liked to call his students' attention to those sparse textual clues that made it possible to deduce what kind of "monstrous vermin" it was Gregor Samsa had changed into during the night. Precisely why Nabokov did this might not have been immediately obvious to his charges. Perhaps it was only a brief, pardonable moment of ostentation, like casually drawing an exquisite watch from one's waistcoat pocket not because one really has any need to check the time, but only to dangle it for a glittering instant before the eyes of the hired help. It certainly allowed him to flaunt his considerable entomological expertise before a captive audience. It even allowed him to demonstrate that he understood aspects of the story better than its author ever had (Kafka might have been able to describe the insect in question, but it is doubtful he could have named it). In fact, however, Nabokov's motives were largely both pure and high. For him, there was no such thing as a merely incidental feature in any text — at least not in any text truly worthy of notice. He regarded it as of the very essence of reading that one know as exactly as possible what one is reading about at any instant. He approached every text in this way. He would lavish loving, sometimes obsessive scrutiny on every concrete detail of the story: trees and butterflies, the designs of drawing rooms and gardens; whatever flora might be springing up in the margins of the page, whatever unguiculate or sleekly squamous fauna might be slinking between its lines or scurrying from one paragraph to the next; the angles of shadows, the songs of birds; and so on. For him the special delight of literature, and in fact its special coherence, lay always in the particular: in the discrete details the author had gathered up into his prose and in the texture produced by their interweaving. And no one was more brilliant at noticing those details. Nabokov was an absolute master of — in the parlance of earlier ages — *literal* exegesis.

That, though, is not how we would tend to think of it today.

HISTORIANS OR HERMENEUTICIANS frequently assert that what most alienates modern readers from the methods of premodern exegetes is the latter's passion for allegory. But this is false. If anything, we today are much more culturally predisposed than our forebears to an unremitting allegorization of the tales we tell or books we read, no matter how elaborate or tedious the results. True, we may prefer to discover psychological or social or political or sexual narratives "encoded" in the texts before us, rather than spiritual or metaphysical mysteries; we might find it impossible to believe that a particular reading could be "inspired" in a more than metaphorical sense; but the principle of the metabolism of the fictions we read into the "meanings" we can produce is perfectly familiar to us. The same critic who might prissily recoil at the extravagances of a patristic figural reading of the book of Numbers might feel not the slightest dismay at the transformation of Prospero into an ironic indictment of colonialism, or of Horatio Hornblower into an inflexibly erect emblem of the "phallic signifier." What makes the spiritual allegories of ancient pagan, Jewish, and Christian exegetes so alarming to modern sensibilities is not that they were *allegories*, but that they were so disconcertingly *spiritual*.

Where our understanding of what a text is and of how to read it differs most radically from that of our benighted ancestors — those poor slouching brutes who invented philosophy, the plastic arts, the hospital, Doric columns, flying buttresses, stained glass, and all the rest of that savage gallimaufry of gauds and baubles — is in our notion of what a "literal" interpretation is. All the term means to us today is a *literalist* construal of a text: that is, taking a text as an accurate documentary account of real events. Thus to read Kafka's *Metamorphosis* literally would, for us, mean earnestly believing that at some precise moment in the past Mr. Gregor Samsa really did awake in his bed in Prague to find himself transformed into an enormous beetle. For ancient and medieval exegetes, however, the very question of whether the events recounted in the text had ever actually happened was largely a matter of indifference for how to go about reading the text literally — or, more precisely, reading it *ad litteram*: that is, with an exactingly scrupulous attention to what was written on the page, in every detail, and with every discernible shade of significance. For them the difference between the literal and the allegorical was simply the difference between what was there to be seen and what was given to be discovered. And their somewhat insouciant attitude to the question of "fact" can prove terribly confusing to modern readers who do not share their presuppositions.

This is especially true in the case of Christian theology. After all, no one today is likely to imagine that Porphyry believed Homer's Cave of the Nymphs episode to be a true story, in the most reductive sense; surely, though, it should not be impossible to determine what a premodern theologian believed about the historical veracity of the scriptural episodes he commented upon. But really the question rarely arose. Sometimes we can tell. It seems clear that Gregory of Nyssa did not believe that God ever truly slew the firstborn of Egypt, but that Augustine did believe that God sent two bears to mutilate the children who mocked Elisha. Augustine accorded the story of the Garden of Eden a degree of historical substantiality that Origen explicitly denied. There was room for variance of opinion, dependent on temperament, theology, credulity, and moral imagination. But, whatever the case, the historical issue was quite irrelevant to how "literal" any given reading of Scripture was. The documentary value of Scripture was so secondary a matter that often we can only guess what the exegete's "historical" view of any given story was. When Origen pondered the physical dimensions of Noah's ark, was it because he believed the story to be "literally" true in our sense? Who can know? What we do know is that by paying such close attention to the details of the story, he was establishing a basis upon which other, more spiritual readings could be stably raised. Hence Thomas Aquinas's assertion that, among the various senses the exegete finds in Scripture, the primary and most indispensable is the literal. He was not proposing that one should assume the historical veridicality of everything one reads in its pages, but only that one must carefully ascertain what the text actually says before one ventures to say what more may be found there. It is an admonition against constructing some other text that better conforms to the interpretations one wants to produce. The meaning must arise from the actual images and words provided; a rose is a rose is a rose; it is not a lily. Not only is Thomas's principle not an exhortation to modern fundamentalism, it does not even entail a reading of Scripture that we today would necessarily recognize as literal at all. The most effulgently beautiful work of patristic literal exegesis is Augustine's *De Genesi ad litteram (On the Literal Reading of Genesis)*; but scarcely any modern reader could distinguish much of it from an exercise in allegory;

at times, what Augustine presents as the plain meaning of the text reads like a rapturous and brilliant discourse on its metaphors.

ANYWAY, NO NEED to belabor the point. Suffice it to say that we today approach the texts we read with expectations and under categories so different from those of our more distant predecessors that it may not be an exaggeration to say that the books we share with them in common (like the Bible) are not really the same books at all. We cannot inhabit texts as they did, and they would certainly find our ways of reading strange and inhospitable. For them, the various senses of the text were separated by subtly shifting degrees of intelligibility and imaginative resonance and significance, both implicit and explicit; for us, the act of reading often devolves into a stark alternative between, on the one hand, the symbolic or fanciful and, on the other, the documentary or "literal." In either case, interpretation is rendered more impoverished than it might have been, precisely on account of this absolute and unambiguous distinction. Inevitably, so pronounced an antithesis forces its poles toward ever more irreconcilable extremes. We feel we must choose, or at least spasmodically lurch, between the "literal" — which is merely aridly factual — and the "symbolic" — which is merely vapidly illustrative or didactic or edifying or hortatory (or whatever). Occasionally, a reader of genius like Nabokov might be able, instinctively, to fly free from so confining a set of alternatives, but that is an aberration. And the pity of it all — no matter what our critical or theological principles may require of us — is that most of us will never be able to experience, as some of our ancestors could, just how rich, variegated, absorbing, ingenious, and *inspired* the act of reading can be.

# FIFTY-ONE

# *Roland on Free Will*

I n my dream (if it was a dream), I was roused by a soft, suave, gauzily sonorous voice, hauntingly reminiscent of Laurence Harvey's. "Are you doing anything just now?" it said. I opened my eyes to see the face of my dog Roland bent close over my own. Even in the dim light before dawn I could see the intent, pensive expression in his deep brown eyes and in the alert quivering of his coal-black nose.

"Nothing in particular," I murmured after a moment.

He stared at me a moment longer, sighed gently, and turned to retreat farther down the bed; settling by my feet on his haunches, he yawned languidly and said, "I didn't think so."

A few more moments passed in silence. "Is there anything on your mind?" I asked at last.

He lowered his head, heaved a louder, more lugubrious sigh, and said, "Freud."

Another pause ensued, and it became clear he had no intention of elaborating unbidden upon this curt, plaintive syllable.

"Sigmund?"

He looked at me with a hint of impatience. "Well, I certainly don't mean Lucian," he said. "The reason I can't sleep, and probably the reason you can't either, is that I just can't grasp what it was that everyone saw in him. I mean, I know the Freudian superstition has been largely discredited since those heady days — his results were falsified, his psychotherapeutic sorcery doesn't work, and so on — but that doesn't change the fact of the extraordinary hold his model of human motives still has over people's imaginations, or the bibulous excitement his ideas once inspired. Why? Was it because all that blather about the unconscious flatters human beings that they're the deepest mysteries in creation? Or that the key to reality can be found in their gastric or genital functions, or locked away in some little tin box concealed in one of their dreams?"

"Well, I . . . ," I began.

But he had already become too animated to notice me. "I mean, just consider that whole silly psychic triad of id, ego, and superego: What makes it so profound to observe that we find ourselves drawn by opposing motives — the appetites of organism, the dictates of conscience — the glandular and the spiritual — so what? That's as great a revelation as noting that you have both a snout and a tail with a body wedged in between." He paused to gnaw briefly at his left flank and then turned back to me. "Would you like to scratch my stomach?"

"Not just now," I said. "So this is keeping you awake, is it?"

"Naturally," he replied with a slightly perplexed shake of his head. "It's just that it's such an obvious conceit, the whole tripartite psyche thing. You just notice that the self comprises contrary impulses and intentions, desires and drives, and *voilà*, there it is for you, ready-made. I want to do this, I feel compelled to do that, and here I am in the middle, poor chap. A dreary dialectic, thesis and antithesis oscillating back and forth across a gap spanning roughly the distance between epigastrium and cerebellum. The hierarchical picture is so obvious, such an immense banality. And it's all bound up with such a tawdry notion of persons' deepest drives."

"Yes, I see what you . . ."

"Now," Roland continued, "if you want to talk about the tripartition of the soul, repair to Plato. There you have something that really seems to make sense to me. The portrait is psychologically true: the perennial tension between the animal ecstasies of the flesh, which bind one to unthinking material necessity, and the rational freedom of the spirit, which is always striving to subdue the brute. What's that line from Yeats about the soul? 'Fastened to a dying animal'? Can't recall. Anyway, there's something truly free there, which is never the creature of an unhappy childhood or a frustrated hunger — spirit, *nous*, *Geist* — something that can convert the countervailing tempests of physiological urges into the elations of reason set free. Well . . . this is something dogs understand very well."

He fell silent and stared at me expectantly. The air about us had begun to grow more lustrous in the pearl-hued light. After several moments, though, he sighed yet again, as if despairing of my capacities, then turned and leapt down to the floor. A moment later, however, his face reappeared over the foot of the bed and, after three more seconds, he leapt back up and seated himself again. "It's all about freedom, you see," he said. "That's what this whole late modern psychomachy is about. It's a passion for determinism, physiological or subconscious or socioeconomic or what have you. It's all to do with the final triumph of the mechanistic philosophy in every sphere, even that of consciousness. How silly. As if machines could delight in bacon, or in the *chasse sauvage* when some impudent rabbit scampers past one's nose, or in that romp that amuses you so — what's it called? Fetch? But nothing so excites the modern materialist as the possibility of proving that consciousness is reducible to physiology, that freedom is an illusion, that mind is a ghostly epiphenomenon of unconscious metabolisms. Every aspiring young materialist dreams of growing up to be a robot."

"I expect you're right," I said.

"Think of those experiments where a subject is instructed to twitch a wrist or push a button whenever he feels moved to do so, and then to report when he consciously made the choice to do it. Then electrodes on the scalp or an MRI can show that a neural impulse precedes the conscious choice by anywhere from one to ten seconds, and the researcher can predict when the subject will perform the action about 70 percent of the time. So the scientist concludes that the *real* decision is just some autonomic electrical flicker in the brain, while the conscious decision is just a posterior accretion. One scientist, that Haynes fellow, even said this renders the existence of free will an 'implausible' hypothesis."

"I've never heard of him."

"But it makes no sense," Roland continued, more emphatically. "There's absolutely no logical connection between that experiment and that conclusion. It's an eisegetical non sequitur. It just shows that a scientist's interests frequently dictate what he thinks he's observed. He goes looking for a mechanical transaction, so he artificially extracts his data from their actual context, and then miraculously discovers what he has predestined his experiment to disclose. The far more sensible conclusion would have been just the opposite: that these results confirm the *reality* of rational freedom. My only hesitancy is that, if the subject were absolutely free, one should be able to predict his actions in that situation with 100 percent accuracy."

I did not want to admit that I was not following his argument, but after several seconds had to: "Why, exactly?"

Roland gazed at me tenderly and shook his head. "Because the subject did exactly what he had freely undertaken to do. He was asked, of his own volition, to act whenever he felt the impulse to do so, and that's what he did. He wouldn't have been twitching a wrist or pushing a button otherwise. But the researchers work by the bizarre fiction that they are witnessing an isolated mechanical process without any prior premise, rather than a premeditated act prosecuted intentionally, so they produce the monstrous fantasy that they have proved that the whole act is reducible to a spontaneous physical urge. I mean, the experiment they imagine they've run isn't even logically possible, because there's no visible intentional content in any given electrical impulse that identifies it with any particular act. You have to know what is freely intended beforehand in order to know what the original neural event might portend. You have to know that the subject chose *in advance* to translate the impulse into an action. The urge doesn't go directly to its goal without crossing the interval of consciousness. So what's the point? That we often feel an urge before we freely decide whether to act on it? Well, you don't need electrodes on the scalp to prove that. But the urge is never isolated, because at both ends there's a decision of the conscious mind: undertaking to act in accord with a prompting, then choosing to submit to that prompting. In between there's some raw physiological agitation, which those free intentions have shaped into an accomplished deed. Let's just say that that's the material substrate, and that the intellect that makes the choices is a kind of formal cause: it's always shaping impulse into intentional action — prospectively, retrospectively . . . synoptically."

"Yes, all right," I said.

"I mean, there's always some prior and final act of the mind, some more capacious realm of intention for any impulse that's embodied and enacted. Yes? So you can't ever arrive at a deeper foundation. The researcher can never retreat to a more original moment, some discrete instant when a physical urge exists wholly outside that free movement of the mind. That object just isn't found in nature. Just you try to find it and you'll see."

"No, I believe you," I said.

But then, as the morning light was becoming positively silver, and as Roland began thoughtfully licking his left shoulder, I fell asleep again, or dreamed I had.

# *Coda: C.B.*

*Merci, Mesdames et Messieurs. Je suis enchanté d'avoir été invité à ce rassem-*
*blement, malgré ma condition actuelle. Mort, c'est à dire. Mais tout d'abord,*
*permettez-moi de proposer l'exhortation suivante:*

Enivrez-vous!
    Il faut être toujours ivre. Tout est là: c'est l'unique question. Pour ne
pas sentir l'horrible fardeau du Temps qui brise vos épaules et vous penche
vers la terre, il faut vous enivrer sans trêve.
    Mais de quoi? De vin, de poésie ou de vertu, à votre guise. Mais
enivrez-vous.
    Et si quelquefois, sur les marches d'un palais, sur l'herbe verte d'un
fossé, dans la solitude morne de votre chambre, vous vous réveillez,
l'ivresse déjà diminuée ou disparue, demandez au vent, à la vague, à
l'étoile, à l'oiseau, à l'horloge, à tout ce qui fuit, à tout ce qui gémit, à tout
ce qui roule, à tout ce qui chante, à tout ce qui parle, demandez quelle
heure il est et le vent, la vague, l'étoile, l'oiseau, l'horloge, vous répon-
dront: "Il est l'heure de s'enivrer! Pour n'être pas les esclaves martyrisés
du Temps, enivrez-vous; enivrez-vous sans cesse! De vin, de poésie ou de
vertu, à votre guise."[1]

---

1. All references in notes are to works by Baudelaire; here *Le Spleen de Paris*, XXXIII:

    Make yourself drunk!/It is necessary always to be drunk. That is the all of it: the
    sole question. In order not to feel the horrible burden of time, which breaks your
    shoulders and presses you down to the earth, you must be inebriated without
    surcease./But on what? On wine, poetry, virtue, as you please. But make yourself
    drunk./And if sometimes, on the steps of a palace, on the green grass of a ditch, in

*Coda: C.B.*

# I

The great virtue of the dead is their silence. Having passed beyond the boundaries of the utterable, they are henceforward deprived of the privilege of utterance, and so can no longer bore us with tedious inventories of their regrets or, worse, burden us with the fruits of their wisdom. They keep their quiet vigils in some inner sanctuary, into which we cannot peer and from which not so much as a whisper should escape. So I beg your kind indulgence in thus presuming to address you from beyond the veil that hides that last and most terrible mystery from view. I was summoned hither, by a power I find I cannot resist. How I shall be received back into the society of the deceased, having cavalierly disregarded the cardinal rule of their etiquette, I cannot foresee; but I never was much bound by custom. And I find that, at my present remove from the undulating inconstancies of our personal and collective histories, I can see many things — concerning both myself and the world where once I dwelt — far more clearly than I could from the more limited perspectives afforded the living.

I am not, however, given to systematic formulations, so forgive me if I should wander somewhat from topic to topic.

So, then, what are the chief predicaments of modern man? I would say, first, disbelief in original sin and, consequently, an inability even to imagine what it would mean to strive against it. And by disbelief I do not mean a coarse but perhaps pardonable rejection of the doctrine on the part of a man who, shaking his puny fists at the unavailing heavens, demands possession of his own soul; that is the disbelief of the rebel, whose act of defiance remains, *contre cœur*, an affirmation of the divine, or at least a confession of a *divine* discontent. I mean rather the impotence of an imagination that finds the very notion of sin incomprehensible and a little absurd; I mean the barren conscience of a man who is quite sure that, whatever sin might be, it surely lies lightly upon a soul as decent as his own, and can be brushed off with a single casual stroke of a primly gloved hand; I mean a habitual insensibility to the illuminations and chastisements of beauty, a condition of being wholly

---

the dismal solitude of your room, you awaken, your drunkenness already diminished or vanished, ask the wind, the wave, the star, the bird, the clock — everything that flees, everything that groans, everything that rolls, everything that sings, everything that talks — ask them what time it is, and the wind, the wave, the star, the bird, the clock will answer you: "It is time to make yourself drunk! So as not to be Time's martyred slaves, make yourselves drunk; never cease making yourself drunk! On wine, poetry, virtue, as you please."

at home in a world from which mystery and sin and glory have all been banished, and in which spiritual wretchedness has become material contentment. To that man, the bliss that calls to him in the beautiful would seem only an intolerable accusation, its gracious invitations only a perverse condemnation of his well-earned and lavishly vegetal happiness. So he does not see it, he cannot hear it. And thus the ancient compact between the world above and that below has been forsaken; the glittering scale of natural and supernatural sympathies — of analogies and symbols, of revelations and memories of paradise — has been shattered, its starry fragments scattered in the dust; the way of ascent has been lost.

Forgive me for saying so much in so small a space, but I am a poet, and therefore lazy.

What, though, am I to make of the world into which I was born? How else can I make sense of that complacent love of moral squalor, that luxuriant banality, that is the single spiritual achievement of our age? Here where every bourgeois has been poisoned by the triteness of Voltaire — that philosopher of the concierges — and where every good citizen hears the voice of progress and enlightenment in the inane prattle of journalists, with all their childish laicism? Progress — the doctrine of idlers and Belgians, content to let their neighbors do their work for them — the oafish belief that civilization lies in steam or turning tables rather than in reducing the marks of original sin upon the soul.[2]

I was often rebuked for the insufferable pride I sometimes took in my baptism, as though that constituted some rare and special pedigree; but, in our time — when every bourgeois is a rationalist, when every aristocrat is servile in his eagerness to become as enlightened as the bourgeois, and when even the tradesman or the peasant aspires to be a modern man of reason — to what more ennoblingly antique lineage may one lay claim than that of the baptismal font?

## II

How did they ever come to this place, these desolate multitudes, gathered here under Satan's ashen skies? It is no use asking them: they cannot recall. They remember only, as in a dream, departing from frozen harbors bathed in twilight, sailing over dark waters lit by a sickly moon,

2. See *Mon cœur mis nu*, XXXVII, LXXXI.

their groaning barks borne on torpid currents past shores where sheer granite cliffs or walls of iron-gray thorns forbade any landing, and at last drawing up into these oleaginous waters, alongside these dreary quays wanly gleaming with rime. If they could cast their minds further back, they might recall a lost paradise: green and yellow meadows stirred by tender winds, umbrageous woodlands and emerald groves, glass-blue mountain peaks melting into azure skies, glittering bays whose diamond waters break in jade and turquoise surges on sands like powdered alabaster — there the rain falls gently, and is transformed by the setting sun into shimmering curtains of gold — there, beyond the valleys and the limestone caves, lies a palace filled with every delight the senses can endure, enclosing garden courtyards where crystal fountains splash in porphyry basins, intoxicating perfumes hang upon the breezes, and unwithering flowers of every hue shine out amid the greenery's blue shadows . . . If only they could recall. But, of course, they do not wish to do so. Occasionally they hear a distant dolorous echo, a faint fading rumor of that forgotten bliss, carried to them over the purple sea, but they only turn away and thrust their hands into their pockets, anxiously feeling for their purses. Their triumph is their diabolical drabness, their pitiless sobriety. (And what is perfect sobriety other than the rejection of love, of communion — the refusal of the God who *is* intimate communion, the love that gives itself with the recklessness of a drunkard?) They wish for no paradise more opulent than the contentment they have already achieved; they will not hear of such a thing.

Herein, I submit, lies the small moral quantum within my own dissipations, which were never so extravagant as I made out in my poems. To play the flaneur, the dandy delicately glistening upon the boulevards, can be an act of principled defiance against an age in which dreariness has become the face of sensualism, in which men cosset their appetites precisely by coarsening and deadening them. It is an ambiguous defiance, I admit. The poet, as I once observed, is like an albatross bound down to a ship's deck, all its floating grace reduced to comic awkwardness, confined to an element it cannot master and above which it should forever soar. He is also, I might add, a peacock among the pigeons.

Here, I have written a sonnet, which I call "Genus Pavonis." (Excuse the roughness of the verse, I entreat you. For all I can tell, it is little better than doggerel. The dead are masters of every language, having entered into that silence that is in truth the fullness of all sound and every utterance, enfolding every language within itself. But, even so, as a poet my only true idiom is French.)

The gorgeous opalescence of your tail,
　　Your shrilling voice upon the evening air,
　　Orgulous cock, *mon semblable, mon frère,*
Your delicate crown — sapphires upon frail
Stems of silver light — your glimmering mail
　　Of green and jet, your bearing debonair. . . .
　　A mirror that deceives me I am fair —
The envy of all animals more pale.

And yet I dare not gaze too long, bright jewel
　　Of burning beauty, strange unearthly bird:
You strip all rivals of their plumage, cruel
　　And jealous; harsher cry was never heard. . . .
Obscure angel, enigma, nature dual:
　　A heavenly splendor . . . vain and absurd.

## III

I admit, there is some peril in resisting Satan's world by seeking to outshine one's fellows. Can one ever then become more than a greater Satan among lesser Satans? But, surely, if we are fallen, we should at least strive to be children worthy of an apostate angel. Perhaps our vanquished god prefers we should not — indeed, prefers we have no thought of him at all. For what the modern age has taught us is that the kingdom of hell is essentially a respectable place, where the devil is best served by remaining incognito, where sin and remorse and penitence trouble no one with their curbside importunities — "Please, sir, only a *sou!*" — where no one frets about angels or devils, where all good men apply themselves virtuously to becoming machines among machines, without sin because without souls. What world, after all, could be more respectable than one without sin? Where the only transgression anyone truly deplores is to deny that the highest happiness is prosperous mediocrity? Where the only indecency is to suggest that, among the ashes of the modern heart, there might linger a spark of divinity that, blown upon with but a little breath, could be kindled into flame?

In such a world, those who uphold public morals and serve the public weal do so only for Satan's ends. They can rise to no higher god than he. They are guardians of the world of commerce, where everything is valued only as it might be bought or sold, where all giving and receiving are governed by the satanic law that each must try to take more than he gives, where any creed but the worship of Plutus must be brought into ridicule, where everything is plunged into the abysmal shadow of that insatiable Typhon called America — that gaslit desert of barbarism, with its infantile, gigantic, exuberant vulgarity, its monstrously guileless delight in affluence, its omnivorous vacuity.[3] For these good citizens, the highest good is that machines should wholly Americanize us, that progress should impoverish us of everything spiritual in our natures, until life can no longer intrude upon us with its fitful energies. Yes, respectable men, men of commerce, men of the most unimpeachable rectitude: under their vigilant gaze the youth will flee his home not when he is eighteen, but when he is twelve, not to seek a hero's adventures or liberate a beautiful captive from a tower or immortalize a garret with sublime thoughts, but to establish a business, enrich himself, surpass his father in avarice and cunning, and perhaps buy a journal for the propagation of enlightened ideals.[4] They shall see to it, that is, that he becomes as virtuous as they.

Against such decency, such respectability, it is necessary to rebel. Only thus can one extirpate the devil from one's heart. And yet, in rebelling, one cannot help but tread the path for a time of the great master of rebellion. Here — another poem, one called "The Fall of Lucifer":

No darkness falls across this golden noon,
And here no cloud or shadow mounts the wind;
Softly falls the dragon, through a ruined sky,
The region of the sullen southern stars.

A meteor, a silver strand of lightning
Upon the hazel dusk, he fell and fell,
Gold his hair and gold his eyes, such bright beauty
In sheer descent upon the languid breeze. . . .

When, still delighting, sang the angels, sang
The stars. . . . The son of morning, fallen where
None can find him, who in the evening of
That age slipped down along the seam of night. . . .

3. See *Edgar Poe, sa Vie et ses Œuvres*, I.
4. See *Fusées*, XXII.

Gone now, all glory, all that lovely bright
Magnificence: become the ember's glow,
The aftermath, the deep reproach of those
Cold, bleak, disconsolate, and empty heavens;

And now, amid a race who crave a God's
Miraculous sadness, terrible mirth,
The tawdry splendor of his glory's waste
Must wear another aspect than its own,

And he must walk the dismal floor of earth,
And range the fallow reaches of the sea,
And rule the turbulent and lifeless winds,
And hide in secret chambers in their hearts.

Do not be appalled if I observe that a truly beguiling beauty still sometimes smolders in his eyes, a virile grandeur still adorns his limbs and shoulders. One cannot arraign modern men for their unconscious diabolism, really, until one reminds them that the devil exists — even if, at times, one must do this by worshiping him. The explicit service of Satan, after all, is more honorable than the brutish servitude to him in which the modern soul labors. By openly adoring the delectable ruins of the fallen angel's beauty, one thereby casts oneself upon the mercy of God. It is a transgression that implores the love of heaven, and is thus a reproach to those whose lifeless consciences know nothing of either the devil or God. Better a forthright Satanist than a complacent bourgeois rationalist, sired by Voltaire in some tidy, comfortably appointed, and aseptic sty. The former can, at least, still revere beauty, even if it be only a corrupted beauty; there remains the possibility of good taste. I, at any rate, was never a complacent rebel. How little the first critics of *Les Fleurs du Mal* understood this, or understood the vacillations of the soul that produced that book, or grasped the meaning of the various impersonations through which that soul told of its wanderings. All my sins I confessed there *as sins*; all my recalcitrance, my every revolt, was directed against God *as God*. It was he from whom I was cut off, he whose absence provoked my misery and loneliness. I never abjured divine love, and certainly enjoyed none of the despicable ease of the contented atheist. When I spoke in the voice of rebellion, I also proclaimed thereby my passionate longing for God's mercy. Voltaire could not be seduced by the devil's shattered glory, true, and could not love what he should not love, but only because he was incapable of rapture before God, and could not love what he should love. That was not moral heroism, but only sterility of imagination.

I beg you to understand that within all of us two allegiances struggle against one another: one to God and one to the devil; one the desire to ascend, the other the desire to descend.[5] And there is no middle way: we yield to one inclination or the other in all that we do and say and think. One cannot therefore reject God but remain otherwise uncommitted. That we might receive mercy, then, and even perhaps absolution, we should acknowledge, without reserve, that when we transgress we do so as Satanists — and so acknowledge also the God from whose gaze we are far removed.


# IV


In the end, however, rebellion must exhaust itself. We grow weary of our paltry carnal transports, our ebulliences of defiance, our abortive expeditions to the frontiers of the respectable world. All this too, in the end, we must give up, or we will have achieved nothing but to bind ourselves more securely to the flesh. This, however, is the greatest trial we can undergo. When defiance dies in our breasts, there follows a fruitless season of the soul; we at first find ourselves deserted, caught in a ghostly twilight between two worlds, a winter of the soul, like a man whose marriage has grown cold or whose garden has grown bare. Nothing we do can prosper at first. We can but wait.

Which brings me, incidentally, to this verse, which I have entitled "Patient Husbandry":

> The violet of twilight, and the pale brittle gold
> Of poplars, the brilliant bleak silver in the fold
> Of the dark ailanthus leaf, and the dying fury
> Of the last late bloom, limp upon the copper briar,
> All like the lovely son of the morning's dimmed glory,
> He who once walked like a god in the stones of fire:
>
> Bitter. Beneath the traces of birds' fading songs
> The sinuous dragon, still lovely, though he is fallen,
> Slips through red thorns, a fugitive shimmer of bronze,
> Then disappears — a ghost in the twined fires of autumn.

5. See *Mon cœur mis nu*, XLI.

The thunder echoes distantly, low walls enclose
The tangled waste where you dream of the absent rose.

The bare ruins of your garden still betray the signs
Of vanished beauty, and the spent year yet declines. . . .
But what of that? As the hardened earth sinks in shadow,
Assume the dove's gentleness, the sweet serpent's guile —
You have wedded yourself to a woman of sorrows
And must live every day for her infrequent smile.

One must always endure the briar while the rose sleeps
In the sap's oblivion; gaze then upon her head,
Lowered, lips describing a silent phrase: she weeps
Rarely. Her pain is your sacrifice. With the dead
The seeds of fallen fruit lie dormant for a time.

But the vision thrives in the still earth. In a flood
Of silence, Simon heard a sweet supernal rhyme,
And fled to desert wastes that he might live apart,
And feed its promise with the fever of his blood,
And hold its secret in the fastness of his heart.

I have always felt a certain affection for the Stylite, I should mention, though not on account of his piety. Was he not, I wonder, the truest flaneur of all, the subtlest sensualist, the supreme dandy? Was not his asceticism really a kind of wanton revel, the voluptuary's craving for the excitement of absolute abandon, an ecstasy so intense it carried him beyond even the boundaries of pleasure?

Who can say? Mortification is one path to transcendence, I suppose, but not the one I best understood, until perhaps the end. I knew instead the venerable, the sacred paths of wine, women, and song — the blessed delirium of the pure heart's yearning for a forsaken Eden.

And when I speak of wine, I mean just that. Not narcotics, not hashish and opium, both of which I tasted in my time; therein lie only the illusory paradises whereby the wily lord of this world leads astray our natural hunger for the infinite.[6] I mean that ruby or golden nectar by which we resist the tyranny of circadian time and loosen the fetters of daily care. I

6. See *Le Paradis Artificiels*, I: *Le Poème du Haschisch*, especially chs. 1 and 5; *Du Vin et du Haschisch*, ch. 7.

mean that noble, pure, enlivening draught from the springs of paradise. Children and savages understand what we good citizens have forgotten: by their delight in things that shine and glitter, their love of feathers and bright threads and beads, they declare their contempt for the real and hence their spiritual natures.[7] The disinherited child, under the tutelage of some invisible angel, yet tastes only heaven in all he eats and drinks, and is made drunk by the sun — and by colors, splendors, iridescences — and he sees all things in their newness, and by his play he instinctively remakes paradise.[8] And we, when inebriated, return to the child's estate; drunkenness is the festival of innocence; in the land of the *philosophes*, the drunkard is a prophet. Blessed wine — our moral protest against the arid sobriety of the devil's kingdom of respectability. Wine, which creates communion, which is poured out in us like God's love. Wine, the first holy sign by which Christ revealed himself at Cana — our true Dionysus, the risen lord of indestructible life, of vitality and abundance, great *choregos* in the orgies of innocence.

## V

Now, conversely, when I speak of woman, I confess, I am often guilty of a certain dividedness. I was always capable of a more exalted view of woman, if not quite the fawning gynecolatry of some of my contemporaries. Here, a poem:

"*The Dancing Girl*"

No soft memory of living flesh can,
Within the crystal lattice of the mind,
Recall her grace, *sa tendresse, sa luxure,*
Or summon up her body's frail complaint,
Its moan of doves and flutes, its mirroring
Of moon's blue light, which seemed to shine in her....
All melts into this dreary anomie
In which all thought is lost; and all the sweet
And ardent turmoils of those distant nights
Are just a fragrance or a voice recalled.

7. See *Le Peintre de la Vie Moderne*, ch. XI: *Éloge du Maquillage.*
8. See *Le Peintre de la Vie Moderne*, ch. XI: *Éloge du Maquillage*; "Bénédiction," in *Les Fleurs du Mal.*

One here must speak in mysteries and say,
The dark reflection of her passing form
In all the gleaming facets of the night,
Between white pillars of the marble earth,
Must indicate what is more real than flesh;
The world is mirror, where the spirit moves
In symbols, glitters, echoes, dreams, and signs,
Fatidic gestures from a nameless world
Beyond time's fragile surfaces, beyond
This labyrinth in which her absence roams.

The glory of her long, unceasing dance
Grows grander in the limpid well of space,
And endlessly her gentle form withdraws
And endlessly draws near, as in all things
That shine and all that, shining, still conceal,
Her motions echo on, and on redound,
Though body is but dream and memory;
And now her dancing fills the frigid world
With figures cast in fire, immersed in night,
More various and strange and true than life.

And yet, one might well ask, why was my principal image of woman
so often that of the prostitute? Again, though, when social order is the regime of mechanism, of bodies without souls, of the market, of materialist
prudence — when this is decency, is respectability — then transgression
becomes a necessary piety. And, in such a world, it is the prostitute — the
rejected and reviled, the suffering servant of an age that knows no sin
and seeks no expiation — who corrupts the logic of acquisition and consumption with the subversive possibility of a tenderness that exceeds the
price remitted; thereby she becomes the emblem of the holy, the sign of
love's patient vulnerability. How often I was considered most blasphemous
when, in truth, I could scarcely have been more devout.

"The Heathen's Apologia"

I
Consider Phoebe, how she goes
Down paths of utter decadence,
For well this carnal pilgrim knows
That God — all opposites' coincidence —

*Coda: C.B.*

Is found upon the left-hand way
Just as upon the right. And so
Let honeyed hungers have their sway,
And appetite be infinite yet grow.


II
Consider Phoebe, how she calls
That virile ephebe to attend her:
God draws the longing from her soul
That prompts the gentle service she will render.
The vastness of creation spills
Into the ocean of her heart,
The tumult of the cosmos stills —
She finds divinity in every part.


III
Consider Phoebe, how she weeps
For hearts that have grown hard and cold:
The knowledge that her sorrow keeps
Discreetly hid from men will not be told.
From chaos the great hand of Zeus
Drew forth the worlds as fruits of love:
These scorching passions he set loose,
These pains, return a glory from above.


IV
Consider Phoebe's ecstasy:
The writhing clutching of her hands
Is God's eternal majesty
Weft on the loom of time with shining strands.
For Phoebe in her agony
Of joy and canticle of sighs
Embraces all of earth and sea,
And clasps infinity between her thighs.


You may disapprove. Perhaps I do as well. But you must see that God himself is the most prostituted of us all, since he is the highest friend of all, the most shared in common, the inexhaustible reservoir of love.[9] Here,

9. See *Mon cœur mis nu*, LXVIII.

where all is sold and nothing given, love can find us only by the supreme
condescension of selling itself, of divesting itself of its glory and descending into the brothels of our hearts, where all our loves are purchased loves,
thus taking us unawares precisely where our lust reigns supreme. Christ
kept company with harlots out of the abundance of his compassion, yes,
but also perhaps because he found them holier — more blameless —
than the righteous. And was not the dereliction of the cross like the self-
abnegation of a lupanar? Was it not there that God gave himself — sold
himself cheaply — to those who could not hope to win his love, requiring
nothing in return but the paltriest pittance of their faith?

## VI

As for song — that, for me, is perhaps the final mystery of divine mercy.
I mean the way of beauty, the ambiguous raptures of art. I expect we all
hope that divine mercy will come to us in the surprise of an annunciation,
the invasion of a splendor that does not wait upon us, but that suddenly
seizes us to itself. But, O Lord, could we really bear to meet your gaze
in the gaze of your angel? Is any but the purest soul prepared for that
encounter?

 I was much taken once, at the museum, by one of those childish but
oddly touching sacred pictures of the Byzantine Greeks. I half sketched
out a poem about it, in fact.

*"Annunciation"*

Beneath a canopy of gold — tempera's sky,
Through which smooth gesso's luminosity still breaks —
Her figure, cowled in dark vinaceous purple dye
Marked with three stars, set off against brown hills, bice lakes,
Is turned to meet the lush farrago of his wings:
Soft lavender, cornelian red, and green imbue
His plumage with prismatic splendor, from which springs
An arc of amethyst, a fringe of fiery blue;
And there an edge of silver frosts his pinions' tips.
He stands erect — his brow's the color of the moon,
His incandescent eyes are indigo, his lips
Are coralline — but bent escarpments seem to swoon
Above the scene. Time cannot comprise him: the day
Wears on, indifferent to eternity's press

*Coda: C.B.*

Of glory; the dark world looks stubbornly away
From his rude revelations of time's changeless depths.

But she in rapture gazes on this presence, bright
With dreadful beauty, at the air about him stained
With iridescence where his wings shed their cool light.
The space between them faintly trembles with its pained
And constant tensions: face to face, the deepest wounds
Of being pass between them. Nacreous and cold,
The gesso's glow still penetrates the trees and stones.
She quickens in life's sleep, and knows that he could hold
Her here forever with his gaze, trapped in his eyes.

Beyond, a fabulous coiled world of ochre lies.

Perfect beauty would be terrifying. We could not bear it; it would con-
vict us of the squalor we have gathered around our souls in our attempts to
shield ourselves from remorse. We must labor, therefore, amid imperfect
beauty, knowing that therein — inasmuch as beauty is the realm of the
spirit — our loyalties to God and to the devil vie with one another. It is the
angel within us, after all, that the devil within us seeks to corrupt. Here,
amid the darkness of this world, the burning embers of true beauty lie
scattered, gleaming jewels of golden fire, sparks of divine glory, and we can
only strive to gather them up again. But there also Satan hangs his lures
and sets his snares, for he too knows the uses of beauty. Some of these lost
splendors were once gems brightly shining in his diadem of stars.


## VII

I end where I began. I cannot — we cannot — poor philosopher, above all
you cannot — erect again that glorious scale of eminence and analogy that
once rose from earth to heaven, but which modern man has pulled down.
In my last days on the earth I learned that, in the end, I knew only the way
of dereliction, of seeking God's mercy in all the final, frailest gestures of
abandonment. In this age, we can find no other path of ascent than that
of our last descent into the penury of a strangely disconsolate hope. There
is only one who can create for us, in our broken solitude, that star-strewn
way of return — and he seems so remote in this age that sometimes it is
as if we only dreamed him. One last verse —

*"John on Patmos"*

My tongue was as a golden bird
   Tangled in an emerald net,
My eyes were diamonds, my ears heard
   His voice in silver echoes; yet
I knew no way to join the dance
   Until the dancer took my hand,
And led me in a floating trance
   When I could scarcely rise to stand.

Or so, when visions seized my soul,
   It seemed; or when his gentle form
Amid the garden shadows, cold
   And still (as when he calmed the storm
Upon the waters), fixed in prayer,
   Became as pure and strange as light
Departing from the evening air
   Before the melting blue of night.

I am as gold or emerald,
   As twilit gems or moonlit silver,
Beyond all grief, transformed, and held
   Within a cage of stars, and never
To leave this island washed by dreams;
   I can recall as none else can
The otherness in him: he seemed
   A shape more beautiful than man.

Thus, in the end, I learned to pray, constantly, out of my deepest despair, my incessant thirst for that boundless love: O God, you whose name I scarcely dare pronounce, blessed be you for the gift of my suffering: the suffering you impart as a remedy for our impurities, to make the strong fit for holy delights.[10] O, have pity upon me, my God, my God, and upon us all. See what innocent monsters throng the city, O creator both of law and of liberty, you the judge who forgives, who perhaps taught me my taste for horror in order to cure my heart as it were at sword's point. Have pity on all men and women who are mad. Can any be monstrous in your sight, you who created them, who alone know why they exist and how

10. See "Bénédiction," in *Les Fleurs du Mal*.

they made themselves and how they might not have done so?[11] Teach me to extend my charity, without so much as a grimace of disdain, to the poor, the abased, the suffering, so to spread a triumphal carpet beneath the feet of Jesus.[12] Teach me also to see how my humiliations have been graces sent by you.[13] Recall, O Lord, how as a child I spoke constantly to you,[14] and forgive me now. I implore your pity, you whom alone I have loved, out of the abyss wherein my heart lies entombed.[15] O, my God, my God, let me not dwell forever far from your gaze.

So I prayed . . .

In this age of broken covenants, we can offer only these whispered supplications, these uncertain prayers, not always knowing if we are heard. As we have lost the path, we must for now make our way in darkness, groping helplessly, till we learn again how to be led by faith.

AH, WELL . . . The reflections of a forlorn ghost or of a soul in bliss — I cannot tell you which. That secret it is not given me to disclose.

So, then — *alors* — *Agréez-vous, je vous en prie, l'expression de mes sentiments distingués. Merci, Mesdames et Messieurs, merci beaucoup. Maintenant je dois partir — je dois retourner à ce terrible mystère qui attend chaque homme — alors je vais dire: "Adieu. Adieu."*

11. See *Le Spleen de Paris*, XLV.
12. See "Le Rebelle," in *Les Fleurs du Mal, poèmes supplémentaires.*
13. See *Mon cœur mis nu*, CXV.
14. See *Mon cœur mis nu*, CIV.
15. See "De Profundis Clamavi," in *Les Fleurs du Mal.*

Made in the USA
Coppell, TX
01 March 2022

74300888R00184